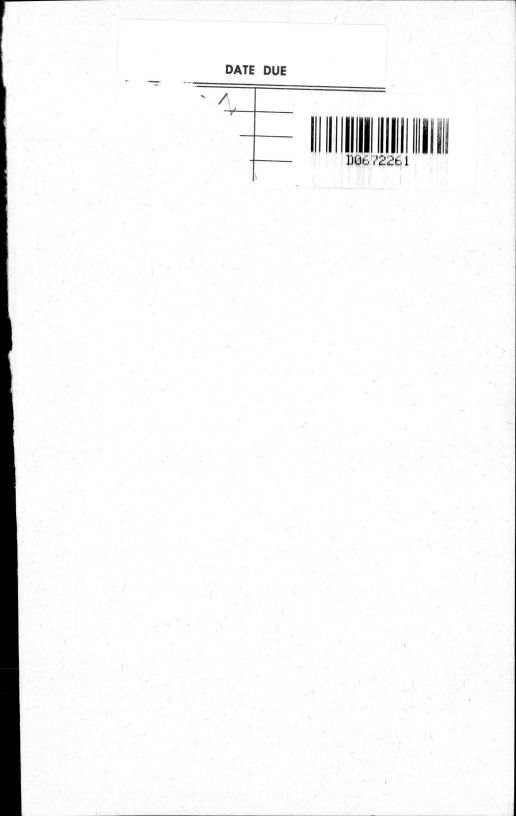

The English
Madrigal Composers

The English Madrigal Composers

BY

EDMUND HORACE FELLOWES

SECOND EDITION

LONDON

OXFORD UNIVERSITY PRESS

NEW YORK   TORONTO

Oxford University Press, Ely House, London W. 1

GLASGOW   NEW YORK   TORONTO   MELBOURNE   WELLINGTON
CAPE TOWN   SALISBURY   IBADAN   NAIROBI   LUSAKA   ADDIS ABABA
BOMBAY   CALCUTTA   MADRAS   KARACHI   LAHORE   DACCA
KUALA LUMPUR   HONG KONG   TOKYO

FIRST EDITION 1921
SECOND EDITION 1948
REPRINTED 1950, 1958, 1963, AND 1967

REPRINTED LITHOGRAPHICALLY IN GREAT BRITAIN
AT THE UNIVERSITY PRESS, OXFORD
BY VIVIAN RIDLER
PRINTER TO THE UNIVERSITY

PREFACE

THERE appears to be no published work dealing exclusively with the subject of the English Madrigal. It is hoped, therefore, that this volume may supply a want, and may prove of interest to many among that large body of singers who are constantly engaged in the practice and study of madrigals, either as members of choral societies or in the privacy of their homes. It may also be found to have some value as a book of reference, as it contains a complete index of the first lines of the whole series of English madrigals, and also separate lists of works of this class at the conclusion of the biographical and critical notice of each composer.

The vast number of organizations which serve to encourage part-singing of all kinds in this country bear testimony to the inherent love of vocal music which has been characteristic of the British race unintermittently for the past 500 years and more ; and there must be many choral singers who would care to know something further about the famous Tudor School of Music which is one of the proud heritages of our race. Possibly this latter consideration will cause the present volume to make a wider appeal to the interest of that large circle of English people who, although they may not engage in the active pursuit of any particular art, nevertheless value highly all the great national achievements of their race, not confining their interests alone to glorious feats of arms or triumphs of states-manship, but extending them to the realms of Literature and Art in its many branches. For it is utterly deplorable that so few Englishmen should even be aware of the bare fact that at the close of the sixteenth century a school of composers flourished in this country who held the first place in European music.

The book has been designed primarily for the amateur and the student rather than for the expert musician, although it deals with certain facts and subjects which may be new to all classes of musicians. For example, the outline of the life of

John Wilbye has not hitherto been printed elsewhere except in the preface to the present author's edition of Wilbye's works and in his paper in the Proceedings of the Musical Association for 1914–15 ; and new biographical details are also given concerning Weelkes, Farnaby, Tomkins, Cavendish, and other composers of this School.

The volume is divided into two parts, the first of which deals with the history and meaning of the Madrigal with special reference to its position in English musical history, and, further, with a general explanation of the technicalities connected with the text of the original editions of the English madrigals, together with some important features bearing on the proper method of singing madrigals. The second part treats briefly of the life and works of the individual composers of the School.

The original spelling has been retained when passages are quoted from early authors, but in all other cases modern spelling has been adopted. This course is rendered desirable by the variety and inconsistency of Elizabethan spelling. Nor has any exception been made in the case of the word *Air*, although most modern writers, in dealing with the compositions of the lutenists, have preferred to retain the spelling *Ayre*, which was usually, but not invariably, the form in which it was spelt on the original title-pages. But with reference to this particular word it may be stated that the use of the *y* in place of the modern *i* was very general, especially when followed by an *r*, as, for example, in *byrd, syr, fayr, yre, wyre, attyre*, &c. This peculiarity was as much a convention as the addition of the final *e* in *childe* or *worke*, and no logical case can be made out for the exceptional retention of Tudor spelling in the case of the word *Air*. Such names as Cornysshe and Fayrfax may reasonably be spelt in the modern manner ; but, on the other hand, *Byrd*, rather than *Bird*, has reluctantly been retained, as also the final *e* in Wilbye and Kirbye, for the reason that by familiarity and constant use the names of these composers have now become stereotyped in that form, albeit the usual custom is to spell Farnaby without a final *e*.

The terms Tudor, Elizabethan, and sixteenth century in relation to music are here used in accordance with the precedent in dealing with the Literature of the same period, as applying to the whole of this School of Composers. For although much of the music was published after the close of the century, and in the early years of the reign of James I, it retained the character and style of the sixteenth century.

The author desires to express his sincerest thanks to Miss Evelyn Heaton-Smith for much valuable help and advice given during the compilation of this volume. He also acknowledges with gratitude his indebtedness to Mr. W. Barclay Squire for the loan of manuscript scores made by him of madrigals of Peter Philips and Robert Jones ; [1] the only known complete set of part-books of Jones's madrigals was, before the outbreak of the European War, at Brussels, and is therefore inaccessible at the present time. The author's thanks are also due to Lord Ellesmere and to Mr. S. R. Christie-Miller for facilities so kindly extended to him for examining and transcribing extracts from unique books in their possession ; also to Dr. A. H. Mann for information with regard to Carlton and Cobbold, and to Sir Ivor Atkins for some of the fresh details concerning Thomas Tomkins and Nathaniel Pattrick.

Acknowledgement must also be made of information obtained from various well-known books of reference, notably, among others, the Oxford History of Music, Grove's Dictionary of Music, articles in Mr. Godfrey Arkwright's *Old English Edition,* and in Mr. Kennedy Scott's *Euterpe* Series ; and also Rimbault's *Bibliotheca Madrigaliana.* Dr. Rimbault's little book has long been out of print, and is therefore not available for general use, but, in spite of sundry inaccuracies of detail, it is a reference book of no small value, and has formed the basis of much of the present author's work.

E. H. F.

THE CLOISTERS, WINDSOR CASTLE.
May 1, 1916.

PS.—The publication of this book has been unavoidably delayed owing to the abnormal conditions brought about by the war.

[1] Mr. Squire also kindly placed at his disposal a transcript of the title-page and contents of Morley's First Book of Airs, 1600.

PREFACE TO THE SECOND EDITION

THE issue of a reprint of this book has been unavoidably delayed by the exceptional conditions brought about by the war that have so seriously affected the whole business of book publishing. For similar reasons the author's opportunity for free revision of the text is severely restricted, because the photographic process of reproduction must necessarily replace that of re-setting if reprints in any form are to be contemplated as a practical proposition.

In the present instance it has been found possible to revise and correct a few details, notably those concerning Orlando Gibbons, who is now known to have been born at Oxford and not Cambridge.

It is very impressive to consider how widely the popularity of the Madrigal, together with all forms of music associated with the Tudor period, has spread throughout the English-speaking world since this book was first published. The names of Morley, Byrd, Wilbye, Weelkes, and the rest were almost unknown at that time except to specialists, and madrigal-singing was limited to members of a few isolated groups and Societies.

All that is now changed, and it is hoped that in its republished form this book may continue to be a means of providing information and guidance to madrigal-singers, as well as to students of the Golden Age of English music.

E. H. F.

THE CLOISTERS, WINDSOR CASTLE.
Feb. 11, 1948.

CONTENTS

APPENDICES

CHAPTER I

THE ENGLISH MADRIGAL IN RELATION TO OTHER FORMS OF CHORAL-SONG

IN one sense music ranks as the youngest of all the Arts. But this statement is true only so far as we limit the subject to the history of musical development in the Western World, the basis of which is the simultaneous employment of two or more musical sounds, that is to say, the combination of melodies. The contrast to such combination is, of course, the bare utterance of melody unadorned by any accompanying sound whatever, unless it be a pedal or drone, an important feature, for instance, in Indian music, the most highly developed system of exclusively melodic music that has yet been evolved.

Music is, in fact, as old as the human race, for Song must be classed with Speech and Dance as one of the natural forms of expression of primitive man. Instrumental music of an elementary nature made its appearance very soon after Song, and as a necessary sequel to it in the process of the evolution of this primeval instinct. But, for countless generations, music throughout the world remained absolutely and solely melodic in character. Two exclusively melodic types of music that have survived to the present day are Folk-song and Plain-song ; and consequently, from the standpoint of pure Art, these should preferably be rendered without musical accompaniment ; but when accompaniment is employed, as it often must be for reasons somewhat similar to those which induce us to mount our pictures in frames, such accompaniment should be so designed that it may work the least possible harm to the melody ; nor should it ever be employed with the smallest idea of adding any material that might distract attention from the melody in all its natural simplicity.

Apart from purely melodic music there are two other distinct phases in the history of musical development, namely, the polyphonic and the harmonic. And these are to be found exclusively in the music of the Western World.   Polyphony, as Mr. Wooldridge so well expressed it,[1] represents the adjustment of 'the mutual relations of the separate melodies so as not only to elicit the full effect of their combination, but to preserve a relative dependence for each ;   the outcome is a complete union maintained upon the principle of an absolute equality between the individual and collective elements of the composition '.   The early experiments in polyphonic music were of a very crude nature, and indeed, until about the year 1400, little can be said to have been done towards raising it to the level of a high art, but subsequent to that date rapid progress was made, and in the great creative period of European Art, from 1520 to 1600, polyphonic music reached the very height of perfection.   On the other hand the harmonic, or, as they are sometimes termed, the homophonic principles, upon which musical development has pursued its course since about the year 1600 until the present day, are not founded primarily upon the recognition of equality of interest in the collective elements, but upon individual melody which is usually limited to a single part ;   the function of the other parts is subordinate to that which sustains the melody, and their main purpose is to reinforce and support it with harmony.

But although the harmonic development led eventually to the revelation of the glories of the Opera, the Oratorio and Cantata, the Symphony, and the string Quartet, yet this fact must be emphasized, namely that the simple beauty and pure grandeur of the vocal music which the sixteenth-century composers wrote for the Church has never since been approached, while the Madrigals of the same period, whether Flemish, Italian, or English, represent the most perfect expression in secular polyphonic song that has as yet been achieved.

Before attempting any detailed consideration of the subject of the English Madrigal it is necessary to say something about English secular Choral-song as a whole, seeing that the Madrigal occupies but one section of the main subject.

In the history of the origin and growth of language, speech was first of all evolved by a series of natural and inevitable processes, while at a later epoch the scientific analyst appeared

[1] The Oxford History of Music, vol. i, pp. 1, 2.

who was able to harness the wild product with the regular laws of syntax and grammar. So also in the history of Choral-song, and, indeed, with that of every class of musical utterance, different forms, typical of the era in which they had their origin, have been evolved by a series of natural processes, and it has been left to musical grammarians at a subsequent period to assign to them distinguishing names, and to define the laws which govern their construction.

Thus musicians in comparatively recent times have stereotyped the use of certain terms in the department of Choral-song, and, in doing so, they have largely obscured the general view of the subject by the employment of the term Part-song for one particular type of composition, instead of reserving it as the generic term to cover this entire class of vocal composition, as distinct from solo, or unison, song. It is difficult to discover the origin of this restricted use of the term Part-song, but it does not seem to have involved such limitations as it now implies before the Victorian era. Nor can such limited use be supported on logical grounds. Song, as a musical term, and as applied to the secular branch of vocal music, must necessarily be subdivided into (a) Solo, or Unison song, and (b) Part-song. Part-song should, in its turn, be subdivided again under the headings of Polyphonic part-song and Harmonic part-song, the polyphonic and harmonic being, as we have already seen, the two main distinguishing phases into which must be separated the musical history that deals with the development of the principle of simultaneous employment of more than one musical sound. In the Polyphonic period we have a variety of terminology in connexion with secular song that will be discussed in detail in a later chapter ; and the definite exclusion of the word Part-song from among such terms cannot be supported in argument, for the madrigalists themselves made use of terms that are in fact identical with it. Thus Byrd, for example, among many others, classified the compositions in his earliest secular volumes in the Table of Contents as ' Songs of 3-parts ', ' Songs of 4-parts ', and so on. Again, in the year 1597, by which time the term Madrigal had come into general use among the English composers, Weelkes used the word Madrigal on the title-page of the volume which he published

that year, yet he headed the sections in the Table of Contents
' Songs of three parts ' and so on.   Similarly Wilbye, who
entitled each of his volumes a ' Set of Madrigals ' to so many
voices, added at the conclusion of each section in the body of
the book the quaint formula so commonly to be found in the
works of all the English madrigalists, ' Heere endeth the songs
of 3. parts ', and so on.   A large number of similar examples
might be quoted to show that in actual practice, apart from
theory, the Elizabethan composers regarded the word Madrigal,
with all its kindred terms, as synonymous with a song of so
many parts, or, in other words, a Part-song.   The Madrigals
constituted indeed the normal part-songs of the sixteenth
century, written as they were in the natural musical idiom of
their own time whether as regards tonality, verbal treatment,
or musical device ; moreover, it must not be forgotten that they
extended over a wide field of design, and were by no means
confined to the elaborate contrapuntal methods which are so
often to be found in them.

Yet some distinction must admittedly be drawn between the
actual Madrigal and that form of composition evolved by
the lutenist composers which they usually described as an Air.
This type of composition was treated in two different ways ;
sometimes it was left in the simple form of melody with lute
accompaniment, and sometimes it was also adapted for an
alternative method of performance, that is to say harmonized
for four voices.   This harmonized arrangement for combined
voices not only closely resembled the Harmonic part-song of
later days, but may be regarded as its direct ancestor.   This
subject will be more fully considered in a later chapter,[1] but
two points may be incidentally mentioned here.   In the first
place the term Air was also employed in Tudor times as being
synonymous with Canzonet ; and secondly, the term Madrigal
has in the past been commonly used in association with the
works of such lutenist-composers as Dowland and Ford, whether
in programmes or in the catalogues of the leading music-publish-
ing houses.   To such a degree has the terminology of the subject
been confused.

Passing on now to the Harmonic phase of musical develop-

[1] See p. 60.

ment, secular Part-song has had a varied and interesting history. Like its predecessor in the polyphonic style, it has assumed several different forms. Developing rapidly and extensively in one direction, it grew into an elaborate type of Choral-song, with instrumental accompaniment, and thus, in the process of time, took a shape so largely magnified and so widely different in scope and design from its original pattern as eventually to be regarded, when combined with Solo-song and purely instrumental interludes, as a completely separate species of musical composition, under the classification of Cantata. This aspect of the subject is clearly outside the scope of our present consideration, although it calls for a passing allusion. The two principal types of part-song proper which have been evolved since the year 1600 are the Glee and that form which might more logically have been termed the Harmonic or Homophonic part-song, but which is commonly known among musicians to-day by the term Part-song alone. The Catch and Round, although they date their origin far back into the polyphonic period, managed to retain their popularity when other forms of polyphonic music were forgotten ; and even at the present time both composers and singers have a use for them. They were especially popular at the period of the Restoration, but unfortunately the depraved taste of that time has so entirely coloured this type of song that scarcely any of the catches of that day could now be reprinted. This circumstance is all the more to be regretted because it excludes not a little of Purcell's music as well as that of the remarkable band of his contemporaries. The Catch Club, which was founded in 1761, was formed with the object of encouraging the Glee as well as the Catch and Round ; and it may be mentioned here as providing further evidence of the popularity of this particular musical form in the eighteenth century also, a popularity which it still largely enjoys.

The Glee, like the Air of the lutenist-composers, is an exclusively English form of vocal composition and has no parallel at all on the Continent in its own line. It followed the Madrigal after an interval of almost two hundred years and was at the height of its popularity in the latter years of the eighteenth century. The word glee is derived from the Saxon *gligg*, which simply means *music* without any reference whatever to cheerfulness or joy; for in point of fact the Glee, like the Madrigal, was frequently set to a subject of a serious character. Though the Glee is the direct successor of the Madrigal, it cannot in any sense be considered as a development of that form of composition. The Tudor Madrigal had reached the limit of possible development in its own particular line, and the Glee represents an independent growth. The Glee was undoubtedly intended to be performed strictly by one singer only to each vocal part and not by a larger body of voices. It differs from the Madrigal in the first place in the matter of tonality. Written, as it was, in the eighteenth century and early nineteenth, no attempt was made by the glee-composers, and quite rightly, to reproduce either the modal features of the sixteenth century, or any of the other special peculiarities of the Tudor musicians.

Moreover, the Glee was constructed, as might have been expected at this later date, on a much more definite design than that of the Madrigal, and in consequence it was capable of much fuller treatment. It was often characterized, too, by a very florid style of vocalization, a feature which shows the direct influence of Handel upon this, no less than upon all other branches of English composition throughout the eighteenth and early nineteenth centuries. But although the Glee, like the Madrigal, offered considerable scope for contrapuntal ingenuity, yet large masses of harmony are much more common in the Glee. Cadences, conspicuous by their rarity in the Madrigal, occur incessantly in the Glee, with the effect of detracting from the strength and unity of these compositions. In spite of these defects the English Glee, though much inferior to the Madrigal in artistic value, will almost certainly hold the permanent place that it deserves side by side with the productions of the English Madrigal School so long as English music is practised at all.

It remains briefly to consider the class of composition which has succeeded in appropriating to itself the generic term of Part-song, but which, as was suggested above, would have more logically been distinguished by the term Harmonic part-song if no better word could have been found for it. It is scarcely necessary to say here anything about that kind of

Part-song which has an indispensable pianoforte accompaniment. This type of composition first became popular in England in the days of Sir Henry Bishop, and it has been successfully exploited by many composers since his time.

The Part-song proper should be rendered without accompaniment of any kind, and in this respect it resembles the Madrigal and the Glee. It should also be performed by a considerable body of voices, yet not by so large a number as to preclude clearness of utterance or delicacy of expression. It is commonly asserted that a Part-song should not be performed by single voices to a part, but it would be difficult to point to a written statement by any composer laying down a rule in this matter. The performance of some Part-songs by single solo-voices can, indeed, lead to very high artistic results, and it is surprising that this delightful kind of music for the home is so little in vogue, although it can be organized with far less trouble or expense than is required for arranging a string-quartet party. Yet it is a fact that there is more string-quartet playing than part-singing in private London houses at the present time, even though there is a far larger number of competent singers for this purpose than of instrumentalists with sufficient skill to join in chamber music.

The Part-song, as we have seen, may be considered to be the lineal descendant of the harmonized Air of the Tudor lutenists the design of which was almost entirely devoid of elaborate contrapuntal device ; but as an Art-form it does not really seem to have taken root in England until the beginning of the reign of Queen Victoria. It owed its renewed popularity in this country at that period very largely to the influence of Mendelssohn, whose Part-songs until almost the close of the nineteenth century occupied an important share in the programmes of most choral and madrigal societies ; and this, often to the prejudice and exclusion of the genuine English Madrigal, which just at that very same period had begun to show signs of gradually winning back its proper place in the affections of English singers. But in dealing with the early Victorian Part-song one important composer must be mentioned who successfully resisted the prevailing influence. This was Pearsall, who, as a notable exception, had sufficient genius and strength of character to strike out a line of his own without regard either for the convention or the fashion of the moment. It must not, of course, be forgotten that a good deal of Pearsall's work was admittedly not much more than the adaptation of music of an earlier period ; but in this particular line of work he was singularly happy and showed the hand of a true artist. It is a common mistake to ascribe wholly to Pearsall's authorship some of the pieces that were no more than adaptations, however skilfully treated ; a notable example of this is his exquisite arrangement of the old Carol *In dulci jubilo*. Several of Pearsall's original compositions were styled Madrigals, and this provides yet another example of the loose usage of that term. Not a few of them were, however, planned to some extent upon madrigalian lines, being written in contrapuntal style with points of imitation and other such devices ; but Pearsall did not tie himself down to the idiom of the sixteenth century, and this was perhaps the secret of his success in enriching the literature of English Part-song with such fine music as *Lay a garland, Great god of Love, Sir Patrick Spens,* and a number of other compositions of this class.

Yet it was to Mendelssohn and not to Pearsall that the English Part-song writers of that day, and for many years after, looked for their lead ; and the influence under which they thus came was a source of weakness rather than of strength. For Mendelssohn's Part-songs are little more than harmonized melodies, the rhythm of which is scrupulously followed by the lower voice-parts with scarcely any variation. A good example is the once popular *An old Romance.* These melodies bear little or no relation to the words to which they are attached, in remarkable contrast to the intimate and subtle connexion between the music and the words of the English madrigalists, both as regards their general and their individual sense. In the case of Mendelssohn's Part-songs almost any other words of the same metre might be substituted for those actually employed without seriously affecting the merits of the composition. Yet, considered solely as melodies, they had an undoubted charm of their own which was found irresistible by English musicians of Mendelssohn's day ; and this resulted in their being sung at every opportunity and heard with undisguised pleasure, while neither singers nor audience seem to have paused to consider upon what an inadequate foundation their enjoyment was built. English composers in large numbers set themselves to imitate this popular but unsatisfactory model ; and this amply explains the poverty of the bulk of English Part-song literature in the mid-Victorian era.[1] It was only when the influence had expended its force that a modern school of English composers arose who lifted Part-song, as well as other branches of composition, to a level so much more worthy of their musical ancestry. Thus in the best work of our contemporary English Part-song writers we now recognize a keen literary appreciation on the part of the composers, as exhibited in the choice of words as well as in the details of their methods, and also in their taste and discretion in clothing those words with sound. We see them aiming at something much more interesting and valuable than a harmonized tune. We find them employing the whole of their art and imagination for the purpose of giving an added beauty to the words instead of using those words as a mere medium for musical expression. These are some of the legitimate methods by which the modern Part-song writers seek to charm their hearers, and in employing them successfully many of our leading English composers to-day are following in the steps first marked out by their great Tudor predecessors. They play, it is true, upon a different kind of instrument, because necessarily it is a more modern and elaborate one ; and the technique that they employ is essentially of another character. But the appeal which they make is to the same instinct, which, at all periods alike, seeks for gratification in the experience of beautiful sound uttered with a due sense of proportion and with an accurate estimate of its suitability to its individual setting and surroundings.

[1] Since this chapter was written the author's attention has been drawn to an article written by Pearsall and printed in Farley's *Bristol Journal* shortly after his death, in which he specially deprecated the inclusion of Mendelssohn's Part-songs in the programmes of the Bristol Madrigal Society, on the ground that they did not belong to the class of music for the study of which the Society had been constituted.

CHAPTER II

THE PROLONGED NEGLECT OF THE MADRIGAL

THERE can be but few so-called educated persons in this country who would not admit that the glory of English Literature is that of the Tudor Period. For although many writers of the sixteenth and early seventeenth century are little more than names to that large majority who have not made English Literature a subject of special study, yet the works of Shakespeare are at least familiar to Englishmen in general, and his greatness is universally recognized ; while the names of Sidney, Spenser, Ben Jonson, Marlowe, Michael Drayton, and a host of others, are not altogether unknown to the average individual, even if a knowledge of their writings is limited, as a rule, to a few popular verses, such, for example, as Marlowe's *Come live with me*, or Ben Jonson's *Drink to me only with thine eyes.* The literature of the period has been rendered accessible to modern readers in complete editions, not only of the great writers, but also of the minor poets of the time ; and such ample annotation and commentary has been provided as is needed for securing the appreciation of these works by all classes of students.

Now, it is an equally true fact, although known and recognized by a very small fraction of English-speaking people, that the high excellence of Tudor Literature has its parallel in the music of the same period; for the music of the Tudor composers, whether in the department of ecclesiastical, of instrumental, or of secular vocal writing, ranks as Art of the first class. It may even be asserted that this English School of Music surpasses that of its contemporaries on the continent of Europe, although such an assertion does not involve any depreciation of the greatness of the Flemish and Italian schools of the sixteenth century, including, as they do, such names as Willaert, Arcadelt, Verdelot, Lassus, Palestrina, Marenzio, Festa, and many more.

Yet, in spite of this fact, it must be stated, in deplorable contrast with the case of the Elizabethan poets and dramatists, that the large majority of educated people in this country still know very little about the existence of such a school of musical composition, and still less about its literature and its leaders. Moreover, there are some, even in the ranks of those who have specialized in the study of Tudor Literature, who do not hesitate to express frank astonishment on being informed of the existence of this great school of musicians, men who were living at this same glorious era of English History, and with whom many of the poets must have been on terms of intimate friendship when they were working side by side at their sister Arts. And such expressions of astonishment are frequently accompanied with some further observation, perhaps with something of a sneer, to the effect that it is widely accepted as a fact that no school of English music has ever attained any importance at any period of history.

It must here be stated frankly that since the decay of the Tudor School, little of first-rate merit has been produced by British composers, as compared with the great continental schools of the seventeenth, eighteenth, and early nineteenth centuries, with the important, but sole, exception of the work of Henry Purcell and some of his contemporaries, notably John Blow and Pelham Humphreys. For it is obviously too early as yet to estimate with a true sense of perspective the relative value of the British music which has been composed within the past forty years or so, even though much of it may seem to provide ground for high hopes. But general statements condemning the inferiority of the English schools of composition are often made owing to utter ignorance of the great achievements of the Tudor musicians ; and such statements have created a formidable barrier of prejudice, both in this country and on the Continent, particularly among those whose learning and education have lain outside the limits of practical musical instruction.

Various causes are accountable for the comparative ignorance that prevails on the subject of the great English madrigal-composers, and of Tudor music in general. One of these was the actual lack of printed editions of the music itself ; and to this cause must be added, as a necessary corollary, the very meagre amount of the music of this school that was given a hearing

either in the concert-room or in the cathedral and collegiate
choirs of this country. Any bookseller can, at short notice,
supply the complete works of almost every Elizabethan poet,
and it was more than a little discreditable to English musicians
that it was impossible to comply with a similar request for the
complete works of Tallis, Tye, Gibbons, Dowland, or Byrd—
to quote those names only—for the reason that definitive
modern editions of these Tudor composers were practically
non-existent. It could not be regarded as satisfactory if, for
instance, but one or two plays of Shakespeare and perhaps
half a dozen of Sidney's sonnets, with a correspondingly
minute selection from other Elizabethan writers, were alone
accessible to the modern reader ; yet such was precisely the
state of things with regard to the musical literature of the period.
Only a small portion, chosen almost at haphazard, had been
published in modern form, while the great bulk was allowed to
remain hidden away in very scarce original editions of the
separate part-books in such libraries as those of the British
Museum and the older universities. The instrumental music
of this period, though of rich artistic interest and great historical
importance, stands on rather a different footing from the vocal
music of the same day. Indeed, owing to the antique character
and idiom of the writing, and more especially to the fact that
the instruments for which this music was designed are practically
obsolete, there would be affectation in suggesting that, except
to a specially chosen audience, much of it could be employed
for performance to-day just as it stands and without explanation in the programme. But with the Church music and the
madrigals the case is very different : these compositions still
remain for us to-day with all the vigour of life actually glowing
in them, and in spite of such antiquity of style, of design, or of
phraseology, as they undeniably possess, they can be presented
just as the composers left them without the slightest need of
apology to a modern audience.

  Until the works of the Tudor musicians, both sacred and
secular, could be printed in complete and accessible form it was
idle to talk of their greatness, almost impossible to attempt
a satisfactory criticism of their works, and useless to suggest
their performance. The prophecy made thirty years ago has

come true, that if this music should become readily accessible it would quickly win for itself a wide appreciation among English choral singers and cathedral choirs.

The neglect of Tudor music must also be examined from a historical point of view. Very shortly after its original production this music fell into complete disuse in England, with the result that much of its actual literature suffered destruction and loss, while its traditions were absolutely obliterated. This lamentable fact was due to the marked decay in public taste which set in rapidly as regards music at the beginning of the seventeenth century, although in other branches of Art this decay was delayed until the later years of the Stuart dynasty. The deterrent influence of the Civil War, coupled with all the distorted ideas which prevailed among certain classes in the middle of the seventeenth century as to the wickedness of any form of singing or dancing, and finally the livelier tastes of the Court of Charles II, due to French education and experience, put an almost complete end to the cultivation of polyphonic music in England. In place of this was substituted in course of time a more florid style of work interspersed with orchestral interludes. The very greatness of Henry Purcell and his contemporaries was in itself further fatal to the general performance of the Tudor music, because their prolific output almost immediately precluded any necessity for its continued use. Incidentally it happened that this reaction told with more force against the madrigals than against the Church music of the Elizabethans, for there is evidence that in the majority of the provincial cathedrals, away from Court influence, certain anthems and services held their place, in a limited degree, side by side with the newer types of composition, until some of them were given a fresh lease of life in the middle of the eighteenth century by the energy of Maurice Greene and the publication of Boyce's ' Cathedral Music '.

It is not easy in these days to realize fully the immense degree of popularity attained by madrigal-singing in this country at the close of the sixteenth century ; nor yet the wonderful standard of musical skill which prevailed among all persons of education at that time. It was regarded as an essential part of the training of a gentleman that he should be able to take part, at sight, in the singing of a madrigal or in a ' consort of viols '—the Elizabethan equivalent to the string-quartet of more mòdern days.[1] Thomas Morley's fascinating description of the discomfiture of a young man whose musical education had been neglected, may be given here in full, as illustrating this statement. The passage is from the opening chapter of Morley's ' Plaine and Easie Introduction to Practicall Musicke '. This book is written in the form of a dialogue between two friends, whom the author named *Philomathes* and *Polymathes*, and their master, *Gnorimus*, who however does not take part in the preliminary passage quoted here.

Polymathes. Before you goe I pray you repeate some of the discourses which you had yesternight at master *Sophobulus* his banket : For commonly he is not without both wise and learned guests.

Philomathes. It is true indeede. And yesternight there were a number of excellent schollers, both gentlemen and others : but all the propose, which then was discoursed upon, was Musicke.

Pol. I trust you were contented to suffer others to speake of that matter.

Phi. I would that had beene the worst : for I was compelled to discover mine owne ignorance, and confesse that I knew nothing at all in it.

Pol. How so ?

Phi. Among the rest of the guests, by chaunce, master *Aphron* came thither also, who falling to discourse of Musicke, was in an argument so quickly taken up and hotly pursued by *Eudoxus* ·and *Calergus*, two kinsmen of *Sophobulus*, as in his own art he was overthrowen. But he still sticking in his opinion, the two gentlemen requested me to examine his reasons, and confute them. But I refusing and pretending ignorance, the whole company condemned me of discurtesie, being fully perswaded, that I had beene as skilfull in that art, as they tooke me to be learned in others. But supper being ended, and Musicke bookes (according to the custome) being brought to the tables, the mistresse of the house presented me with a part, earnestly requesting me to sing. But when, after many excuses, I protested unfainedly that I could not : every one began to wonder. Yea, some whispered to others, demaunding how I was brought up : so that upon shame of

---

[1] In making this comparison it should be mentioned that a complete ' chest of viols ', such as formed part of the outfit of all musical establishments in Tudor times, consisted of six instruments of the viol family.

mine ignorance, I go now to seeke out mine old friend master *Gnorimus*, to make my selfe his scholler.

In spite of the general proficiency to which this quotation seems to bear testimony, madrigal-singing soon fell into abeyance ; in fact it appears doubtful whether madrigals were much sung after the year 1640. This suggestion is borne out by reference to Pepys's diary, in which the author, a man of undoubted musical taste and accomplishments, made no mention whatever of the great composers of the English madrigal school or of their works. Morley alone was mentioned in the diary, and that in connexion with his ' Introduction to Musique' which Pepys studied for an hour and described as ' a very good but unmethodical book '.[1]   In another interesting entry [2] Pepys recorded his opinion, after having ' sung several good things ' with three of his friends, that he was ' more and more confirmed that singing with many voices is not singing but a sort of instrumental musique,the sense of the words being lost by not being heard, and especially as they set them with Fuges of words, one after another, whereas singing properly, I think, should be but with one or two voices and the counterpoint '. Pepys's opinion is in sharp contrast with that of Byrd, who, in the Address to the Reader in his 1588 volume of compositions, said ' There is not any Musicke of Instruments whatsoever, comparable to that which is made by the voyces of Men, where the voices are good, and the same well sorted and ordered.' Pepys was no doubt reflecting the prevailing opinion of his day, and his statement argues a definite disapproval of the madrigal style of composition, as well as of concerted singing in general.

Thus, with the lapse of no more than sixty years after the prosperity and fame of the English madrigal school had reached its height, madrigal-singing had practically come to an end, and the traditions associated with it were completely severed.

In the eighteenth century there was something of the nature of a revival of interest in Tudor music, and madrigals were occasionally sung by a few enthusiasts to whom warm praise is due. Notable among them was that little band of amateurs who in the year 1741 founded the Madrigal Society in London, an institution which has never ceased its activities from that

---

[1] Pepys's Diary, March 10, 1667.   [2] Ibid., September 15, 1667.

day to this, though at one time it was perilously near failure through lack of adequate support. But the atmosphere of the eighteenth century was not favourable for the cultivation of madrigal-singing, especially in the latter half of that century when the influence of Handel was supreme in England, and when but little English music had the chance of a fair hearing. This will account for the extraordinary criticism to which Dr. Burney subjected the Tudor madrigalists. Writing in 1789 [1] he says :

'The harmony of these *Minor Musicians*, or second class of English masters of the sixteenth century is pure and regular ; but however well received and justly admired by their cotemporaries, they are in general so monotonous in point of modulation that it seldom happens that more than two keys are used from the beginning to the end of a movement, which renders the performance of more than one or two at a time insipid and tiresome. " If ", says an enthusiastic admirer of Handel, " some of that great master's oratorio choruses were well performed by voices *only* in the manner of madrigals, how superior would their effect be to the productions of your Bennets, Kirbys, Weelkes's, and Wilbyes ! " The idea was so just that I wish it put into execution : as there is more nerve, more science and fire in the worst of Handel's choruses than in the greatest efforts of these old madrigalists.'

The nineteenth century witnessed a growing taste for madrigal-singing in this country, and it was marked in the early years by such publications as those of Holland and Cooke, who edited in complete form the two- and three-voice sets of Morley's Canzonets and the same composer's Set of four-part Madrigals. This effort was eclipsed by the members of the Musical Antiquarian Society, who in the middle of the century reprinted both the Wilbye Sets, Gibbons's Set, Bennet's Set, Bateson's first Set, and one Set of Weelkes, and the somewhat inferior *Fa-las* of the younger Hilton. The ' Triumphs of Oriana ' had been already printed in 1814 under the editorship of W. Hawes. But it is only in the past quarter of a century that English madrigals have shown signs of recovering the wide popularity which they enjoyed three hundred years ago ; and even to-day there exists a great deal of ignorance and prejudice upon the subject, both within and without musical circles.

[1] Burney's General History of Music, vol. iii, p. 131.

CHAPTER III

ENGLISH PREFERENCE FOR VOCAL MUSIC

BEFORE dealing with the origin and history of the English Madrigal School, it is important to make it clear that the natural bent of English musical taste is in the direction of vocal rather than of instrumental music. This is not only the case in the present day, but a careful examination of the subject will show that it always has been so ; and the fact has a very direct bearing upon the whole subject of the madrigals of the Elizabethan era, not only from the point of view of a critical consideration of the madrigal music itself, but also from that of its origin and history. It is this fact too that makes the regaining of whole-hearted popularity for the madrigal in this country a matter of absolute certainty. In England choral music has ever been the most marked feature of the national musical genius, and it is this more than anything else that has given the stamp of nationality to British music in all stages of its development. The continuity of the existence of an English school of composition for no less than five hundred years cannot be denied, even if it must be admitted frankly that at several periods our composers did not rise above mediocrity. Now this unbroken continuity, which is without a parallel in the history of any other European nation, is to be traced almost entirely in the fields of vocal music.

It is noteworthy that the decay of the taste for polyphonic music in the seventeenth century, which was mentioned in the previous chapter, is also to be observed at the same period on the Continent, if only in a less degree than in England, where special causes did so much to hasten it. In foreign ecclesiastical circles it is the case that a good deal of polyphonic music continued in use, but the madrigal, by contrast, did not long survive the harmonic innovations which are usually associated with Monteverde and his disciples in the early years of the century, and which led to such rapid developments in new fields of invention that their very novelty swept away, as in a flood, the devotees of the older types of music, and led also to the sudden rise of the great instrumental composers. When once instrumental music attained its great importance, the cultivation of secular vocal music, outside the range of Opera, and, to a less extent, of Cantata, no longer continued to hold quite the same position among musicians of any nationality ; and in making these exceptions it must be remembered that instrumental music constitutes an all-important feature in their construction. It is difficult to speculate upon what might have happened in England, musically speaking, if the Civil War had never occurred, or if all the prospect of musical development, both vocal and instrumental, on national lines, as laid down by Henry Purcell upon the true foundation of the earlier English schools, had not been completely wrecked a generation later by the coming of Handel to live and work in England. The name of Purcell naturally overshadows those of his contemporaries, such as Pelham Humphreys and John Blow, the importance of whose instrumental work is not generally recognized at its true value ; for example, the harpsichord works of Blow are almost wholly unknown to modern Englishmen, yet it is not too much to say that one set of his pieces closely foreshadows the English Suites of J. S. Bach. It is therefore possible to suppose that giants in instrumental composition might have arisen in this country to compete with the great continental musicians of the eighteenth and nineteenth centuries ; but, be that as it may, it is worth while to emphasize the fact that the English composers at all times, whether in success or only in mediocrity, have in reality been following consistently the normal trend of the national genius which has hitherto always lain chiefly in the direction of singing and of vocal composition.

And not at the close of the Tudor Period alone was English music supreme in Europe. If there are comparatively few English people who appreciate the fact of the supremacy of English music in Elizabethan days, there are far fewer who realize that in the first half of the fifteenth century, also, this country was in the forefront of European music, and that England may be regarded as the cradle of the Art of modern music. And in this connexion it should be recalled that the famous Reading Abbey manuscript which contains the Round *Sumer is y comen in* has absolutely nothing to compare with it in the contemporary musical literature of the Continent; and the date of this composition, so marvellously modern in character, is now usually fixed at about the year 1226. Seeing then that we can trace the lineal descent of the Tudor musicians from the English composers of the early part of the fifteenth century, of whom by far the greatest figure was John Dunstable, it becomes a matter of some importance to mention the remarkable influence which Dunstable and his contemporaries exerted upon the foreign musicians who immediately followed them. For it is agreed that the early Flemish school of composers, under the leadership of Okeghem and Josquin des Pres, owed much to English influence. Johannes Tinctoris, the Flemish theorist (1445–1511), paid a high tribute to English music in the early fifteenth century. He regarded England as the *fons et origo* of the Art, a state of things which he ascribed largely to the rise of the choirs of the Royal chapels in this country, and to the honour and emoluments attached to those institutions, which had the effect of encouraging the study of music. Tinctoris also stated that it was directly due to English influence that the science of the Belgian school of music received so wonderful an enlargement as to make it seem a new Art. The scientific study of music in England at this period is further reflected in the granting of Degrees in Music at the Universities of Oxford and Cambridge, which first took place in the fifteenth century, many generations before similar academic recognition was given to the Art of Music at the leading foreign universities. Tribute to the influence of Dunstable and his English contemporaries is provided in a poem by Martin le Franc, who, about the year 1440, ascribed the superiority of the French school of that time, led by Dufay and Binchois, as compared with that of their predecessors, to the adoption of English methods ; and the following couplet occurs in this poem :

> Et on pris de la contenance
> Angloise, et en suivy Dunstable.

Thomas Ravenscroft in the opening page of his ' Briefe Discourse ', published in 1614, mentions Dunstable as ' the man whom Joan: Nucius in his " Poetical Musicke ", and divers others affirme to be the first that invented composition '. Such a statement undoubtedly goes too far, for indeed no single individual could rightly be termed the inventor of musical composition, and the statement gains little on the assumption that *composition* stood for *counterpoint*. Yet it does serve as evidence of the high esteem in which this early English musician was held on the Continent.

Returning now to the Tudor Period, it can truly be said that in the latter part of the sixteenth century and until a short time after the year 1600 English music stood first in Europe ; and this was all the more indisputably the case after the death of Palestrina in 1594. The Elizabethan musicians added no little lustre to that glorious page of our history which records the deeds of great explorers and the defeat of the Armada ; and the golden age of English Literature was also the golden age of English Music. But quite early in the seventeenth century, as we have already seen, the English school of composers and singers suddenly crumbled away. Now the year 1600 is commonly regarded as constituting the dividing line which separates ancient from modern music, while it also marks the conclusion of the era in which music was developed almost exclusively upon purely vocal lines. Thus the two hundred years or more which preceded 1600 had witnessed the growth of the Art of Music, as it were, from its infancy to its first manhood ; they had also seen the development of the polyphonic type of music from the very embryo to that perfect form of expression that is to be found in the work of Palestrina and of Byrd, and which in its own line has never since been surpassed. But the remarkable point to notice in connexion with all these facts is this : that when the decay of the polyphonic type of music set in, and when, simultaneously, the rise of the great schools of instrumental composition was heralded, English music suddenly ceased to be in the front rank, nor has it ever regained the proud position which it then lost. In fact, just so long as instrumental composition occupied a subordinate position in the scheme of musical development, English musicians were found in the foremost place, but so soon as the relative position of vocal and instrumental music became reversed, the music of this country ceased at that same moment to occupy a position of the first importance. The genius of the race found expression most readily and naturally in vocal music ; when that class of music ceased to monopolize the field, the nation failed to produce composers capable of competing successfully under conditions that were less suited to their traditional instincts. At the same time, though we are forced to acknowledge that England at the close of the Tudor Period ceased to be one of the chief centres of musical composition, we may reflect with pride upon the fact that our own countrymen played the most important part in the nurture of the Art of Music from its infancy up to years of full maturity.

And to this day 'the British nature seems to be adapted to choral singing to a degree which is without comparison on the Continent. No foreign chorus could to-day be found to approach the excellence of some of the famous Yorkshire choirs. The national predilection for, and predisposition to, vocal music is as conspicuous to-day as it has always been. It was this national genius for vocal music that may be said to express itself spontaneously even so early as the thirteenth century in *Sumer is y comen in*, while it was conspicuously evident in John Dunstable's time. Again, it was the recognition of the same inherent taste for this particular class of music that made for the greatness of the Tudor composers. It was this national tendency, too, which showed itself in Purcell's work ; for, important as Purcell is as an instrumental composer, his most valuable work, by far, is in the realms of vocal music. And it may be noted that this fact was appreciated by his contemporaries ; thus, Henry Playford in the ' Address to the Reader ' at the beginning of *Orpheus Britannicus*, the famous collection of Purcell's songs, published in 1698, says as follows : ' his extraordinary talent in all sorts of Musick is sufficiently known, but he was especially admired for the vocal, having a peculiar genius to express the Energy of English words, whereby he moved the Passions of all his Auditors.' It was, again, the same national predilection that rendered Handel intensely popular in his adopted land, and that caused England above all other countries to become the home of Oratorio. In more modern times the tendency may be clearly observed, for instance, in the work of Pearsall and of the younger Wesley. Again, it appears in the present generation in the best work of Parry, of Stanford, and of Elgar—not to mention the names of several other living composers ; it is, moreover, in the vocal department of composition that these musicians have indubitably displayed their most distinctively national characteristics. And, once more, it was this same inherent instinct for vocal music which inspired the founders of the original Madrigal Society in London, and which is chiefly displayed at the present time in the multiplicity of choral and madrigal societies throughout the country, as well as in the competitive-festival movement of recent years, a movement that has led, more than anything else perhaps, to a widespread and growing appreciation of the madrigals of the Elizabethan period.

CHAPTER IV

THE ORIGIN OF THE ENGLISH MADRIGAL
SCHOOL

THE origin of the English Madrigal School is traceable partly to the work of the continental madrigalists, and partly also to that of our own national composers of earlier generations. The practical history of English secular Polyphonic Song may be regarded as dating approximately from 1530, in which year the first known printed set of books of this character was printed by Wynkyn de Worde. The choice of this date as a starting-point must not be taken to imply that nothing of the nature of secular Song for combined voices was attempted before that date, for we have already seen that *Sumer is y comen in* was written as much as three hundred years before that date, and many other compositions could be mentioned to show that secular Polyphonic Song was not wholly unknown in England before 1530. Yet it is only subsequent to this date that it may be regarded as having a continuous history.

Several of the leading English composers in the middle of the sixteenth century wrote some secular vocal music. Among these, Cornish, for example, although most of his important work was written for the Church in the old contrapuntal manner, composed a considerable number of secular pieces, mostly for three voices and in a style much more nearly resembling the Harmonic Part-song than the Madrigal. Very often these compositions took the form of the plain harmonization of some simple old song-tune, well known and popular in its time. This style of secular composition, which was sometimes set to words of a light and humorous character, found a good deal of favour with many of the most prominent English composers until as late a date as 1580 or thereabouts. And even such austere musicians as Tallis and Tye have left some examples of this lighter kind of work ; for instance *Fond youth is a bubble* is one of Tallis's compositions surviving in the Mulliner MS.[1] In this same collection is *In going to my naked bed*, the words of which are by Richard Edwards ; no name is appended to this song in the Mulliner book, but there is no real obstacle to the theory that Edwards wrote both the words and music of this beautiful little work. A correct edition of this song is now available to replace the garbled versions formerly in use.[2] The MS. is as early as 1564 and possibly earlier, and the musical text in its original form is quite in conformity with the style of that date. When this class of secular work was undertaken by the Church composers in the middle of the century, they evidently regarded it as something quite apart from their more serious efforts and as of an experimental nature. Much of it when compared with work of the succeeding generation, as represented by Morley, Weelkes, and Wilbye, is decidedly crude and immature, but Dr. Burney's censure of Whythorne's music as being ' truly barbarous '[3] is wholly unwarranted. It is unfortunate that many subsequent historians have, in various forms, reiterated this censure without, apparently, troubling to score any of Whythorne's compositions ; or in doing so they may have misread the clefs or fallen into some such error as alone could explain their sneering criticism.

Historically speaking, Thomas Whythorne occupies an important position in the development of the English Madrigal ; for his ' Songes of three, fower, and five voyces ', printed in part-books and published in 1571, is the only secular English Set of books of this kind between the twenty songs printed by Wynkyn de Worde in 1530 and Byrd's 1588 Set. Whythorne's Set contains as many as seventy-six compositions. These are very far from approaching the interest and value of the great English madrigalists of a quarter of a century later, but they are not by any means to be dismissed with contempt. To take an illustration : *It doth me good when Zephyrus reigns* (No. 27) shows a great deal of merit and contains several interesting features. The closing bars of the first section may be quoted :

---

[1] Brit. Museum. Add MS. 30513.
[2] Edited by E. H. Fellowes. *Stainer and Bell Ltd.*
[3] Burney's General History of Music, vol. iii, p. 119.

At the conclusion of the whole piece, which is of some length
and has a section in triple time expressing a joyful sentiment,
there is a very interesting little *Codetta*. The song might very
well have ended without these additional three bars, but they
add a good deal in rounding off the form of the composition.

It is improbable that any one has scored many of these songs
of Whythorne, and judgement must be reserved until that has
been done. The present writer scored half a dozen of them
chosen at random ; and the conclusion framed upon this limited
experience is, that this composer has undoubted claims to be
regarded as an important pioneer in the history of English

Part-song, even though his ability cannot be considered as approaching the first class.

But the value of pioneer work is not necessarily to be gauged by its intrinsic merit. The English composers of the middle of the sixteenth century do undoubtedly deserve recognition on the ground that they paved the way for the systematic development of this class of secular music in the form of the Madrigal and the lutenists' Air. Incidentally these composers provide another interesting comparison between Tudor music and Tudor literature, since the position of the earlier madrigalists like Whythorne, when viewed in relation to Wilbye or Dowland, is analogous, in many respects, to that of such pioneers in literature as Wyatt and Surrey when considered in relation to Shakespeare, Spenser, and Sidney. For at this same period, a time of eager intellectual curiosity and endeavour in so many directions, ' when Dawn's left hand was in the sky,' Wyatt and Surrey, spurred on by the ever-widening interest of the day in literature, were attempting new forms of expression in the Sonnet and in various lyric measures. Surrey, too, was making trial of that 'strange metre' blank verse, which Sackville, another innovator of a few years later, was to adopt as the best vehicle of dramatic poetry. And if none of these three were completely successful, they at least, as was the case with their musical contemporaries, laid a sure foundation on which the poets of the next generation built up their enduring verse.

But if the English Madrigal School owes something to its predecessors in our own country, its sudden rise to pre-eminence in the closing decade of the sixteenth century must be ascribed mainly to the influence of the Flemish and Italian schools of madrigalists. It does not seem to be realized, by most of those who indulge in the practice of singing English and Italian madrigals, that the music of the Italian school belongs to a generation that was many years older than that to which the work of the English madrigalists belongs ; the earliest Sets of Arcadelt and Verdelot were published before the year 1540 and were followed by a steady output throughout the century, while very little made its appearance later than 1590. The date of the first Set of secular compositions that can be classed as English Madrigals was 1588, quite fifty years later than the opening of the Flemish-Italian school, and the life of the English school may be said to have extended until about the year 1622, the date of the publication of Tomkins's Set, though two or three Sets were indeed published subsequent to that date. It has already been said that the Flemings owed much to the English composers of Dunstable's time ; thus in dealing with the influence of the foreign madrigalists of the sixteenth century upon our own school at the close of that century we are really tracing back to an influence which emanated originally from England.

The first leader of the great Flemish madrigalists was Adrian Willaert, who was born in Flanders about the year 1480. Like his great followers Arcadelt and Verdelot, who may possibly also have been his pupils, Willaert left his native country to settle in Italy, and he is commonly regarded as the founder of the Venetian school of musicians, while Arcadelt made Rome the centre of his influence. As far as can be ascertained, the earliest actual composer to publish madrigals of the type which the term now generally denotes to musicians was Verdelot, whose first works appeared in a set bearing the title of *Madrigali* in 1535. Another great Fleming at this time was Roland de Lattre, or Lassus, who was born at Mons early in the sixteenth century ; he spent his early manhood in Italy, where he came to be known as Orlando di Lasso, but he lived subsequently at Antwerp, and later at Munich, where he held a Court appointment. But by far the greatest figure in the Italian school was Palestrina, who was born about the year 1528 ; but his fame necessarily rests upon his Church music rather than on his madrigals. In a long life he composed an immense quantity of music the greater part of which was for the Church, yet it includes at least four Sets of madrigals, two of which he described on the title-page as *Madrigali spirituali*. The names of Festa, Marenzio, Anerio, Gastoldi, Converso and others will be familiar to modern madrigal-singers, many of whom will, at some time, have sung English versions of the work of these representative Italian madrigalists.

Madrigal-singing must have been in vogue in England for many years before the appearance in 1588 of Byrd's ' Psalmes, Sonets, and songs ', but it was of course mainly

confined to the work of the foreign composers as being practically the only music of the kind available. And this fashion
was consistent with the Italian influence which showed itself so
conspicuously in all branches of Art and Literature in England
at that time. It has been frequently asserted that the popularity of the Madrigal in this country was entirely due to the
publication of Yonge's collection entitled *Musica Transalpina*
which was published in the same year as, but probably later
than, Byrd's ' Psalmes, Sonets, and songs '. Thus Burney
wrote as follows : [1]

' Our countrymen were not at first taught to admire the
Music of Italy by the sweetness of the language to which it
was originally set . . . but by Italian madrigals with a literal
translation into English adjusted to the original Music and
published by N. Yonge 1588. These being selected from the
works of Palestrina, Luca Marenzio, and other celebrated
masters on the continent seem to have given birth to that
passion for madrigals which became so prevalent among us
afterwards.'

But we have direct evidence that Italian madrigals were
sung in England with their original Italian words at least as
early as 1564. An unusually fine set of four part-books in MS.
exists in the Fellows' library at Winchester College bearing the
date 1564 on one of the initial letters in the Bassus-part of one
of the madrigals. This set of part-books is probably unique.
The original red leather binding is in good condition and each
part-book bears the royal arms of Queen Elizabeth. The
manuscript is beautifully written on vellum, the initial letters
of each composition being illuminated in simple design in colour.
These books contain about seventy four-part Italian *Canzone*
by Willaert, Verdelot, Lassus, Arcadelt, and others, and seventeen French *Chansons* in four parts. They also include, in a later
hand—probably about 1600-5—ten three-part compositions
described as ' Mr. Ford's three parts '; these latter are disappointing from the musical point of view, and it seems unlikely
that the composer is to be identified with Thomas Ford
the lutenist. But the existence of this book, which cannot
have been the only one of its kind, proves conclusively that

[1] Burney's General History of Music, vol. iii, p. 119.

Italian madrigals were being sung in England at the very beginning of Queen Elizabeth's reign.

It is also a fact that many of the compositions in Byrd's 1588 Set are to be found in a very fine set of manuscript part-books in the Christ Church library which bear the date 1581.[1]

On the other hand the popularity of the Italian madrigals in England was evidently stimulated by such publications as *Musica Transalpina*. Nicholas Yonge, who edited this collection, appears to be identical with a lay-clerk of the name at St. Paul's Cathedral; he gathered round him, at his house in St. Michael's, Cornhill, as he tells us in the Dedication of his first collection, ' a great number of Gentlemen and Merchants of good accompt (as well of this realme as of forreine nations) ' . . . for the ' exercise of Musicke daily '. Yonge also furnished them with music-books yearly sent him from Italy. The cult of the Italian Madrigal was further stimulated by a second volume of *Musica Transalpina* compiled by Yonge and published in 1597, and also by the efforts of Thomas Morley, who issued in 1597 a collection of Italian Canzonets for four voices with English words, and another of the same kind for five voices in the year 1598.

It seems strange that madrigal-writing should not have been attempted by English composers till so late a date. The only explanation ready to hand is that the production of Church music fully occupied the minds of Taverner, Tallis, Tye, and Whyte, except for the occasional work of their lighter moments to which allusion has already been made. The upheaval of the Reformation movement naturally touched English music very closely, and the publication of the Prayer-Book, with its greatly changed type of ritual, created a demand for Church music of a new character. The religious reaction which followed the death of Edward VI delayed this demand until the reign of Queen Elizabeth, but it was then met by a liberal output of Church music which must have taxed the time and energies of the composers to their full extent. But, even so, it is remarkable that madrigal-composition remained so long unattempted in England; and it may be noticed that Byrd, who was born as early as 1543, yet did not publish any secular vocal

---

[1] Christ Church, Oxford, MSS. 984–8.

compositions, as far as we know, before reaching the age of 45, even though, as we have just seen, many of them had been composed some years earlier. The one Set of compositions that stands out as a somewhat curious and isolated landmark in this period is Thomas Whythorne's, which, as has already been said, marks a praiseworthy effort on the part of the composer and anticipates the greater successes which were to be achieved a quarter of a century later. The same composer issued a second Set in 1590, but these, oddly enough, resemble the Madrigal less closely in character; they consist of ' Duos, or Songs for two voices . . . The first (part) for a man and a childe to sing, or otherwise for voices or Instruments of Musicke . . . The second . . . for two children . . . otherwise for voices or Musicall Instruments . . . the third part . . . with voices or Instruments.' The first twelve pieces are set to words from the Psalms, and the rest have only the opening phrase of the words printed with the music, a plan which was followed by East in his Fifth Set of Books, and occasionally elsewhere, although a satisfactory explanation of this plan has yet to be discovered.

The coming of the English Madrigal was long delayed; but when once the idea was started, there followed immediately an amazing flow of such compositions. Yet the period of the English madrigal-composers was almost as remarkable for its brevity as for its brilliance, for by far the larger part of the output was issued within the limits of twenty-five years. It is of no little importance in criticizing the works of the madrigalists, and more especially in considering the individual work of any one of these composers in relation to that of his contemporaries, to have a clear view of the order and dates of the various Sets. We are fortunate in knowing with some degree of completeness what Sets were published by the madrigalists; several of these Sets are now represented by only one known exemplar, yet very few seem to have perished entirely. A sheet catalogue of ' Musick bookes printed in England ' was published by Thomas East (or Este) in 1609. This catalogue was afterwards included, with additions, in Clavell's ' General Catalogue of Books printed in England since the dreadful Fire of London 1666', published in 1675.[1] The following is a synopsis showing the

---

[1] Rimbault's *Bibliotheca Madrigaliana*, p. 14.

dates of publication of the strictly madrigalian Sets; such
Sets as those of Martin Peerson do not figure in this list.

1588.	Psalms, Sonnets and Songs for 5 voices . . .	*Byrd*
1589.	Songs of sundry natures, for 3, 4, 5, and 6 parts . .	*Byrd*
1593.	Canzonets to 3 voices	*Morley*
1594.	Songs and Psalms for 3, 4, and 5 parts . . .	*Mundy*
	Madrigals to 4 voices	*Morley*
1595.	Ballets of 5 voices	*Morley*
	Canzonets to 2 voices	*Morley*
1597.	Madrigals to 3, 4, 5, and 6 voices	*Weelkes*
	Madrigals to 4, 5, and 6 voices	*Kirbye*
	Canzonets to 5 and 6 voices	*Morley*
	Canzonets to 3 voices (in Anthony Holborne's Citthern School)	*Wm. Holborne*
	Songs of sundry natures	*Pattrick*
1598.	Madrigals to 3, 4, 5 and 6 voices	*Wilbye*
	Ballets and Madrigals to 5 voices	*Weelkes*
	Canzonets to 4 voices	*Farnaby*
	Airs (exact title unknown), including 8 Madrigals for 5 voices.	*Cavendish*
1599.	Madrigals to 4 voices	*Farmer*
	Madrigals to 4 voices	*Bennet*
1600.	Madrigals of 5 parts	*Weelkes*
	Madrigals of 6 parts	*Weelkes*
1601.	Triumphs of Oriana for 5 and 6 voices . . .	ed. by *Morley*
	Madrigals to 5 voices	*Carlton*
1604.	Madrigals to 3, 4, and 5 parts	*East*
	Madrigals to 3, 4, 5, and 6 voices	*Bateson*
	Songs of sundry kinds (including 6 Madrigals for 5 voices)	*Greaves*
1606.	Madrigals to 3, 4, 5, and 6 voices	*East*
	An hour's recreation.	*Alison*
1607.	Madrigals of 3, 4, 5, 6, 7, and 8 parts . . .	*Jones*
1608.	Airs or Fantastic spirits for 3 voices	*Weelkes*
	Canzonets to 3 voices	*Youll*
1609.	Madrigals to 3, 4, 5, and 6 voices	*Wilbye*
1610.	Pastorals, Anthems, Neapolitans, Fancies, and Madrigals, to 5 and 6 parts	*East*
1611.	Psalms, Songs and Sonnets	*Byrd*
1612.	Madrigals and Motets of 5 parts	*Gibbons*
1613.	Madrigals to 3, 4, 5, and 6 parts	*Ward*
	Madrigals and Pastorals of 3, 4, and 5 parts . .	*Pilkington*
	Madrigals of 5 parts	*Lichfild*
1618.	Madrigals to 3, 4, 5, and 6 parts	*Bateson*
	Anthems, Madrigals, and Songs to 4, 5, and 6 parts .	*East*
1619.	Songs of divers airs and natures of 5 and 6 parts .	*Vautor*
1622.	Songs of 3, 4, 5, and 6 parts	*Tomkins*
1624.	Madrigals and Pastorals of 3, 4, 5, and 6 parts . .	*Pilkington*
1627.	Airs or Fa-las for 3 voices	*Hilton*

The opportunity of the English madrigalists was a very
exceptional one. They enjoyed all the advantage that could

be reaped from the experience of the Italians with their perfect model, their beautifully smooth style, and their faultless technique. Their work followed the Italian design in its main features ; but it bore a distinctive national stamp, and it even surpassed the work of the Italians in vitality and in the fertility and variety of imaginative expression, as well as in the boldness and originality of harmonic treatment. The very fact that the English madrigalists delayed their appearance until this late epoch was in itself a source of liberty which they were not slow to recognize ; for by that time harmonic revolution was in the air, and the fetters which had bound fast the older generation of composers by the rigid rules of the modes were showing the first signs of giving way, albeit modal characteristics are abundantly evident throughout the music of these English composers. They were also singularly fortunate in being able to draw their inspiration from contemporary poetry at a moment when the national literature reached its actual high-water mark. But if their opportunity was a great one, it was certainly grasped to the very full, and they left behind them an imperishable and priceless inheritance for English musicians of all time.

CHAPTER V

ETYMOLOGY AND USE OF THE TERM
MADRIGAL

THE meaning and origin of the word Madrigal seems to have baffled etymologists of all nationalities for at least three centuries. The term was first employed, as far as can be ascertained, by the rustics of Northern Italy possibly as early as the twelfth century, and it first found its way into Italian literature about the beginning of the fourteenth century. At that period also the term was employed in connexion with musical compositions of a somewhat elaborate style, as examples of which Mr. Wooldridge printed in the ' Oxford History of Music '[1] three important pieces by Francesco di Landino, Maestro Piero, and Zacharias.

The term, as denoting a form of musical composition, subsequently fell into abeyance for considerably more than a century; but in the meanwhile the Madrigal, though apparently no longer set to music, seems to have survived in the form of poetry, and hence the explanation of the ultimate use of the word for a particular type of lyric, although it had an exclusively musical significance. Variant forms of the word in use in this interim period were *madriale* and more commonly *mandriale*. The word was revived as a musical term in Italy by the Flemish composers soon after the year 1530, and the earliest known volume of musical pieces at the period of that revival to bear the definite description of *madrigali* was published in 1533. This volume consisted mainly of the works of Verdelot. The Flemish and Italian musicians built upon the foundation laid two centuries earlier by Landino and his contemporaries; they retained something of the characteristics of their design, although their style was necessarily more modern as regards detail and more fully developed; also their principles in setting words to music were different. But in reviving the old term they preserved the continuity of idea and thus added much to the historical interest of their

[1] Oxford History of Music, vol. ii, p. 51 et seq.

own work. After the year 1533 the name *madrigale* was used consistently by the continental composers, and it found its way to England in the form of *madrigal* in the latter part of the same century. The original meaning of the word had evidently been completely forgotten before it was recalled into use by the Flemish and Italian musicians, and it would seem that the madrigal-writers of the sixteenth century, whether English or foreign, regarded the term primarily as denoting a musical composition set to words of a pastoral character even though their madrigals were by no means limited to pastoral subjects.

The word was first used of an English composition in Nicholas Yonge's first Set of *Musica Transalpina* in 1588, for by including a composition of William Byrd, Yonge thus classed it definitely as a Madrigal. The term was not employed by Byrd himself in his 'Psalmes, Sonets, and Songs of Sadnes and Pietie', published earlier in the same year, yet this volume may be fairly regarded as containing the earliest specimens of original English madrigals. For Byrd divided the volume into four sections, the second of which he called 'Sonnets and pastorals'. Now in this section is Byrd's original Italian version of *La Virginella*, the English translation of which was inserted in Yonge's collection, and it was there classed as a Madrigal ; and in this same section we also find such characteristic madrigals—though they are not actually so styled—as *As I beheld a herdman wild* (No. 20), *Though Amaryllis dance in green* (No. 12), and other thoroughly madrigalian pieces. Presumably Byrd used the term *pastoral* as being the English equivalent of the Italian *madrigale*, but *madrigal* very quickly superseded *pastoral* and established itself as a recognized word in our language.

It was Thomas Morley who first used the term on the title-page of a set of original compositions of this type. His 'First Booke of Madrigalls to Foure Voyces ' was published in 1594. Yet even Morley confessed that he was wholly at a loss to explain the etymology of the word.[1] And since Morley's time until latterly no better success was achieved in this direction, although several ingenious theories have been put forward at

---

[1] Morley's Plain and Easy Introduction to Practical Music, p. 178.

different times. The eighteenth-century historian Hawkins confessed himself unable to give any satisfactory derivation to the word.[1] This writer tells us further that Kircher laboured in vain to find an etymology for it ; and that Huet, Bishop of Avranches, in his treatise *De l'Origine des Romans* supposed it to be a corruption of the word *martegaux*, a name given to the ancient inhabitants of a part of Provence, who, so Huet averred, were probably the inventors of, or excelled in this particular species of composition. Hawkins added the caustic comment that had Huet known that there is a small town in Spain named Madrigal, it is likely he would have ascribed the origin of madrigals to the Spaniards. The same historian also cites Doni, a writer on music in the early seventeenth century, as suggesting the derivation from the Italian word *mandra*, a flock, but adds the objection that ' pastoral manners are not peculiar to this kind of poetical composition '. And, once again, Hawkins states that Crescimbeni, and some years later Mattheson, took up the inquiry but left the matter nearly where they found it. In more modern times neither Rimbault [2] nor Oliphant [3] could throw any new light upon the subject, their researches amounting to little more than a repetition of Hawkins's information. Rimbault, however, quoted from Salvadore Corticelli's work *Della Toscana Eloquenza*, in which is given the derivation from *mandra* on the ground of the pastoral character of the compositions, with the additional information that the songs were also called *madriale* and *mandriale* in early days.

Comparatively recently the much-disputed subject of the derivation of the word Madrigal has been handled in so complete and convincing a manner by Signor Leandro Biadene,[4] who, as Professor of neo-Latin Philology in the University of Pisa, is, of course, qualified to deal with the question with the full weight of authority, that it is not too much to say that the problem has at length been solved.

[1] Hawkins's General History of the Science and Practice of Music, vol. ii, p. 463.
[2] Dr. E. F. Rimbault's *Bibliotheca Madrigaliana* (1847), Preface, p. vi.
[3] Thomas Oliphant's A short account of Madrigals (1836), pp. 5–6.
[4] Article by L. Biadene in the *Rassegna bibliografica della letteratura italiana*, vol. vi, pp. 329, &c. (Pisa, 1898).

Discussing, in the first place, the traditional and stereotyped view that the word was derived from *mandra* and that its earliest form was *mandriale* which subsequently became *madriale* and finally *madrigale*, Biadene mentions that this opinion was accepted by all the earlier Italian writers and that it was incorporated in all the principal dictionaries, including the *della Crusca* and that of *Tommaseo* as well as in the less important works of the kind, not only in Italy but also in other countries. Unfortunately the New English Dictionary, although it has been published since Biadene wrote this essay, followed the same line. Littré, whose French dictionary appeared in 1872, also gave *mandra* as the derivation, but nevertheless made the noticeable observation that the primitive form in low Latin was *matriale*, and he quoted a Latin writer of the fourteenth century who described a remarkable boy who could sing 'matrialia etiam difficillima'. Scheler, in his Dictionary of French etymology, published in 1873, went so far as to state that all the theories as to the derivation of the word *madrigal* had become suspect since the discovery of a Latin writer of the fourteenth century who employed the word *matrialia* to denote a species of musical composition.

Biadene goes on to prove by carefully reasoned argument not only that the traditional theory of the derivation of the word from *mandra* through the successive forms *mandriale*, *madriale*, and *madrigale*, was in conflict with all the rules of Italian etymology, but actually that the reverse order of successive development of these different forms of the word was in strict accordance with facts that can be cited. Thus, he argued, if *mandriale*, derived from *mandra*, was the original form of the word, the excision of the *n* to make it *madriale* has no parallel in the Italian language. The writer says it is remarkable that Covarruvias was the only authority who appears to have noticed this fact and to have appreciated the difficulty constituted by it, while unfortunately the explanation which Covarruvias attempted to offer was founded upon error. Again, the addition of the *g*, by which *madriale* has usually been supposed to have turned into *madrigale*, cannot be explained by any known rule of Italian etymology, although the reverse process is simply accounted for. Moreover, Biadene states that he knows of no other Italian word with the termination *igále*.

So much for destructive criticism. On the constructive side this writer then develops his own theory. The earliest recorded examples of the word in any form are, he says, to be found in the writings of Francesco da Barbarino and Antonio da Tempo in the early years of the fourteenth century. Barbarino, in a work entitled *De variis inveniendi et rimandi modis* which was reprinted in recent years by Signor O. Antognoni,[1] says, in defining distinctions between various kinds of composition, ' Voluntarium est rudium inordinatum concinium, ut matricale et similia '. Shortly afterwards, in the year 1332, da Tempo[2] wrote ' mandrialis est rithimus ille qui vulgariter appelatur marigalis '. After explaining that the term *mandrialis* was independently employed as being derived from *mandra* for the reason that this kind of rhyming and singing came originally from the shepherds who sang and played to simple words of an amatory and rustic character, differing from that of the ordinary kinds of rhyme, da Tempo proceeds, ' Sonus vero marigalis secundum modernum cantum debet esse pulcher et in cantu habere aliquas partes rusticales sive mandriales, ut cantus consonet cum verbis.' In writing the word *marigalis* da Tempo, as a Venetian, would have naturally omitted the *d*, for it was the custom throughout all northern Italy both to pronounce and hear *madre* as *mare*; thus the word *marigalis* quoted by da Tempo as the term ordinarily employed to denote this class of song in his day was none other than *madrigalis*. When we recall Barbarino's use of the word *matricale* in the passage just quoted and recognize that this word exactly corresponds to the Italian form *madrigale*, we may reasonably infer that the word *madrigale*, with its variant form *marigale*, was in common use among the rustic people of Italy at least as early as the thirteenth century, even though it may not have found its way into literature before the fourteenth.

From *madrigale*, Biadene proceeds, it is but a short step to *madriale* as used by Sacchetti, Soldamieri, and others in the second half of the fourteenth century, for there are numbers of

[1] *Giornale di filologia romanza*, vol. iv, pp. 93 et seq.   [2] Op. cit., p. 139.

similar instances of the elimination of the g : for example, *legale—leale*, and *regale—reale*.

We have yet to account for *mandriale*, the term which was undoubtedly used in the fourteenth century to denote short pastoral poems, as for instance, by da Tempo in 1332 in the passage just quoted. Signor Biadene is of opinion that this word originated in the fusion of the words *madriale* and *mandria* and thus had quite an independent origin ; he suggests that this fusion was brought about by the *letterati* of the time, seeing that pastoral songs of a particular type were called *madriali* and that the Italian word *mandria* meant a herd (Latin *mandra* and Greek μάνδρα, a fold). The true etymological order of succession of the forms of the word is : (1) *matricalis* ; (2) *madrigale*, with the variant *marigale* ; (3) *madriale* ; (4) *mandriale* ; and it is noteworthy that the musicians in 1533 revived the original form *madrigale*.

It only remains to deal with the question as to how the neo-Latin word *matricalis* came to be applied to this use. Signor Biadene goes fully into the use of this adjective and shows how it acquired a meaning which was virtually synonymous with *materna* ; and as *lingua materna* means the mother tongue, or the vernacular or simplest form of language, so *cantus matricalis*, which is not far removed from the use of *matricalia* for songs, may reasonably be taken to stand for the simple and primitive songs of the rustics. In this matter the words of da Tempo are much to the point : [1]

' Primo modum illum rithmandi et cantandi habuimus ab ovium pastoribus. Nam pastores tamquam rustici et homines grossi primo coeperunt amoris venerei circa compilare verba grossa et ipsa cantare et in suis tibiis sonare modo grosso sed tamen naturaliter.'

Before leaving the subject of the origin of the word Madrigal, it is interesting to observe how near the true solution of the problem those etymologists came who suggested that it was derived from *madre* ; and further, how they lost the scent by pursuing the theory that these songs might originally have been addressed to the Holy Virgin.

The obscurity which veiled the etymology of the word

[1] *Giornale di filologia romanza*, vol. iv, p. 139.

Madrigal for so long a period, may perhaps be held accountable for the loose and indefinite manner in which that term has been employed, not only by musicians, but also in English literature. Poets and other writers have frequently treated the term as no more than an euphonious synonym for Song. In this simple sense Marlowe wrote the couplet :

> By shallow rivers to whose falls
> Melodious birds sing madrigals.

The pastoral character which is a feature of so many madrigals was plainly alluded to in Sir William Alexander's line :

> Those madrigals we sing amidst our flocks.

Neither Marlowe nor Alexander, who wrote in 1614, would have had in their mind the technical meaning with which the term was invested by the musicians who were their contemporaries. Another contemporary writer, Robert Greene, used the expression ' doleful madrigals of sorrow '. Here again the word is no more than a synonym for song, and the quotation must not be pressed in reference to the serious and sad type of madrigal such as is so often overlooked by those who in more modern days use the term. Nor can the word, as used by Jackson in 1640 in the following rather startling passage, be taken for more than an alternative for song, although the imitative character of madrigal-music may have been present in the writer's mind in regard to the repetition of the word *crucifige* :

' Changing their late joyful hymns of Hosanna to the Son of David into sad madrigals of Crucifige, crucifige.'

Milton might appear to have had solo-song in his mind when he wrote the couplet :

> Who shall silence all the airs and madrigals
> That whisper softness in chambers.

But Milton would have known the exact technical meaning applied to the word by musicians, for his own father was one of the contributors to Morley's famous collection of madrigals known as the ' Triumphs of Oriana ' ; and the association of ' airs and madrigals ' in this passage must carry with it a reference to the special use of both those terms by musicians at the beginning of the seventeenth century.

And poets of later days undoubtedly used the attractive word as a mere alternative for Song in such passages as Campbell's :

> And oft amidst the lonely rocks
> She sings sweet madrigals.

Or Henley's description of the May thrush's song as :

> Gay golden-vowelled madrigals.

Charles Dickens may have been thinking of the 'Triumphs of Oriana', made 'in praise of Elizabeth', when he used the phrase in ' Dombey and Son ' : ' And gentle Mr. Toots . . . likewise hears the requiem of little Dombey on the waters, rising and falling in the lulls of their eternal madrigal in praise of Florence.'

The history of the Madrigal as an Art-form can be discussed in very few words. Dealing with the earliest type as represented in the work of Francesco di Landino and his contemporaries, Mr. Wooldridge has described in the ' Oxford History of Music '[1] a very definite and somewhat elaborate form that governed this species of composition in the fourteenth century, when it first assumed a position among musical compositions of a scientific kind and had been raised far above the rustic type of song of which da Tempo wrote. The following quotation from the madrigal *Tu che l'opera d'altrui*[2] by Francesco di Landino, the blind organist of San Lorenzo in Florence, who was born in 1325 and was leader of the Florentine school of musicians, will give an idea of the type of madrigal in vogue at that period. This piece, which is printed more fully in the ' Oxford History of Music ', is for two voices, and in spite of the length of the notes it should be performed at a fairly fast *tempo* of four minims in a bar. There were, of course, no bars in the original version of this music. The imitative passages foreshadow those of the sixteenth-century madrigalists in a remarkable manner ; but it will be noticed that the principles which governed the setting of the words differ even more widely from those of the sixteenth-century musicians than do those of the Tudor madrigalists from those of our own time. The practice of employing but one syllable over a very lengthy

---

[1] Oxford History of Music, vol. ii, p. 49.
[2] Florence, *Bibl. Mediceo-Laurenziana*, Cod. Ned. Palatino, 87.

musical phrase, or even a series of phrases divided by rests, was strongly condemned by Morley,[1] who quoted from the music of Dunstable in illustration of his point, and condemned such passages as the work of a dunce! Morley in this instance was guilty of the error of criticizing the art-work of one generation by the standard of another.

---

[1] Morley's Plain and Easy Introduction, p. 178.

In discussing the Flemish revival of the Madrigal in the sixteenth century Mr. Wooldridge states [1] that the composition was studiously simple both in form and style of melody, the music following the metrical structure closely, yet enriching it with graceful points of imitation and the simpler forms of ornamental cadence. The Flemings pursued a cautious way and kept within the outlines of the original models ; but the Italian madrigalist Constanzio Festa opened out a new path which led to the broadly ornate form in which madrigal-writing eventually arrived at perfection. It would not be easy to improve upon Mr. Wooldridge's sketch of the outline of madrigal-structure, for it never was bound by any such rigid or regularly moulded shape as could be prescribed by a formula or a schedule of rules like those associated with later forms of musical composition.

The English madrigalists followed very much upon the same lines of design and construction, such as they were. They too dealt with the metrical structure of the words line by line, or phrase by phrase, thus often dividing up the work into well-defined sections ; and each short phrase within the section was itself usually repeated ; a very general, but by no means strict, practice being for each voice to repeat such a phrase three times. And this principle is certainly one of the most distinctive features of the stricter kind of Madrigal as compared

<hr />

[1] Oxford History of Music, vol. ii, pp. 286, 290.

with its kindred Art-forms. Yet they rarely allowed all the voice-parts to come to an end simultaneously at any one point except to enforce some well-defined close in the poetry, but by a process of skilful dovetailing they joined section to section. They adhered to the convention of the day in using the major triad at all full closes of importance. They displayed a keen sense of accurate verbal accentuation, together with a fine appreciation of the poetry which they wedded to their music. They employed a great variety of texture and rhythm. They expressed every kind of mood, whether of joy or sorrow, by the employment of suggestive harmony or discord with never-failing resource. By semi-pictorial methods they gave colour to ideas of motion or flight through the use of rapid musical phrases ; and by lengthy and sustained notes and by strongly suspended harmonies they suggested repose or languishing despair. This was the type of detail which they studied and cared for, rather than any conventional subserviency to musical rule or formality of design ; and it was this feature which enabled them to achieve such glorious success.

CHAPTER VI

ELIZABETHAN MADRIGALS AND KINDRED CONTEMPORARY ART-FORMS

IT is more than a little remarkable that the Elizabethan composers themselves were quite inconsequent in applying the titles to their published works. For this purpose they made use of a large number of terms besides Madrigal ; among these were Canzonet, Ballet, Fa-la, Motet, Air, Song, Pastoral, Neapolitan, and others.

Before discussing these terms in detail it may not be out of place to refer to Morley's remarks on some of the different types of composition of this class.[1] But Morley was dealing with the subject from the point of view of Italian music rather than English, although he does not actually say so, for he was writing before the great bulk of English madrigals had been produced. Thus, for instance, he concludes with the *Villanella* and the *Vinate*, which he describes as representing ' the last two degrees of gravity, if they have any at all ' ; and neither of these forms are to be found among the published works of the English madrigalists. Morley makes a quaint comment in reference to the *Vinate* :—' They have framed this to be sung in their drinking : but that vice being so rare among the Italians and Spaniards I rather think that musick to have been devised for the Germains (who in swarmes do flock to the University of Italy) rather than for the Italians them selves.'

Morley dealt in the first place with the Motet, which he described as ' properlie a song made for the church either upon some hymne or Antheme or such like '. But he did not limit the term to Church music, as some writers have since done, for he included under this heading ' al grave and sober musicke ' ; and his definition explains the use of the term by Orlando Gibbons, whose one volume in this class of composition bore the title ' Madrigals and Mottets of 5. Parts '. No further indication appears in the body of this book by which to determine how

---

[1] Morley's Plain and Easy Introduction, p. 179.

these alternative titles were to be applied to the individual
pieces ; but it may be assumed that the compositions of
a specially serious and introspective character, of which
several examples occur in the Set, suggested the employment
of the term Motet as being more suitable than the alternative
Madrigal. And Martin Peerson gave the title to his volume
published in 1630 ' Mottects, or Grave Chamber Musique '.

Passing from Motet to Madrigal, Morley says, ' The light
musicke hath beene of late more deeply dived into, so that
there is no vanitie which in it hath not been followed to the
ful : but the best kind of it is termed Madrigal, a word for the
etymologie of which I can give no reason : yet use sheweth
that it is a kind of musicke made upon songs and sonnets, such
as Petrarcha and manie Poets of our time have excelled in. . . .
As for the musicke it is next unto the Motet the most artificial,[1]
and to men of understanding the most delightfull. If therefore
you will compose in this kind you must possess your self with
an amorous humor . . . so that you must in your musick be
wavering like the wind, somtime wanton, somtime drooping,
somtime grave and staide, otherwhile effeminat, you may
maintaine points and revert them, use triplaes and shew the
verie uttermost of your varietie, and the more varietie you
shew the better shal you please.' It will be seen that in this
delightful sketch of what a madrigal should be Morley did not
give any kind of definition as to its structure. There is no
doubt that the English composers took a wider view than the
Italians of what a madrigal might be. They did not limit its
meaning to pastoral subjects or to the lighter type of conceit,
but, desiring to express themselves in a more serious vein, they
included all subjects, both grave and gay, among their Sets ;
yet the term Madrigal was retained without discrimination in
this matter, and so it came to have a much more comprehensive
meaning. Morley's 1594 volume has already been mentioned as
being the first English Set in which the actual title of Madrigal
was used ; and this was the only Set so entitled at the time
when the Plain and Easy Introduction was written. The only
other Sets published with that title before Wilbye's first Set
appeared in 1598 were Kirbye's Set and Weelkes's first Set,

[1] The word is used here in its old sense, meaning full of artifice.

both of which were published in 1597. This Set of Weelkes's included his wonderful three-part madrigal, *Cease, sorrows, now* (No. 6), which was not only an entirely new departure from a harmonic point of view, as we shall see in a later chapter, but was probably the earliest example of the serious type of English madrigal to bear the name. But from 1598 onward, when Wilbye established the serious madrigal as a recognized form of composition, the term was much more generally used on the title-pages. Thus it came to denote almost any secular composition written at that period in the imitative contrapuntal style, and this enlargement of its meaning accounts partly for the very indiscriminate use that came to be made of it by the English composers in describing their works.

' The second degree of gravitie in this light musicke ', said Morley, ' is given to Canzonets, that is little short songs (wherein little art can be shewed being made in strains, the beginning of which is som point lightly touched, and every strain repeated except the middle) which is in the composition of the Musicke a counterfet of the Madrigal.' Here is all the appearance of a strict definition ; yet an examination of the canzonets of Morley himself, as well as of other Elizabethan composers, shows that the form of the Canzonet was shaped upon no fixed rule. In accordance with his own definition, Morley always added in the title-pages of his Canzonets the words ' or Little Short Airs ', thus implying that they were designed on a smaller scale than Madrigals. Yet his *I follow lo the footing*, and *Stay, heart, run not so fast* (Nos. 17 and 18 of his Canzonets to five and six voices) are classed as Canzonets, while *April is in my mistress' face* (No. 1 of Morley's Madrigals to four voices) is a Madrigal, although the last named is on a much smaller model. Again, Farmer and Farnaby each published a volume of compositions of very similar calibre within a year of each other ; but whereas Farnaby gave his pieces the title of Canzonet, Farmer's were called Madrigals. The Canzonet was, of course, borrowed from the Italian *Canzona* and the *Chanson* of the Flemish School. *Chanson,* as denoting a composition for several voice-parts, seems to have been employed even before the revival of the term *madrigale* by the early sixteenth-century musicians on the Continent.

The term Pastoral has already been mentioned as having been used by Byrd in his first secular volume in 1588 as an English equivalent of the Italian *madrigale*. But the word continued in occasional use long after Madrigal had come to be generally employed. For example, it occurs in Michael East's third Book in 1610; and Pilkington used it in both his Sets of ' Madrigals and Pastorals ', though there is nothing in the music of those Sets that marks any distinguishing characteristic between the several compositions.

Neopolitan was a term commonly employed by the Italians, but rarely to be met with in the English madrigal-literature. East employed it in his third Book, but the style of the pieces so named is in every respect similar to the Madrigals and Pastorals in the Set. Morley speaks of ' Neapolitans differing from canzonets in nothing save in name '.

The most distinctive term used by the madrigalists was the Ballet, for which *Fa-la* was sometimes substituted as a more colloquial alternative. The Ballet had its origin as far back as the fourteenth century and was known in all musical countries ; thus the Italian *Ballata* of that period corresponded to, and was perhaps derived from, the French *Chanson balladée*. An essential feature of the Ballet of the English madrigalists, like that of their Italian predecessors in the same century, was the introduction, at the end of each section, of a florid and rhythmical passage vocalized to the syllables *Fa la la*. This type of refrain was employed with great effect in this unaccompanied vocal music for much the same purpose as that for which short instrumental interludes are introduced in contrast to vocal passages in other types of choral composition. With rare exceptions the *Fa-la* formed no actual part of the poem itself; but it provided the material for these vocalized sections in the simplest and most suitable shape. Occasionally some other syllable or word was substituted. Weelkes used *No, no, no* in *Say, dainty nymphs, shall we go play?* (No. 9 of his Ballets); and Morley gave *Lirum lirum* for the refrain of *You that wont to my pipes' sound* (Morley's Ballets, No. 13). The Ballet was of a much more regular and simple rhythm in all its sections than the other types of composition of the period. This was due to the fact that in its more primitive form it was a combina-

tion of singing and dancing. Morley mentioned this feature
of the Ballet:[1] 'There be also another kind of Ballets, commonly called Fa las . . . a slight kind of musick it is, and I take
it devised to be danced to voices.' It is evident the Ballets
were not danced by Elizabethan singers; but the dance-
rhythms were ever present in the minds both of the composers
and singers, and this should be remembered by modern singers
in performing these old vocal ballets. Morley stated that
Gastoldi, the Italian madrigalist, was the originator of the
Fa-la. It is possible that Gastoldi did much to popularize it,
but there are earlier examples than his.

A large number of English people at the present day regard
the *Fa-la* refrain as the distinguishing feature of the Madrigal.
This erroneous idea may be due to the comparatively large
number of Elizabethan ballets that have been reprinted,
a number out of proportion to the madrigal-compositions of
all other types which have survived from that period. Sulli-
van's part-song or so-called 'madrigal' in *The Mikado* has
done much to perpetuate this error in modern days.

Only three complete Sets of Ballets with this actual title were
published by the English madrigalists in their own time, one
by Morley in 1595, and one by Weelkes in 1598. The Airs or
Fa-las of the younger Hilton, published in 1627, have only
a small artistic importance. Several other madrigal-Sets
included a small proportion of *Fa-las*. Tomkins ranks with
Morley and Weelkes as a writer of *Fa-las*. He had the advantage of writing at a later date than these, but he had sufficient
genius to add something new to the Ballet; his *See, see the
shepherds' Queen* (No. 17 of the Set) has three distinct sections,
each with its *Fa-la*, as compared with the conventional two
sections of the earlier English and Italian model. Some very
fine specimens of Tomkins's work are entirely madrigalian in
character, even though a *Fa-la* refrain is introduced. For it
does not necessarily follow that the presence of a *Fa-la* makes
the composition a Ballet; in the true Ballet a regularly defined
dance-rhythm must be maintained throughout all the sections.
A very fine example of the use of the *Fa-la* refrain in a composition that cannot possibly be described as a Ballet is Weelkes's

---

[1] Morley's Plain and Easy Introduction, p. 180.

O care, thou wilt despatch me (Nos. 4 and 5 of his Madrigals for five voices). There the careworn man appeals to Music to cheer him, and the subtle imagination of Weelkes led him at this point to write a *Fa-la* in the usual merry rhythm of crotchets and quavers, but at a slower *tempo* and clothed with harmonies which vividly depict the unsuccessful effort towards gaiety.[1]

A good illustration of the indiscriminate use of their terminology by the madrigalists is provided in Morley's Book of Ballets; this book contains several pieces which cannot possibly be styled Ballets and have no *Fa-la* refrain; yet nothing is said either on the title-page, or elsewhere in the volumes, drawing any distinction between these and the rest.

The Catch, or Round, was alluded to in Chapter I of the present work, but it calls for further mention here as having been in vogue in the Tudor period, although it is quite distinct from the Madrigal even in the most comprehensive meaning of that word. The form of the Round was designed for three or more voices singing the same melody, each voice entering at an independent point, and the overlapping effect resulting in musical harmony. The earliest known Round is *Sumer is y comen in,* but the form itself is so popular that it has continued to enjoy a vigorous existence ever since the thirteenth century. It is not strictly correct to apply the term Canon to this form of vocal music, for that word has in later days acquired an exclusive meaning of its own ; but Canon was in fact used by Ravenscroft, as well as by other Tudor musicians, as a synonym for Catch or Round. Between the years 1609 and 1611 Ravenscroft edited three volumes, consisting mainly of Rounds, but including also some folk-songs and tavern-songs ; they were entitled *Pammelia, Deuteromelia,* and *Melismata.* The contemporary versions of such traditional Rounds as *Three blind mice* and *Frog he would a wooing go,* besides many other well-known nursery rhymes, are to be found in these books. A manuscript collection of Rounds, made by one David Melvill in the early years of the seventeenth century, has recently been printed for the Roxburgh Club ; it contains a large number of examples that are also to be found in the Ravenscroft volumes.

The Air, so often spelt Ayre in the original editions of these

---

[1] This madrigal is more fully analysed on p. 198.

works, is the only term that remains for consideration. This word was used by the Tudor composers with greater variety of meaning than any other of these terms. Morley [1] regarded it as being applicable to Ballets 'and all other kinds of light musick saving the madrigal ', and he was quite consistent in using it as an alternative to Canzonet in his title-pages. Weelkes called his last volume ' Ayeres or Phantasticke Spirites '. But since, as we have already seen, many Canzonets are indistinguishable from Madrigals, and that madrigal-form is itself indefinite, it is difficult to follow Morley in his statement, more especially as his own *Hark! Alleluia* (No. 21) was classed by him as a ' Canzonet or little short air to six voices ', for it would be ridiculous to describe this particular composition as a ' kind of light musick '.

At the same time a close study of the whole subject shows that this term denoted very much what it does in modern days, namely, a tune. For the Airs of the lutenists involve little if any verbal repetition ; and the same thing may be said in a general way about the Canzonet, and even of the Ballet. Though the terminology was so loosely employed, yet this main distinction between the Madrigal and the Air or Canzonet was evidently understood by these composers, repetition being considered an essential feature of the Madrigal.

But the word Air was used by the Tudor musicians in another sense, as denoting a type of composition which is to be very clearly distinguished from the Madrigal. For purposes of differentiation this may be called the Lutenists' Air, for it was the creation of the lutenist-composers who were the contemporaries of the Tudor madrigalists ; and the distinguishing feature of this species of Air was the invariable presence of a lute accompaniment in the original printed editions. The history of lute-playing and of lute music in England is somewhat outside the scope of the present volume, but it is fully dealt with in an admirable article in Mr. Kennedy Scott's Euterpe Series,[2] in which the causes are carefully explained which led to the appearance of this new Art-form in the very last years of the sixteenth century as the product of the creative

[1] Morley's Plain and Easy Introduction, p. 180.
[2] Lutenists and Lute-playing in England by J. D., Euterpe Series, vol. vii.

genius of John Dowland. The lutenists' Air in its harmonized
form for combined voices much more nearly resembles the
modern Part-song than the Madrigal. This is to be accounted
for by the natural instinct of the lutenist to write a solo-song,
usually with several stanzas of words and with an accompaniment for the lute reinforced by a bass viol or viol da gamba ;
and in many instances, though by no means invariably, the
solo-song was adapted to use for combined voices by the
comparatively simple process of harmonization in four parts.
No positive evidence can be cited to prove whether the lutenists
intended these Airs, when arranged for combined voices, to be
sung with accompaniment as an indispensable part of the whole
effect. The harmonies of the lute-part do not quite invariably
agree with those of the voices ; and in certain rare instances the
simultaneous performance of the two would produce cacophonous results. There need be no hesitation as to the artistic
correctness of singing such pieces as Ford's *Since first I saw
your face* (Music of Sundry Kinds, No. 8) or Dowland's *Awake,
sweet love* (First Book of Airs, No. 20), for four voices without
accompaniment.

Another type of composition is occasionally to be met with
among the lutenists' Airs. For example, Dowland's *Come when
I call* (Book III, No. 21) is a dialogue for two solo-voices,
concluding with eight bars for five-part chorus ; each of the
solo-voices has its separate lute accompaniment, while the
First voice has in addition a string accompaniment of three
viols. And another device was to write a solo-song with lute
and string accompaniment and to repeat the refrain with
a chorus of combined voices. Dowland's wonderful *From
silent night* (A Pilgrim's Solace, No. 10) is for solo-voice, with
accompaniment for lute and bass-viol and also what is virtually
an *obbligato* for treble-viol or violin.

One other use of the term Air must be mentioned. It was
employed by Morley to denote what in modern phraseology is
described by the word *colour* in relation to individuality of key.
Thus he speaks of ' the ayre of everie key ' being different,[1]
and in reference to what he calls ' going out of the key ', and
especially ending in another key, which he condemned as ' one

[1] Morley's Plain and Easy Introduction, p. 147.

of the gravest faults which may be committed ', Morley gives one of his delightfully quaint illustrations : ' every key hath a peculiar ayre proper unto it selfe so that if you go into another then that wherein you begun, you change the aire of the song which is as much as to wrest a thing out of his nature, making the asse leap upon his maister, and the Spaniell beare the loade '.[1]

In spite of the loose terminology of the Tudor musicians, the lutenists clearly recognized the difference between the Madrigal and the Air.   Robert Jones and Pilkington, each of whom published work in both of these classes of composition, noted the difference in a distinct manner on their title-pages.   Jones, after having published two books of ' Songes and Ayres ', entitled his next volume ' *First* Set of Madrigals '.   Similarly Pilkington produced a 'First Booke of Songs or Ayres', and afterwards a First and a Second ' Set of Madrigals and Pastorals '.   This is all the more noteworthy in Pilkington's case, because in his work, more than in that of any other of these composers, the two styles overlap.   Many of his Songs and Airs are somewhat madrigalian ; yet the presence of the lute-part leaves no room for option in classifying them.

Before leaving the subject of the terminology it may be stated that although attempts have been made since Tudor days to assign exact meaning to terms which were vaguely used by these old musicians, it is now customary in concert programmes or in music catalogues to apply the term Madrigal rather than Part-song or Air to such pieces as *Awake, sweet love* or *Since first I saw your face*.   Meanwhile both Part-song and Air have become vested with a technical meaning which disqualifies them for employment in these particular instances, and in consequence Madrigal offers itself as the only alternative ; so that it may not be unreasonable to suggest, as a matter of general expediency, if not on more logical grounds, that the word Madrigal should now be adopted as the generic term covering the entire field of the unaccompanied secular vocal part-music of the Tudors.   The difficulty that has to be confronted in any attempt to classify these pieces of music under the several titles is greatly increased by the fact that the forms which these terms denote are also very indefinite, and that there

Morley's Plain and Easy Introduction, p. 147.

is a considerable overlapping of their style. Nor must it be forgotten that the term Madrigal, whether rightly or wrongly, has already acquired this generic significance in the minds of a large section of the community.

There is one further point that must be made clear. It has been frequently stated by those who have attempted definitions of madrigal-form that one of its essential features is the modal character of its tonality ; and this statement is made, apparently, with the intention of covering compositions that have been written, designedly in the madrigal style, since the Tudor period. As referring to the sixteenth-century Madrigal such a statement is of the nature of a truism, for it means no more than that these madrigals, whether English or Italian, were written in the idiom of their own time. To lay down a rule making it imperative that any composer who since the Tudor period should desire to set a pastoral lyric to contrapuntal music, perhaps introducing a *Fa-la* refrain, must necessarily confine himself to one of the ancient modes, all for the sake of calling it a Madrigal, is to distort the whole historic sense. Certainly the would-be madrigalist will succeed in attaining to Morley's ideal in one respect, for his work will be extremely ' artificial ' ; but the meaning of that adjective has changed since Morley used it. If such a composition lacks the modal character, the true Elizabethan flavour will, of course, also be wanting ; but this will still be the case if the composer fails to reproduce the curious antique methods of underlaying the words, or still more the peculiar principles of rhythmical treatment, not to mention other special characteristics so commonly ignored at all periods by aspiring imitators of the great madrigalists. Moreover, the Tudor composers lived and wrote at an epoch of rapid transition in the history of musical development. This fact had a direct influence on their methods of word-setting, for the old principles which governed Plain-song were beginning to give way to the more regular mensurate rhythms, and both these influences are apparent in the English madrigals. And as regards the modes and the tonal principles which they controlled, the differentiating characteristics were at this time in the actual process of disappearing or becoming merged in those two survivors among them which virtually constitute the ordinary major and minor scales of more modern times. There are many madrigals of the Tudor School which cannot be said to have any distinctively modal character. Once again, this was the period at which many traditional conventions associated with part-writing were being defied and overthrown, with the result that in this music we find chords employed and progressions used which would have been sternly condemned by the older theorists. All these details contribute towards making the musical idiom from about 1590 to 1625 in a very special degree peculiar to its own time. Yet the madrigal-composers of that day employed it with absolute spontaneity ; and such irregularities as they frequently introduced, by way of harmonic experiment or otherwise, were written with a natural freedom that cannot conceivably be counterfeited by a modern imitator.

All imitative Art is liable to be wrecked upon the rocks of artificiality (in its modern sense), and the copyist's work never fails to betray a lack of the spontaneity and vitality which may be present in the work from which the copy is made ; but imitation under the very peculiar conditions just described is foredoomed to failure. Moreover, it cannot be too strongly stated that if it be just possible at the present time, by slavish care, to make a passable imitation of an Elizabethan madrigal, yet even the best imitative work has practically no inherent value as compared with that of a purely creative kind ; for in Literature and Music alike it is a principle of vital importance that the contemporary idiom should be exclusively used as the vehicle of expression.

On the other hand, the sixteenth-century madrigals still stand in the realm of true Art to-day with their vitality unimpaired by the lapse of three centuries. Though they are clothed with a phraseology and idiom which have long since passed out of fashion, and though they have, in a sense, grown antique, yet they are ready for use exactly as they stand, with all the full vigour of life glowing in them, even in the changed circumstances and conditions of the twentieth century.

CHAPTER VII

THE TUDOR PART-BOOKS AND THE VOICES EMPLOYED

THE original editions of the works of the English madrigal writers are now extremely scarce and command very high prices on the rare occasions on which they appear in the market. Thus, for example, at the Huth sale in 1916 a copy of the 'Triumphs of Oriana' fetched as much as £89, while Morley's Ballets sold for £68 and the second edition of his three-part Canzonets for £82. Even higher prices ruled at the Britwell sale in 1919, when Pilkington's Sets realized £100 and £125, and Bennet's £98; while single voice-parts, practically useless when separated from the rest of the parts, fetched £10 and more.

It is not known what number of copies were printed in each edition, and no more than an approximate conjecture can now be made on the subject, but it would seem that there could not have been more than 250 copies to an edition, and possibly there were not more than 100. We know that it was customary not to have more than one, or, at the most, two complete sets of the part-books of any one volume of madrigals in the library of even a music-loving household. At Hengrave Hall, for instance, where Wilbye lived, the inventory of the music books,[1] made in 1602, shows no example of a duplicate copy of any one work. Moreover, it is unlikely that manuscript extracts were made from these books for the use of further singers, because that would have involved an infringement of the terms of the printing licence successively owned by Tallis, Byrd, Morley, East and others. Incidentally the scarcity of copies, even in Elizabethan days, raises the question as to whether the madrigals were usually performed by single voices or by several singers to each voice-part; and it seems probable that no strict rule was observed in this matter, the only necessary limitation being that not more than two or three persons could

[1] See the Author's Paper on Wilbye, Musical Association Proceedings, 1914–15.

have sung with comfort while sharing one part-book.   The
best musical effect would often have been secured, especially
in the more complex types of madrigal, by single voices.   But it
must be remembered that no such thing as a public performance
or anything even remotely resembling a modern concert was
given until long after Tudor times.   Chamber-music, in its
strict meaning, was the only form of playing or singing that
was then in vogue.   And there were no conductors in the
modern sense ; indeed the custom of conducting with a *bâton*
did not come into general use until the nineteenth century.

The music at this time was never printed in score after
the manner of modern part-songs, but each voice-part was
printed by itself in a separate book.   We may presume that
the composers in the first place wrote their music in score, but
that they discarded or destroyed the score as soon as the
separate part-books had been prepared from it, and the part-
books alone passed through the printers' hands.   It may
readily be imagined that under such conditions singers had to
exercise their attention to the utmost in such matters as the
counting of rests, and the strict observation of the values of
notes and rests alike, seeing that they had no conductor to give
them their cue of entry or to correct any error ; while they also
lacked the guidance provided by a simultaneous view of all the
vocal parts as shown in a score.   These early singers had to
meet yet another difficulty, the measure of which can scarcely
be apprehended by the modern performer whose music is
regularly intersected with bar-lines to assist him in keeping his
place, for the music in these old part-books is printed without
any bar-lines whatever, except in the case of the lutenists'
Airs, in which a certain amount of barring, often of an irregular
kind, was rendered necessary by the system of lute-tablature.
The accompanying facsimile of a page of the Cantus part-book
out of Wilbye's ' First Set of Madrigals ' will illustrate the fore-
going remarks.

It was the usual custom of the madrigalists to issue a volume
consisting of a good number of pieces together, rather than to
publish isolated compositions of this kind in accordance with
the method of more modern times.   Their volumes most commonly comprise from 20 to 24 madrigals ; but Byrd's ' Songs

Of 5 voc.   XXII.   CANTVS.

Flo-ra gaue me fayreſt flowers, :||:   none ſo fayer, :||:

:||:   In Floras treaſure, none ſo faier:||:   :||:   In Floras treaſure: Theſe I

plaſt on Phillis Bowers, She was pleaſd, :||:   :||:   And ſhe my pleaſure,

She was pleaſd, :||:   :||:   And ſhe my plea- ſure: Smiling meadowes ſeeme to

ſay, Come yee wantons, heere to play.   Smiling meadowes ſeeme to ſay, Come yee

wantons, heere to play, Come heere to play. Come yee wantons heere to play, to

play, Come yee wantons heere to play, :||:   :||:   to play, come ye

wantons, heere to play, to play. Come, come yee wantons heere to play.

Heere endeth the ſongs of 5. parts.

of sundrie natures ' includes as many as 47 numbers, and the
two Wilbye Sets contain 30 and 34 madrigals respectively.
The longer compositions are not infrequently divided into two,
and occasionally more, sections, these being numbered as
independent pieces in the Set. Wilbye's *Sweet honey-sucking
bees* is a case in point ; the first section figures as No. 17 (in the
second of Wilbye's volumes) and the second section, which
begins at the words *Yet, sweet, take heed,* is printed as a separate
composition and numbered 18 in the Set. The connexion
between the two sections in such cases is indicated by the
heading ' The first part ' and ' The second part ' respectively.
Weelkes's *My flocks feed not* is in three sections, numbered as
2, 3, and 4 of his first Set of madrigals. And Gibbons's *I weigh
not Fortune's frown,* which extends to as many as four sections
(Nos. 3 to 6 of his ' Madrigals and Mottets '), forms, as a whole,
a composition of considerable length. The consecutive sections
are usually, but not invariably, designed for the same combinations of voices. Occasionally the time-signature, and sometimes
even the key-signature, of the second section differs from that
of the first. In *And think, ye Nymphs* (Nos. 42 and 43 of ' Songs
of sundrie natures ') Byrd set the first part for five voices and
the second for six. In some instances either section is sufficiently
complete to admit of performance by itself, and such separate
use is perfectly consistent with the clear intention of the composers.

The composers never specified to what particular class of
voice the parts were to be allotted, for the names given by
them to the part-books afford no indication as to the actual
pitch or class of voice which should most suitably be employed,
whether soprano, alto, tenor, or bass. A variety of names was
given to the part-books, but the name, when once given, held
right through that particular book, regardless of the different
classes of voice which were often required to sing the music
contained in it. For example, the Altus and Tenor-books
contain music by no means exclusively intended for the use
of those individual voices. In the case of a Set of four-part
compositions the part-books might be named respectively
Cantus, Altus, Tenor, and Bassus, but if the Set should happen
to include a composition, say, for two sopranos, an alto, and

a tenor, the second soprano-part, regardless of compass, would be printed in the Altus-book, the alto in the Tenor-book, and the tenor in the Bassus-book. A part for soprano compass may even appear in a Tenor-book, as in the case of Weelkes's *Three virgin nymphs* (No. 10 of his 1597 Set) which is for three sopranos of equal compass and a bass. Similarly the music in a Contra-tenor part-book, as in Byrd's Sets, is by no means limited to the counter-tenor voice.

The names most ordinarily given to the part-books by the madrigalists were Cantus (*primus* and *secundus*), Altus, Contratenor, Medius, Tenor, and Bassus; while in the case of compositions of more than four parts the terms Quintus, Sextus, and Septimus were also used. Byrd employed the term Triplex instead of Cantus in his 1588 Set, but only for the first four compositions in that book. As another alternative to Cantus the term Superius was occasionally employed. With very few exceptions Cantus is used for the top voice-part and Bassus for the lowest; while Altus, Contra-tenor, and Tenor, when those terms are used at all, always appear in that order as far as the pitch of the voice-part is concerned, even though they may not correspond throughout to the compass of voice usually associated with those terms. The position of the Medius, Quintus, Sextus, &c., in relation to the Altus, Contra-tenor, and Tenor is variable. The choice of voices to which the several parts are to be allotted for performance does not therefore depend upon the original term prefixed to the part-book, but solely upon the compass and general range of the music; and each case must be judged on its own merits and with reference to individual conditions. The choice is consequently left entirely to the discretion of the conductor, and may vary according to the material at his disposal, an important consideration depending upon whether the voices of men, women, or boys are available for the alto-parts.

For practical purposes with modern singers a serious difficulty is presented by the awkward compass of the inner voice-parts of much of this music, both sacred and secular, though the difficulty is much mitigated when male altos are available. For the alto-parts sometimes extend for a compass of nearly two octaves, ranging for an octave on either side of middle C.

And the tenor-parts often lie very high, yet too low for female
alto singers. It seems probable that in Elizabethan days male
singers made very free use of the *falsetto* register. In order to
meet this very real difficulty some editors have introduced
drastic emendations into the text ; such a course of action is
inexcusable unless adequate annotation is printed which may
enable the student to perceive the exact form of the composer's
text, and may also make it possible to perform the music in its
original design when circumstances admit of it. In Wilbye's
Sweet honey-sucking bees, where two counter-tenor voices of
equal compass are employed, the difficulty has been met in
most reprints by a wholesale rearrangement of these two voice-
parts without annotation, but it might be overcome by transposing the music down a tone ; while if counter-tenors are
available, the parts, as they stand in the original text, are exactly
suitable for that class of voice. In many instances this type of
difficulty can be solved by the readjustment of a single phrase
and sometimes of no more than one note. Another plan is to
include a few alto voices among the tenors, and *vice versa*. But
all such minor matters are best left to the judgement of conductors, who must be guided by their own individual requirements, acting always on a wise discretion and with due reverence for the composer's text.

The problem of the voices is closely intertwined with the
question of musical pitch. Nothing approaching a uniform
standard of pitch was in existence in Tudor times, nor is it easy
to arrive at any definite conclusion as to how far the pitch in
those days differed from that which we now use. It must not
be forgotten, too, that a considerable variation, amounting to
nearly a semitone, is still tolerated in our own day in spite of
all the efforts to secure uniformity.

Musical pitch, as is well known, can be formulated with
scientific exactness ; for example, the pitch which is now most
commonly employed in this country, and is usually known to
orchestral players as ' flat pitch ', is signified by the formula
$=435 \cdot 4$. In other words, that this note is produced by
a series of vibrations generated at the rate of $435 \cdot 4$ per second
at a temperature of $59°$ Fahrenheit. Unfortunately the old

musicians left few exact records for our information ; but it is known that the pitch of the organ in Halberstadt Cathedral in the year 1495 was A = 505·8 ; while that of Hampton Court in 1690 was A = 441·7. These facts are naturally of little value in determining the musical pitch in use at the close of the sixteenth century, but it will be noticed that whereas the Hampton Court organ corresponded fairly closely with our modern standard of pitch, the Halberstadt organ was nearly a minor third sharper.

It is very frequently stated, and this opinion is widely supported, that musical pitch in the Tudor period was about a minor third flatter than that of the present day. This estimate is mainly founded on the supposition that the old keyed-instruments, the predecessors of the pianoforte, were tuned to some such pitch, and also on the fact that their frames were not strong enough to stand the increased tension that the higher pitch would involve. It is, indeed, necessary to strengthen the frame of these old instruments when adapting them in modern days to our present standard of pitch. But there are grave difficulties in bringing this theory into line with the compass of the voices employed in the madrigals.

In examining this aspect of the question it will be obvious that the inner parts of a vocal composition give little indication of a definite nature; but very valuable evidence is provided by the soprano and bass parts, for, on the reasonable assumption that the human voice in these two departments has not greatly changed in compass, it would appear that the pitch used by the composers of secular vocal music at this period was very much the same as it is now, even though it was by no means standardized and, no doubt, varied considerably in actual performance. Thus, the soprano parts were never written above A, yet that note was very commonly employed ; and the compass of this voice frequently extended down from A to middle C. These facts do not in themselves militate against the theory that the pitch was a minor third lower, although that would give F sharp as the highest note ever assigned to the top voice-part. But at the other end of the vocal range the bass parts offer an insuperable objection to the pitch having been as much as a minor third below our own ; for very commonly the compass ranges,

as in modern days, from G up to D ; but occasionally it goes
down to low E and even D, which, if transposed down a minor
third, would correspond to B natural in our pitch.

But we possess one other exact record about pitch in England
in the seventeenth century. This consists of an explanatory
note appended to the organ copy of Thomas Tomkins's *Musica
Deo Sacra*.[1] This work was not published till 1668, twelve years
after his death, but the note may be taken to refer to the
life-experience of Tomkins, which covers the first half of the

seventeenth century. The note is as follows : ' 𝄞 sit tonus

fistulae apertae longitudine duorum pedum et semissis : sive
30 digitorum Geometricorum.' In other words, when Tomkins
wrote F it represented to him a sound which stands between
G and A flat in our modern pitch. Thus Tomkins used a pitch
that was more than a tone higher than ours. There is no reason
to suppose that this composer was singular in his experience,
and it happens to agree rather nearly with the known pitch of
the Halberstadt organ in 1495.

In the light of all these facts taken together only one theory
seems possible : namely that three distinct classes of pitch
prevailed simultaneously in this country at the period of the
madrigal school, though none of these was defined with exact
precision ; while it is more than improbable that uniformity
of standard within these three classes was even approximately
observed. Thus, the secular vocal pitch would have been much
the same as it is now; the pitch of Church music (involving that
of organs) was more than a tone higher than modern pitch ;
while virginals and other kindred instruments were tuned
about a minor third below the pitch of to-day. And with a
musical system which, as we know, involved the use of three
different standards of scale,[2] there is nothing inconsistent in the
theory that there were as many as three general standards of
pitch in simultaneous use. It is noteworthy that virginals do
not seem to have been employed for accompanying voices in
Elizabethan times, and indeed they were precluded from such

---

[1] This note is printed in the copy of this work in the library of St. Michael's
College, Tenbury, together with a note on *tempo* (see p. 90). No other known
copies have these notes.   [2] See pp. 97–8.

employment by the important differences of scale to which they were tuned, quite apart from any question of pitch.[1] And there is nothing to show that the lute and instruments of the viol family, which were commonly used with the secular vocal music, might not have been tuned to a higher pitch for purposes of accompaniment ; the pitch of the lute was easily raised as much as a minor third by a mechanical contrivance called the *capo d'astro*.

Returning to the theory that different standards of pitch were in use for Church music and secular vocal music, it is interesting to compare the music of each class ; and on this evidence the theory receives strong confirmation. In the madrigal Set of Tomkins are included a few settings of scripture words, and in these the compass of the voices is pitched lower than in the secular songs. In one case the Cantus-part ranges ♯♭ to ♯ and the tenor-part is exactly an octave lower in compass. If this composition is raised in pitch something over a tone, the compass of these voice-parts becomes normal. On the other hand, those secular numbers in the same Set which take the soprano up to A are not likely to have been conceived at the pitch which Tomkins defined in *Musica Deo Sacra*. It is moreover a fact well known to all English Church-musicians that the greater part of the sacred polyphonic music of this period, as scored, lies too low for satisfactory effect unless it is transposed up at least a tone ; and this circumstance endorses Tomkins's note. But it is remarkable that this difference of pitch is frequently referred to in a slipshod and careless manner by those who should know better ; a well-known cathedral Service of this school was lately reprinted in transposed form, and the editor explained in his Preface that he had transposed the music *up* a tone for the reason that pitch at the beginning of the seventeenth century was *lower* than it is now. He had done the right thing, but the correct explanation was that the pitch for Church music was, as Tomkins records, quite a tone *higher* than modern pitch.

One other matter of importance is closely connected with the consideration of the voice-parts of this music. It is the

[1] Ibid.

question as to whether madrigals should be submitted to transposition for the purpose of bringing the voice-parts into more suitable range or of meeting special needs. Some authorities have declared that transposition should never be allowed; Thomas Morley himself was one of these ; for he says,[1] ' Those songs which are made for the high key be made for more life ; the other in the low key for more gravitie and staidnesse ; so that if you sing them in contrarie keys they will lose their grace and will be wrested as it were out of their nature.' In more recent times Thomas Oliphant endorsed this view, for,[2] after quoting Morley to support him, he says that transposition should never be allowed because it involves serious detriment to the music ; and he adds that every part is well adapted to the particular quality of voice for which it was originally written. In expressing this opinion Oliphant ignored the difficulty which does undoubtedly exist for choirs of mixed voices in relation to the compass of the inner voice-parts ; and one remedy for this is certainly transposition. Occasionally also the soprano parts lie in a very high register, and nothing will be lost, from Morley's point of view, by transposing certain pieces at least a tone down. This is especially the case with some of Morley's Canzonets for two voices, and such madrigals as the same composer's *Ho! who comes here?* or *Hark! jolly shepherds* (Nos. 19 and 20 of Madrigals for four voices).

Yet it is well to bear in mind Morley's instruction. For it is evident from the variety of clefs selected by the madrigalists, as well as from the deliberate limitations of compass which they sometimes imposed upon the voice-parts, that they had a strong feeling not only for differentiating the ordinary four classes of voice, but also for appreciating the variety of compass controlled by singers within the limits of each class. Consequently they provided suitable music for all ranges of voice, including occasionally those of very limited range, and they also wrote for various combinations of voices. In this way they met the needs of almost any casual gathering of singers ; and this feature is not without its advantages in our own day, particularly in country districts. In modern four-part vocal music the

[1] Morley's Plain and Easy Introduction, p. 166.
[2] Oliphant, A Short Account of Madrigals, p. 13.

combination of soprano, alto, tenor, and bass is so very general, except, of course, when male or female voices are being employed alone, that too great a tendency has been shown by editors of madrigals to squeeze the original combinations into the S.A.T.B. mould by means of transposition, regarding this as a matter of presumed necessity, in defiance of the composer's deliberate intention. This method of editing often involves further difficulties connected with the compass of the inner parts, and these are surmounted only too frequently by tampering with the original part-writing.

Transposition may reasonably be employed in certain cases, at the discretion of a conductor, to meet special requirements and circumstances ; but there can be no doubt that these old composers deliberately obtained a contrast in tone-colour by their varied treatment in the selection of voices to be used together, and it would involve a definite loss if this feature were entirely obliterated.

CHAPTER VIII

TITLE-PAGES, PATRONS, AND PRINTERS
OF THE ORIGINAL EDITIONS

It has already been explained that the individual voice-parts of the madrigals were copied from the full score into separate books and printed only in that form. For practical use this was in many respects a convenient method. The lutenists' Airs were printed on a different system, all the voice-parts, together with the lute-tablature, being printed in one book, not in score, but ingeniously arranged on the page so that four persons standing in a semicircle and holding the book in the centre could sing the music from the one copy. The lute-part was always printed in conjunction with the Cantus-part under this arrangement, and for this reason bar-lines, corresponding with those in the tablature, were introduced into the Cantus-part, while the Altus, Tenor, and Bassus voice-parts were printed entirely without bars just as they were in the madrigal part-books.

In the case of the madrigal part-books, with which we are here chiefly concerned, the complete Set of each voice-part was bound as a volume, and the title-pages, together with the dedications, tables of contents, and other such details, were reproduced identically in each of the corresponding volumes ; the only point of difference was the addition of the name of the voice to which the part-book belonged : viz. Cantus, Altus, and so on. This will explain the apparent inconsistency that occurs when, for instance, the voice-part of a third soprano is to be found in the Tenor part-book. As numbers of four-part madrigals were written with a voice of tenor compass as the lowest part, which therefore appeared in the Bassus part-book, it will be readily understood that the name of the part-book implies nothing as to the actual class of voice which should be employed for singing the music throughout a particular part-book. In any Set of madrigals which was not uniformly for the same number of voices, the madrigals were grouped together in accordance with the number of voices, the group for three voices being placed at the beginning of the volume; and at end of each group came the formula 'Here endeth the songs of three parts ' and so on. In such cases the Cantus, Altus, and Bassus books were those in which the three-part compositions were printed ; and in these circumstances the Bassus very commonly contained music for an alto or tenor voice. The Tenor part-book came into use when the four-part group was reached, and the Quintus, or Medius, and Sextus part-books were further added to meet the increase of voice-parts in the later groups of the Set. All the part-books in the Set were numbered in accordance with the Cantus book, thus the Quintus book might begin at No. 13 and the Sextus at No. 19, but the complete table of contents from No. 1 would appear in these books.

The title-pages were frequently ornamented with lace borders of beautiful design. The size of the type on these title-pages varied a good deal, and, unlike our modern custom, the name of the composer was sometimes printed quite small. The musical position and the University degree of the composer were usually added. One curious feature of the title-pages was the use of the term ' First Set ' even in cases when a second Set was not subsequently published or ever contemplated by the composer who employed it. Many of the madrigal Sets are described on the title-pages as ' Apt for the viols and voices '. This formula has given rise to much discussion with reference to its exact meaning. It was Weelkes who first used this formula in his Madrigals for five and six voices, published in 1600, and after this date it appeared on the title-page of almost every madrigal Set. This fact will account for its inclusion in Wilbye's 1609 Set whereas it does not appear in his 1598 Set, a circumstance which had seemed difficult to explain seeing that the music of these two Sets did not appear to differ materially in style. The same fact explains the absence of any such formula from Morley's Sets. Some composers adopted the variant ' apt for viols *or* voices ', and in Robert Jones's Set, published in 1607, the description is : ' for viols and voices, or for voices alone, or as you please.' The

alternative employment of voices and instruments for performing music was no new thing in 1600, because Byrd, in the
' Epistle to the Reader ' of his 1588 volume, speaks of ' expressing of these songs either by voices or instruments '. But
twelve years elapsed after this date before the stamp of general
sanction was given to the alternative practice by the composers
on their title-pages.

There can be little doubt but that Weelkes was influenced
in this matter by the greater importance which instrumental
accompaniment had assumed since the year 1597, when Dowland had introduced an entirely new class of vocal music in his
' First Booke of Songes or Ayres '. For although the instrumental
accompaniment was not regarded as an indispensable feature
in the performance of the lutenists' Air for combined voices,
yet its function and utility were more definitely recognized
after its appearance. Dowland's 1597 book bore the title ' The
First Booke of Songes or Ayres of fowre partes with Tableture
for the Lute : So made that all the partes together, or either of
them severally may be song to the Lute, Orpherian or Viol de
gambo.' The subject of the lutenists' music will be dealt
with in a later chapter. But as regards the music of the
madrigalists proper, it is evident that they perceived in the
growing demand for instrumental music a further and more
general use for the compositions which they had designed
primarily for voices alone ; consequently from this date they
duly advertised the suitability of their music for instrumental
as well as vocal performance. For music composed expressly
for viols was at this period precisely similar in style to vocal
music. We can scarcely doubt that unaccompanied voices
were regarded as the best medium for performing the madrigals,
provided always, as Byrd put it,[1] ' the voices are good and the
same well sorted and ordered '. Yet it seems probable that
the support of the viols was occasionally drawn upon when, at
casual gatherings, it happened that either the singers were
insufficient in number or quality for rendering the whole of
the voice-parts, or that any of the singers lacked the necessary
skill to sustain his own part correctly without support. It must

---

[1] Byrd's Reasons to persuade everyone to learn to sing, Byrd's 1588 Set,
Preface.

not be supposed that the formula 'apt for voices and viols' can be cited to justify or render desirable in modern times the accompaniment of Tudor music for combined voices, whether sacred or secular, by a pianoforte, or an organ, or any other instrument tuned on the principle of equal temperament.

Before leaving this subject it may be mentioned that many of the madrigals can be performed with fine effect upon modern string instruments, especially if due discretion is exercised for securing unanimity in details of bowing and phrasing as well as in the use of expression marks. When madrigal music was played upon viols in Tudor times, as we learn from Ford's 'Musicke of sundrie Kindes', the notes which were reiterated in the voice-parts solely for the purpose of carrying additional syllables of the words were, as a general rule, tied together. Good taste in dealing with all these points will add considerably to the effectiveness of the instrumental performance of a madrigal.

In occasional compositions in the madrigal Sets it will be found that the words are printed in only one, or sometimes two, of the part-books, while the remaining part-books have the music without any words beyond the opening phrase, which was only placed there for purposes of reference. In these conditions the music of these other parts was intended to be played on viols as an accompaniment to a vocal solo, or duet, as the case may be. Sometimes the words of a refrain or chorus appear in all the voice-parts in contrast to the solo with which the composition opens, and in such cases the viols should play right through, the voices joining in only where the words are printed in full. The following are examples of this class of composition : Byrd's *Ah, silly soul* and *How vain the toils* (No. 31 and 32 of his 1611 Set) both of which are for solo with string-quintet accompaniment ; *O God that guides the cheerful sun* (No. 28 of the same Set) is for solo and chorus ; John Mundy's *The Shepherd Strephon* (' Songs and Psalmes ', Nos. 20 and 21) is for solo with instrumental accompaniment. The whole of Martin Peerson's ' Private Musicke ' consists of compositions of this kind ; the best-known number in this set is to Verstegan's carol *Upon my lap my Sovereign sits* (No. 12), which should properly be performed as a solo with a lullaby refrain at the end of each stanza, in which alone the chorus takes part. Peerson's music was not designed on the madrigal model nor intended by him for use as unaccompanied combined song.

On the back of the title-pages of the madrigal Sets it was almost the invariable custom to inscribe an elaborate dedication to some influential patron. These dedications were generally couched in terms of liberal flattery in the style of the day ; but in many cases these dedications record facts or provide clues which have led to the discovery of fresh information connected with the biography of the composers. The complete list of patrons is a wide and representative one, and some of the names figure in more than one of the madrigal Sets. Sir Christopher Hatton was the patron of Byrd's first Set, of Gibbons's Set, and of East's last Set. Robert, Earl of Essex, Queen Elizabeth's favourite, was patron of John Mundy's Set and also of Watson's ' First sett of Madrigalls Englished ' ; while his son, the third Earl, was one of Michael East's patrons. Byrd and Campian each dedicated a volume to Francis, Earl of Cumberland. Sir George Carey, afterwards Lord Hunsdon, was among the many patrons of Morley and of Dowland. Tomkins and Hume both enjoyed the patronage of William, Earl of Pembroke ;　and Mary, Countess of Pembroke— ' Sidney's sister, Pembroke's mother '—was patroness of Morley's Canzonets to three voices. Other notable people to whom the madrigalists dedicated volumes were : Henry, Prince of Wales (Robert Jones) ; Lord Howard of Effingham (Morley) ; Lady Arabella Stuart (Wilbye) ; Edward, seventeenth Earl of Oxford (Farmer) ; William, sixth Earl of Derby (Pilkington) and Robert, first Earl of Salisbury (Morley and Jones).

Some of these dedications are clothed in language that has a peculiar charm. Morley, in the dedication of his ' Booke of Balletts ' to Sir Robert Cecil, afterwards Lord Salisbury, professes the conventional spirit of self-depreciation and adds that in offering to his patron ' these simple compositions ' he is imitating ' the custome of that olde world who wanting incense to offer up to their Godds, made shifte in steade thereof to honour them with milk. Or as those who beeing not able to present a torch unto the hollie Alters ; in signe of their devotion, did light a little candle, and gave up the same. In which notwithstanding did shine more cleerely the affection of the giver then the worth or value of the guift it selfe. May it so therefore please your Honor to accept of this small present with that good intention wherwith I offer it.'

The following is Weelkes's dedication of his five-part Madrigals to Lord Windsor in 1600 :

' My Lord, in the Coledge of Winchester, where I live, I have heard learned men say, that some Philosophers have mistaken the soule of man for an Harmonie : Let the president of their error be a priviledge for mine. I see not, if soules doe not partly consist of Musicke, how it should come to passe, that so noble a spirit as yours, so perfectly tuned to so perpetuall a Tenor of excellencies as it is, should discend to the notice of a qualitie lying single in so low a personage as my selfe. But in Musicke the Base part is no disgrace to the best eares attendauncie. I confesse my conscience is untoucht with any other arts, and I hope, my confession is unsuspected, many of us Musitians thinke it is as much praise to bee some what more then Musitians, as it is for golde to bee some what more then golde, and, if *Jack Cade* were alive, yet some of us might live : unlesse we should think, as the *Artisans*, in the Universities in *Poland*, and *Germany* think, that the Latin tongue comes by reflection. I hope your Lordship will pardon this presumption of mine, the rather, because I know before Nobilitie I am to deale sincearely ; and this small facultie of mine, because it is alone in mee, and without the assistance of other more confident sciences, is the more to bee favored, and the rather to bee received into your honors protection, so shall I observe with as humble and as true an heart, as hee, whose knowledge is as large as the worlds creation, and as earnestly pray for you, to the worlds Creator.'

A good example of the flowers of speech, or, as it seems to our notions, the extravagant flattery, which Elizabethan writers and composers were accustomed to offer to their patrons, appears in John Dowland's ' Address to the Courteous Reader ' in his ' First Booke of Songes or Ayres '. Speaking of favours shown to him on the Continent during his travels, he said : ' I bent my course toward the famous provinces of Germany where I found both excellent masters and most honorable Patrons of Musicke. Namely those two miracles of this age for vertue and magnificence, Henry Julio, Duke of Brunswick, and learned Maritius Lantzgrave of Hessen, of whose princely vertues and favors towards me I can never speake sufficiently.'

Although it is conceived in the same spirit of flattery, there is some poetry in the language which Morley employed in the dedication of his three-voice Canzonets to Lady Pembroke : ' If at any time your Ladiship shall but vouchsafe your heavenly voice ; it cannot be but they will so returne perfumed with the sweetnesse of that breth, as the Ayr wil be made even delightfull thereby, and for that cause to be in request and sought for ever after.'

This extract almost inevitably recalls the lines from Ben Jonson's ' Drink to me only with thine eyes ' :

> I sent thee late a rosy wreath,
>
> .   .   .   .
>
> But thou thereon didst only breath
> And sent'st it back to me ;
> Since when it grows and smells, I swear,
> Not of itself but thee.

Farmer's praise of his patron, Edward, Earl of Oxford, was bestowed upon a man who was really skilled in many of the arts and was a poet of no mean order. Farmer declared of him, with some foundation of truth, in his dedicatory address : ' without flattrie be it spoke, those that know your Lordship know this, that using this science as a recreation, your Lordship have overgone most of them that make it a profession.'

Orlando Gibbons, addressing Sir Christopher Hatton, gave a wise hint to critics of madrigals, which might be more generally remembered by those in our own time who readily condemn the finest Tudor music upon an indifferent performance. ' Experience tels us ', said Gibbons, ' that Songs of this Nature are usually esteemed as they are well or ill performed, which excellent grace I am sure your unequalled love unto Musicke will not suffer them to want, that the Author (whom you no lesse love) may be free from disgrace.' Gibbons probably realized that most of his own madrigals are far more difficult to sing effectively than those of the rest of the school. Byrd breathed a similar sentiment ' that you will be as careful to heare them well expressed, as I have been both in the Composing and correcting of them. Otherwise the best Song that ever was made will seeme harsh and unpleasant.' This extract is from Byrd's address ' to all true lovers of Musicke ' in his 1611 volume. In a similar address ' To the curteous Reader ' in his 'Songs of sundrie natures', the same composer says ' I do now publish for thee songs of 3. 4. 5. and 6. parts to serve all companies and voyces : whereof some are easie and plaine to sing, other more hard and difficult, but all, such as any yong practicioner in singing, with a little foresight, may easely performe.' This statement fully bears out the suggestion that the madrigalists wrote expressly for every variety of voice-combination and had no idea of restricting themselves to the stereotyped S.A.T.B. group of more modern days.

Occasionally short poems in praise of the composer were printed in the preliminary pages. A good example of these is in Morley's ' Madrigalls to Foure Voyces ' :

TO THE AVTHOR

MORLEY ! would any whether MORe LYeth
   In our ENGLISH to merit
   Or in th'ITALIAN spirit
Who in regard of his each wit defieth ?
Lo the cleare proofe then if a man would make it
   (O would some one but try it)
To choose his Song, and Gold enough lay by it
And say to thee : heere, better this and take it.
I know (how ere thou lik'st them) thou could'st doe it
   Wert thou but so put to it.
For if thou sing'st thus when nought doth invite thee
Aware when PRAYSE and GOLD did both invite thee.
                        Incerto

One other preliminary page in these books calls for special notice, because it forms a delightful preface to the whole of this wonderful series of musical publications, and is, in fact, found in the very first of them, namely Byrd's ' Psalmes. Sonets, and Songs of Sadnes and Pietie ' (1588). In addition to the dedicatory address and an ' Epistle to the Reader ' Byrd gave his ' Reasons briefly set down by th'auctor, to perswade every one to learne to sing ' :

' First it is a knowledge easely taught, and quickly learned where there is a good Master, and an apt Scoller.

2. The exercise of singing is delightfull to Nature & good to preserve the health of Man.

3. It doth strengthen all the parts of the brest & doth open the pipes.

4. It is a singuler good remedie for a stutting & stammering in the speech.

5. It is the best meanes to procure a perfect pronunciation & to make a good Orator.

6. It is the onely way to knowe where Nature hath bestowed the benefit of a good voyce : which guift is so rare, as there is not one among a thousand, that hath it : and in many, that excellent guift is lost, because they want Art to expresse Nature.

7. There is not any Musicke of Instruments whatsoever comparable to that which is made of the voyces of men, where the voices are good, and the same well sorted and ordered.

8. The better the voyce is, the meeter it is to honour and serve God there-with : and the voyce of man is chiefely to be imployed to that ende.

omnis spiritus laudet Dominum
Since singing is so good a thing
I wish all men would learne to sing.'

These music-books were produced under an extraordinary series of monopolizing patents. The first licence or patent of this kind was granted by the Crown in the year 1575 ; and it gave to Thomas Tallis and William Byrd the exclusive right in England to print, not only their own compositions but also those of all other composers whether English or foreign. The sole right of ruling and selling music paper was also secured to them. The terms of this licence were as follows :

' Elizabeth by the grace of God, Quene of Englande Fraunce and Ireland. . . . To all printers bokesellers and other officers ministers and subjects greeting. Knowe ye, that we for the especiall affection and good wil that we have and beare to the science of Musicke and for the advancement thereof, by our letters patent dated the xxii of January, in the xvii yere of our raigne have graunted ful priveledge and licence unto our wel-beloved servaunts Thomas Tallis and William Birde two of the Gentlemen of our Chappell, and to the overlyver of them, and to the assignees of them and over the surviver of them for xxi yeares next ensuing, to imprint any and so many as they will of set songe or songes in partes, either in English, Latine, Frenche, Italian or other tongues that may serve for musicke either in Churche or chamber, or otherwise to be either plaid or soonge, And that they may rule and cause to be ruled by impression any paper to serve for printing or pricking of any songe or songes, and may sell and utter any printed bokes or papers of any songe or songes, or any bookes or quieres of such ruled paper imprinted. Also we straightly by the same forbid all printers bookesellers subjects and strangers, other then is aforesaid to doe any the premisses, or to bring or cause to be brought out of any forren Realmes into any our dominions any songe or songes made and printed in any forren countrie, to sell or put to sale, uppon paine of our high displeasure, And the offender in any of the premisses for every time to forfet to us our heires and successors fortie shillinges, and to the said Thomas Tallis and William Birde or to their assignes and to the assignes of the surviver of them, all and evrie the said bokes papers songe or songes, We have also by the same willed and commanded our printers maisters and wardens of the misterie of Stacioners, to assist the said Thomas Tallis and William Birde and their assignes for the dewe executing of the premisses.' [1]

After the death of Tallis, Byrd became the sole proprietor of this monopoly, and he assigned the right of printing the music-books to Thomas East (or Este). The terms of the arrangement between Byrd and East are unknown, but obviously some such compact was necessary between the composer and the skilled artisan. Consequently the earliest English madrigal books were printed ' by Thomas East the assigne of William Byrd, *Cum privilegio Regiae Maiestatis*'. This was the formula as printed on the title-page of Yonge's *Musica Transalpina* in 1588, and in Byrd's Set in the same year. In the latter publication it is added that the books are to be sold at the dwelling house of the said T. East, ' by Paules wharfe.' In the succeeding madrigal books, up till and including 1594,' the reference to the printer on the title-pages remains the same except that East had changed his address to ' Aldersgate-streete, at the signe of the black horse '. The last madrigal publication in which East was described as ' the assign ' of William Byrd was Morley's book of two-part Canzonets in 1595. After that year the original patent expired, and Weelkes's first Set and the second volume of *Musica Transalpina* in 1597 were simply ' printed by Thomas Este '. But in the same year Morley's volume of four-part Canzonets selected from Italian authors was printed ' by Peter Short dwelling

[1] Rot. Pat. 17 Eliz. pars. 7, m. 2.

on Bredstreet hill at the signe of the Star and are there to be sold '.   Other publications in 1597 and the following year were printed both by Short and East.

In 1598 Morley succeeded in obtaining a fresh patent from the Crown granting him a monopoly that was, if possible, even more drastic than the original one.[1]   Under this new licence many of the most important madrigal-volumes were produced ; Short and East were still the printers, while later the name of William Barley began to figure, but all these three acted as assignees of Morley.   The earliest Set of madrigals printed by Barley was that of Farmer in 1599 ; this was ' printed at London in Little Saint Helens by William Barley the assigne of Thomas Morley and are to be sold at his shoppe in Gratious-streete'.   One Set alone, that of Carlton in 1601, was ' Printed by Thomas Morley dwelling in Little Saint Helens '.   Robert Jones's Set, printed by Short in 1607, was ' to be sold at the Inner Temple-gate '.   The last mention of Morley's patent was in connexion with Dowland's ' Third Booke of Songs or Aires ' ; this was printed in 1603 ' by P(eter) S(hort) for Thomas Adams, and are to be sold at the signe of the white Lion in Paules churchyard by the assignement of a Patent granted to T. Morley '.   This unusual form of reference to the patent is, no doubt, to be explained by Morley's recent death.   The patent itself passed into the ownership of William Barley, but none of the madrigal publications refer to him as the proprietor until 1606, in which year at least three Sets were printed ' by John Windet, the assigne of William Barley '.   Windet made his first appearance as a printer of this class of work two years earlier when he was ' dwelling at Powles Wharfe at the Signe of the Crosse Keyes '.   Early in 1606 he was ' at the Golden Anchore in Pater Noster Row ' ;   and later in the same year his books were ' to bee sold at his shoppe in Saint Dunstones churchyard in Fleet street '.   Between 1604 and 1607 Windet printed the large majority of the books of Madrigals and Airs—ten publications as against two by East ;   but after that date his name no longer occurs, and presumably he had died.   In 1608 Barley himself printed Weelkes's ' Ayeres or Phantasticke

---

[1] This lengthy document, dated September 20, 1598 (Rot. Pat. 40 Eliz., p. 10, m. 18) is printed in full in Steele's The Earliest English Music Printing, p. 67.

Spirites' and sold them 'at his shoppe in Gracious street'.
Thomas East then reappeared as the principal printer, though
still as the ' assigne of William Barley '.

The fact that in 1609 Wilbye's second Set of madrigals was
' printed by Tho. Este alias Snodham . . . at his shop in
S. Dunstones Church-yard in Fleet Street ', and that subsequently the name in connexion with this business invariably
appeared as Thomas Snodham, led to the theory that East
had changed his name to Snodham. This theory has been
disproved by Mr. Percival Vivian,[1] who quotes an entry in
the Stationers' Registers under the date of January 17, 1609,
showing clearly that Snodham took over East's business at
the latter's death.

In 1609 Barley printed Ravenscroft's *Pammelia* and one of
Jones's Sets of Airs at the new address of ' Powles Church yard
at the signe of the Crowne '. After this date almost all these
music books were printed by Snodham, and his name appears for
the last time as printer of Pilkington's second Set of madrigals
in 1624. The few subsequent publications of music books of
this class were printed by William Stansby, whose name
had first occurred in this connexion as printer of Corkine's
' Ayres ' in 1610.

Other names of less importance connected with the printers'
notices on the title-pages of the later madrigalian publications
were Thomas Adams, John Browne, and Matthew Lownes,
who acted sometimes as the assignees of William Barley. The
following appear to have printed a few music books on their
own account : Lawrence Lisle ' dwelling at the signe of the
Tigers-head in Paul's Church-yard ' ; Robert Wilson ; Edward
Allde ' dwelling neere Christ-Church ' ; George Latham ' at
the Bishop's head in Pauls Church-yard ; ' and Humfrey
Lownes, the printer of the younger Hilton's *Fa-las* in 1627.

Having regard to the conditions under which they worked,
the printers of these music-books deserve much credit for the
style and accuracy with which they were produced. Taking
the series as a whole the proportion of misprints is exceedingly
small. This same opinion was expressed contemporarily
by Byrd, who paid a high tribute to the accuracy and care

[1] Vivian's Works of Campion, p. 255.

of his printer, and uttered at the same time a word of caution not always heeded by editors of madrigals, so many of whom have hastily sought for explanation of unexpected and puzzling points by accusing the original printers of faulty work.   In his Epistle to the Reader of his 1588 volume Byrd wrote thus : ' In expressing of these songs either by voyces or Instruments, if ther happen to be any jarre or dissonance, blame not the Printer, who (I doe assure thee) through his great paines and diligence doth heere deliver to thee a perfect and true Coppie.'   And it may not be wholly out of place here to quote from the same address Byrd's admirable advice to the critic, advice which will serve for all time and for all subjects : ' If in the composition of these Songs, there be any fault by me committed, I desire the skilfull, either with courtesie to let the same be concealed, or in friendlie sort to be thereof admonished : and at the next Impression he shal finde the error reformed : remembring alwaies that it is more easie to finde a fault then [1] to amend it.'

---

[1] The word *than* was almost invariably spelt *then* in Elizabethan literature.

CHAPTER IX

SOME TECHNICAL FEATURES OF THE NOTATION

A GLANCE at the part-books will show how necessary it was for the Elizabethan madrigal-singers to acquire a complete familiarity with all the technical details of musical notation as used in these books, from which they were expected to sing at sight. The notation of the English madrigal-books does not approach that of the Church music of the sixteenth century as regards intricacy and complexity of detail. And few of the difficulties which confront the student of Tudor Church music, as regards the meaning and value of the actual notes, are to be met with in these part-books, a fact which is largely explained by the late date at which most of the English madrigals were written and printed. Yet there are several matters which should be explained here, and it must be borne in mind that the scope of this chapter is limited to secular English vocal music. In the first place it was important that singers should understand the exact meaning and value of the rests as well as of the actual notes. The semibreve and minim rests were printed perpendicularly, and not horizontally as in modern notation, and therefore they were less conspicuous, but rests of all kinds were usually printed in such a position on the stave as should most easily catch the eye in any particular passage ; this was especially the case in arranging a group of rests, and there was no uniformity such as now is customary as regards their position on the stave. Rests for breves and longs were also used, and were represented thus :

The subject of the ancient note-values does not call for elaborate treatment in this place, but we have one important record as to the *tempo* normally adopted in this country ; for there is a printed note at the end of the organ copy [1] of

---

[1] The organ copy of this work, at St. Michael's College, Tenbury, has this printed note, but it does not appear in other known copies.

Tomkins's *Musica Deo sacra* as follows: ' sit mensura
duorum humani corporis pulsuum, vel globuli penduli, longitudine duorum pedum à centro motus.' The normal beat of
a man's pulse is 72 to the minute, and that of a woman 80,
whereas the beat of a two-foot pendulum is 76·6. Thus the
tempo indicated by Tomkins can be approximately expressed
in terms of the modern metronome as M.M. ♩= 76. It cannot
be supposed, however, that Tomkins, or any other composer,
adhered rigidly to any such standard regardless of the varying
character and style of the words as well as of the music. In this
matter there was probably a far greater variety of use in secular
music than in Church music, and it is to the latter class that
Tomkins's note has special reference.

The time-signatures to be found in the madrigal part-books
are many and various. In the mediaeval period, in which time-
signatures had their origin, the principal signs used were the
complete circle, , and the semi-circle, , which has
in modern days assumed the shape of the letter c,
The former, as being the type of figure that best represented
the idea of perfection, came to be employed for that reason to
indicate what was known as ' perfect ', or triple, time ; while
the latter stood for duple, or common, time. These figures
were also used with a line drawn through them
to denote that the unit of measure was to be a minim
instead of a semibreve. The same figures were used, too, with
a dot in the centre ; this dot denoted the
' Greater Prolation ', a term that indicated the relative value of
a semibreve to a minim as one to three, as opposed to the
' Lesser Prolation ', in which, as in modern times, the semibreve
was equal to two minims. These time-signatures had no such
reference to the number of beats in a bar as they have come to
assume in more modern music.

In the latter years of the sixteenth century numerical figures
came to be used, either with, or as a substitute for, the old circle
and semicircle, to denote triple time. Thus in the compositions

of the madrigalists we find, among other time-signatures, 3 and
$\frac{3}{2}$, or 3·1 and 3·2, both with and without the circle and semicircle in their various forms. Occasionally also we get such
unusual time-signatures as 6·1, which, for instance, Byrd used
in an instrumental Fantasia (No. 26 of his 1611 Set) ; while
Pilkington in *Yond hill-tops Phoebus kissed* (Set II, No. 2) used

the signature ⊘. Morley[1] actually gave 5·1 as a possible
6·1

signature, but no example of this is to be found in the writings
of the English madrigalists, although a phrase or group of five
units is not altogether uncommon in this music. At this period
English composers employed the old signatures without always
attaching much importance to their exact significance, and
numbers of examples might be cited from the works of the
madrigalists to illustrate their indiscriminate use of them. The
Cantus-part of Morley's three-part Canzonets is printed throughout with the barred semicircle, while the Altus and Bassus
part-books have it unbarred. Again, in the first edition of
Morley's four-part Madrigals the barred semicircle was used,
but in the second edition the unbarred semicircle is substituted
for it.

In passages with triple time-signature the madrigalists' usual
practice was to write three minims to a bar rather than three
crotchets, as in modern notation. Occasionally the unit of the
beat in triple time was a semibreve ; several examples of this
occur in Tomkins's Set, and there is one in the concluding bars
of Wilbye's *Lady, your words do spite me* (First Set, No. 18).
Sometimes they wrote in white notation and sometimes in black,
and sometimes they mixed the two types of notation quite
indiscriminately. It is important to distinguish carefully
between black minims and crotchets, for both have precisely
the same appearance ; and the confusion is complicated by the
necessity in this notation of adding tails to the crotchets, with
the object of differentiating them from the black minims, and
thus giving them the appearance of quavers. In such passages
it will be noticed that the black minims and tailed-crotchets
always have their counterpart in the minim and crotchet rests

[1] Morley's Plain and Easy Introduction, p. 91.

of the standard type. For practical purposes, and in the great majority of cases in the English madrigals, when the time-signature in the original text changes from duple to triple, i. e. from C($\frac{4}{4}$) to $\frac{3}{2}$, the time value of the 2 may be taken to be that of the preceding 4 ; in other words the value of the minim may be regarded as being equivalent to the crotchet of the preceding section. From a strict point of view the triple time should relatively be slightly slower, in the ratio of three to four, because the *tactus*, or beat denoting the beginning of a bar, remained constant whether in duple or triple time. The purpose in employing the *tactus* or the *stroke*, as Morley calls it,[1] was solely to give a unit of duration, and not in any sense to establish a bar or unit of rhythm. Thus in the triple time the three minims would occupy the same length of period as four crotchets in the preceding duple time; so that, in terms of the metronome, if the *tempo* of the former passage had been M. M. ♩ = 120, that of the triple time would be 𝅗𝅥 = 90. These exact proportions were almost certainly not observed in secular music by the Elizabethans, and it will generally be found that the natural interpretation of the music will be satisfactorily secured by treating the new minim unit as being of roughly the same value as that of the former crotchet. Moreover, in numbers of instances there is no room for doubt that the unit of time must have remained constant when the measure changed from duple to triple and triple to duple. Such instances occur in Dowland's *Lend your ears to my sorrow* (Book III, No. 11), where there is an overlap in the Tenor-part. Again, in the concluding passage of Wilbye's *Thou art but young* (Set I, No. 29). Exceptional cases, in which a slower *tempo* may seem to be suitable to the words and also to be in conformity with the composer's intention, must be left to individual taste and discretion. The general principle will be rendered clear by the following quotation from Morley's *Arise, get up, my dear* (three-voice Canzonets, No. 20), in which the added pianoforte-part has, for the purposes of explanation, been translated into terms of the crotchet unit in the section that is in triple time :

---

[1] Morley's Plain and Easy Introduction, pp. 9 and 21.

The key-signatures in the original editions were limited to three alternatives : (1) no sharp or flat, (2) one flat, (3) two flats. This third alternative was comparatively rare in the madrigals, but examples of it are to be found in Wilbye's *Flora gave me fairest flowers* (Set I, No. 22), and in Gibbons's *Nay let me weep* (No. 17). A sharp never occurs in the key-signatures of this date.

The madrigal-composers were largely influenced by the old Church modes ; yet they were breaking away from the stricter discipline of the rules which governed modal music and were feeling their way towards the modern scales through the channels indicated by a limited kind of modulation in which they indulged. Thus they treated the modes with great freedom, and by the liberal introduction of accidentals they modernized the harmonic effect, sometimes entirely obliterating the modal character of their music. It was their eager search after new methods of expression in this detail, as in so many others, that paved the way for a system of modulation and key-variety, such as constitutes the groundwork of Form in the Classical period. When a composition was written in a mode in its normal position, that is to say not transposed, no sharp or flat appears in the signature, whatever the mode may be. The simplest practical method of ascertaining the mode of a composition is to look at the bass note of the final chord ; if, for instance, this should be D, the Dorian mode is indicated ; if E, the Phrygian, and so on. Strictly speaking, modal music lies within the range of the octave, but a melody may be either authentic or plagal ; in other words, and in more modern phraseology, a melody in the key of C major may either lie mainly between C and C, as, for example, *The blue-bells of Scotland* and *Barbara Allen*, which are authentic melodies, or between G and G, as in *Men of Harlech*, which is plagal. In the modal system the prefix *hypo* was added to the name of the mode to distinguish the plagal from the authentic melodies. Thus, if there is no flat in the key-signature of a madrigal, and the final bass note is G, and the melody lies mainly between G and G, the Mixo-lydian is the mode in which it is written ; but if under these same conditions the melody lies mainly between D and D, the mode is the Hypo-mixolydian. The following table shows the modes in ordinary use in the latter part of the sixteenth century. The Locrian and Hypo-locrian modes, with B as the Final, are omitted here.

Number.	Final.	Range.	Mode.
1.	D	D to D	Dorian
2.	D	A ,, A	Hypo-dorian
3.	E	E ,, E	Phrygian
4.	E	B ,, B	Hypo-phrygian
5.	F	F ,, F	Lydian
6.	F	C ,, C	Hypo-lydian
7.	G	G ,, G	Mixo-lydian
8.	G	D ,, D	Hypo-mixolydian
9.	A	A ,, A	Aeolian
10.	A	E ,, E	Hypo-aeolian
11.	C	C ,, C	Ionian
12.	C	G ,, G	Hypo-ionian

When a B flat occurs in the signature it shows that the mode is used in a transposed position. Such transposition was to an interval of a fifth below (or fourth above) the normal position of the mode ; hence the true mode in such a case is the fourth below or fifth above. For instance, G with a B flat is the same as D without one. Consequently, to take one such example with a flat in the signature, if the Final is G and the melody is authentic, the music is written in the transposed Dorian mode. In the rare cases in which two flats appear in the key-signature the mode has been twice transposed, namely a fifth lower than the fifth below the normal position, or, in other words, a tone down. Consequently the Dorian mode twice transposed has C for its Final, the range of the melody lies between C and C, and it bears a signature of two flats. The modes were never transposed to other intervals.

The key-signatures employed in the madrigal-period, and indeed until well on in the eighteenth century, frequently present to modern eyes the appearance of having a flat or sharp too few for the key in which the music may, rather loosely, be said to be written. The explanation is not far to seek when the very gradual transition from the modal system to the modern major and minor keys is borne in mind. The Dorian mode, with the minor third and major sixth, contained no flat :

and the transposed Dorian (from G to G) only one ; and so, by
habit, after the modes as such were forgotten, the key of
C minor, for example, continued for some time to bear the
key-signature of two flats only. The transposed Aeolian mode,
with the minor third and minor sixth, contains, it is true,
two flats :

but on the other hand the Lydian mode, from F to F with
B♮, has no flat, and therefore, when transposed, has the
appearance of having a flat too few in the signature :

This provides ample explanation of the apparent irregularity
of the key-signatures. And this explanation applies similarly
to the presence of a sharp too few. This is to be accounted for
by the great prevalence of the use of the Mixo-lydian mode with
the major third :

It is obvious also that the transposed forms of this required
a sharp too few in the signature. It is not therefore surprising
that this practice, as already mentioned, survived long after
the old modes had passed out of general use ; thus, for example,
Handel's *Harmonious Blacksmith* variations, which are in
E major, have only three sharps in the key-signature of the old
editions ; and Bach's so-called ' Dorian ' Toccata and Fugue
in D minor, which is in no sense composed in the Dorian mode,
owes its name to the omission of the flat in the key-signature.

It may seem almost superfluous to mention that the key-
signatures of the sixteenth-century music have a totally
different significance from that which they bear in modern
music ; yet it is all too common an experience to hear choral
singers and others speaking of a madrigal being in such and
such a key because the signature denotes that key in modern
music. It is a fundamental error to say that a madrigal in the
Mixo-lydian mode is in C major for the sole reason that no

sharp or flat appears in the key-signature ; but in Vincent
Novello's manuscript score of Tomkins's ' Songs ', made by
him in 1844, and now in the library of the Royal College of
Music, Novello himself appended a note making that actual
error. On the same principle, the music of the *Harmonious
Blacksmith* is not turned into A major by the omission of the
fourth sharp in the key-signature.

The madrigal-composers made brave experiments in the
direction of modulation, but it was considered by Morley [1]
a ' wonder of nature ' to begin, for instance, in the key of G, to
close in C or D and thence to return to G ; for modulation of
an extended kind was not possible for them. For one thing,
the old ' untempered ' scale, for which they wrote, precluded it,
and it was modulation that eventually created the necessity
for equal temperament.

There were at least three different scale systems in simultaneous use in the days of the madrigalists, and they will be
best explained and compared with the modern scale of equal
temperament by means of a table based upon some figures
given by Professor Wooldridge in a very lucid article upon the
subject.[2] Of these three systems one was that of the natural
vocal scale, another was the old modal scale, and the third was
that employed for the keyed-instruments, such as the virginal.
And each of these was different from the modern scale framed
on the principle of equal temperament.

The octave is made up of twelve semitones, and for the
purposes of comparison each of these semitones is divided into
hundredths, or cents, thus making 1,200 cents in the complete
octave. The modern diatonic scale then consists of five tones,
each of 200 cents and each containing two semitones of 100 each.
It is important, however, to mention that the term *cent* is used
here in a highly technical sense which cannot be discussed in
this brief notice ; it will be sufficient to say that the above
statement must not be taken to imply that all the semitones
in the scale of equal temperament are of uniform measure. In
the old keyed-instrument and in the modal scales the interval
of a whole tone was practically constant ; but in the natural

---

[1] Morley's Plain and Easy Introduction, p. 147.
[2] Arkwright's Old English Edition, Part III, Preface.

vocal scale there were two kinds of whole-tone, apart from the semitones, three of them being slightly larger than the whole-tone of equal temperament and two being markedly smaller ; they were styled major tones and minor tones by the old musicians.   With the object of adding clearness to its meaning the notes and intervals of the scale of C major are given in this table :

	c–d	d–e	e–f	f–g	g–a	a–b	b–c	c–c
1. Modern dia- tonic scale	200	200	100	200	200	200	100	1,200
2. Natural vocal scale	204	182	112	204	182	204	112	1,200
3. Modal scale	204	204	90	204	204	204	90	1,200

4. Old keyed-in-
   strument
   scale
	193	193	117	194	193	193	117	1,200

This table deals primarily with the differences in tones and semitones, but further interesting deductions can be made from it as regards other intervals, and especially with reference to the major and minor third and the major and minor sixth. In the natural vocal scale the major third and sixth are smaller than the same intervals in a scale of equal temperament, whereas the minor third and sixth work out larger.   It is interesting, too, to observe the values of such intervals as the diminished and the augmented fourth and of the diminished fifth in these old scales, whereas these intervals are, of course, uniform in the modern diatonic scale.   The diminished fourth must especially be noticed, because the madrigal-writers were fond of using that interval in such a phrase as : and in the chord . A study of these figures will also make it clear why the Tudor composers could not modulate into extreme keys, and that, when they did make elaborate experiments in modulation, as for instance in one of Bull s virginal pieces, they must have been experimenting also in systems of tuning based upon the principles of equal temperament—an effort truly characteristic of the Elizabethan spirit.

But, reverting to the subject of unaccompanied vocal music, these differences of tonality have an important bearing upon the performance of such music by modern singers.   Among other things, one of the causes of the universal difficulty of securing a sufficiently sharp major third and leading note, when dealing with modern conditions, is made obvious ; for Professor Wooldridge stated [1] that singers, when unhampered by accompaniment, will instinctively revert to the natural vocal scale ; and this fact has been proved by experience. But this does not in itself provide the true explanation of the so-called false relations and clashes between the major and minor thirds, even at the same octave, which are so characteristic of Tudor music. It is impossible to suppose for an instant that these clashes produced anything approaching the cacophonous effect that they do on a modern pianoforte, and the true explanation is to be found in the practice which prevailed in early times of sharpening the major third in the rising scale and flattening the minor third in the falling scale. In such conditions rising or falling cadences came to be known, respectively, as the *terminus acutus* and the *terminus gravis*. It is not too much to say that if this principle is recognized, and the major third is deliberately sharpened while the minor third is flattened, modern musicians can find in these clashes a new sensation of beauty in sound, or rather, will rediscover an old one which their Tudor ancestors evidently enjoyed.

As regards the use of accidentals it must be remembered that the laws of *musica ficta*, which so strictly controlled the music of a generation earlier, were being partially abandoned in the transitional period at which the madrigalists wrote, and things were no longer taken for granted to the same extent as formerly ; so it became imperative to insert accidentals even with notes which had been too obvious in their meaning to need them. This is noticeably the case with the major triad, which by the laws of *musica ficta* was invariably to be used not only in the final cadence but at every cadence of importance throughout a composition (unless the bare fifth or octave were used without any third). In the older music the sharp was seldom indicated in such a place, and indeed it was known as the ' sign of the ass ' in such a connexion, for the reason that no one but an ass required such a reminder ; but in the time of the English Madrigal School it was being very generally inserted.

---

[1] Arkwright's Old English Edition, Part III, Introduction, p. 9.

The principle of using accidentals differed from modern practice. In the first place, the only two signs employed were the flat and the sharp ; the natural was scarcely ever used in the madrigal part-books, although primitive forms of it are occasionally to be met with in the Church music of the same period. In No. 22 of Pilkington's second Set there are two instances of a capital F to signify a natural following an F sharp, and two more in No. 24. These are the only examples known to the present writer in any of the madrigal part-books. Thus, if the piece was written with a key-signature of one flat, the sign of the sharp had to be employed to denote when, by exception, B natural was required in the music. The sharp was, in fact, the only sign available for raising a note a semitone ; and similarly the flat was the only sign to denote the converse. Thus a flat printed before C immediately following a C sharp would denote C natural. But, secondly, such a contradictory accidental was very seldom used at all, because, owing to the absence of any bar lines in the music, it was the practice to print accidentals against each note that required it, even when such a note was repeated consecutively ; for the normal presumption was that any note that had no such accidental indicated was to be taken at its face value. The completeness with which the accidentals were printed varies very much in these books, and no definite rule seems to have been followed. There are instances, as in the example quoted below, in which the accidental is repeated for each of several reiterated notes, and an example of the converse will be found in Morley's *On a fair morning* (No. 22 of his four-part Set of Madrigals), in which one flat only is printed before twelve repeated E's but is intended to control them all. The following passage from the tenor part-book of Ward's *Sweet Philomel* (No. 13) provides a good example of the liberal use of accidentals :

my mournful style which will of mirth your su - gar'd notes be - reave.

As an illustration of the more sparing use of accidentals the following phrase may be quoted from Weelkes's *Phyllis hath sworn* (No. 20 of his ' Balletts and Madrigals '). The accidentals

here printed above the stave are those that have to be added
as being in accordance with the composer's intention, although
not actually indicated. For the purpose of illustration the
text of the Cantus and Quintus-parts in this passage have been
combined :

needs a - gree, Phi - le - mon then must needs a - gree

In the above passage there is no room for doubt as to the
correctness of the added accidentals, but there are numbers of
cases in the text as printed in the madrigal part-books, which
involve difficult decisions on the part of a modern editor, and
these must be left to individual judgement.

Occasionally the accidental was given several notes ahead.
This plan may have been deliberately adopted as a kind of
warning :

Something must be said here to explain the great variety of
clefs which were used in these part-books. The system of
modern notation, as is well known, is founded upon a stave of
eleven lines, called the Great Stave. Staves of thirteen and even
fifteen lines were occasionally employed. But the human eye
has been found able to grasp the position of notes most quickly
when but five of these eleven lines are used ; and, moreover,
five lines are practically enough to take all the notes any voice
could use without leger lines ; a stave includes an octave plus
a fourth, that is to say room for a mode and its plagal variety.
So the matter resolved itself into the question as to which five
lines were to be selected as being most suited for any single
piece of music.

Taking the note that is commonly called middle C as the
central point of the combined compass of human voices, that
note was placed upon the middle line of the eleven, and the
sign ▓, or ▓, which is a corruption of the letter C, ⊆, was
prefixed to the stave at that point to serve as the ' key ' (or its
French equivalent *clef*), thus determining the actual position

in the musical scale which the lines of the stave were to denote. Two other signs were employed upon the Great Stave as additional landmarks to assist the eye in recognizing the position of the notes. One was placed five notes, or two lines, above, and the other five notes, or two lines, below middle C. The signs employed for this purpose were also corruptions of the alphabetical letters of the notes which they signified : viz. 𝄞 for *g*, and 𝄢 for *f*. It is not necessary to speak here of two other signs or clefs which signified, respectively, the D a fifth above the treble G, and the G a seventh below the F of the bass clef, except to mention that this latter obsolete clef-signature was the Greek letter *gamma*, which, since it represented the lowest note of the Great Stave, is the origin of the term *gamut*, a word which is a combination of the two words *gamma* and *ut*, for which latter term *do* has been substituted in more modern times :

| Γ (*gamma*) | A | B | C | D | E |
| *ut* | *re* | *mi* | *fa* | *sol* | *la* |

The three key signs, or *clefs*, mentioned above, figured thus on the Great Stave :

For the purposes of the organ or pianoforte and its predecessors the simple plan adopted was to obliterate the middle line and only to employ a fraction of it temporarily when the note C was required for use. Convenience soon dictated the use of further leger lines between the two groups of five lines in pianoforte score, and this had the effect of obscuring the origin of the system and straining the link that connects the ' treble ' and ' bass ' clefs.

For the purposes of voices or of those instruments which require the use of no more than five lines of the stave at one time, these two signs for the G and F clefs have come into use exactly as they stand in the pianoforte stave, and in modern music they are almost exclusively employed. But they do not adequately satisfy the requirements of the Alto and Tenor voice, or of such an instrument as the viola, because the compass of the music ranges about the middle of the Great Stave in varying degrees. Thus for the viola the middle five lines have been selected from the Great Stave of eleven. Acting upon this principle of pure expediency the musicians of the madrigalian era selected whichever five lines most nearly included within their limits the notes written for the particular voice-part in hand. In this way they almost entirely avoided the use of leger lines. It is very important to emphasize the fact that the C clef signature, or any other, remains absolutely constant in its position on the stave, and that it is simply a matter of which six lines of the eleven are eliminated and which five remain in use. Students and pupils are far too frequently misled, and needlessly confused, as to the actual principle which governs the use of clefs.

The following scheme should make this principle clear :

1 and 10. The Great Stave of eleven lines.
2. Treble clef ; sometimes known as violin clef.
3. Soprano clef.
4. Mezzo-soprano clef.
5. Alto clef ; sometimes known as viola clef.
6. Tenor clef ; much used also for violoncello music.
7. Baritone clef with C signature ; very rarely used.
8. Baritone clef with F signature ; the more normal form, but denoting the same selection from the stave as No. 7.
9. Bass clef.

It is unfortunate that modern musical terminology in England has confused the meaning of the words *clef* and *stave*, and has led to their being misapplied. It would have been more correct, having regard to their original meaning, to speak of the

Treble or Alto stave rather than clef, and for the word clef to have been reserved exclusively to denote the sign, or figure of the signature.

Every one of the eight possible varieties of selection of stave or clef is to be found in the English madrigal part-books, but the baritone clef with C signature was very rarely used, and there are no examples in the madrigal books of the F clef on the top line or of the G clef on the middle or the fifth lines, though these are to be found in sixteenth-century music. For the rest the choice was mainly governed by the compass of the voice-part, yet in this matter, as in so many others of the same nature, very curious inconsistencies are to be met with ; whether these were due to the handiwork of the printers or of the composers cannot now be determined.

No expression marks were printed in these books, nor are there any indications to be gathered from the text to show whether any individual phrase was to be sung loud or soft. Yet it must not for a moment be inferred from this fact that the madrigals were sung, or are to be sung now, without a consider-able amount of light and shade as well as freedom of *tempo* ; on the contrary, every available resource must be drawn upon so that the music may be rendered with suitable expression. There is a danger in printing expression marks in modern editions of Tudor music because, as Mr. Arkwright was one of the first to point out,[1] they have the deceptive appearance of authority, and because, moreover, conductors ought to be left entirely free in this matter. It is astonishing how commonly, even among trained musicians, printed expression marks in modern editions convey the false impression that they were the work of the composer himself. They also force upon the performers the interpretation of one single individual, namely, that of the editor, whose taste and opinion alone they represent upon this important matter of discretion, as to which, in many instances, scarcely two persons would think alike; and so they may stereo-type the expression and rob the performance of that interest which an unfettered individuality of treatment cannot fail to impart.

[1] Note upon Accent and Expression by G. E. P. Arkwright, Old English Edition, Part XXI.

CHAPTER X
THE METHODS AND IDIOM OF THE
MADRIGALISTS

THE only legitimate purpose in setting words to music is to increase their beauty and add to the clearness of their meaning. This fundamental truth was appreciated to its fullest extent by the English madrigalists, and it was because they built upon so secure a foundation that their work still lives with such enduring vigour. But the methods and idiom which they used had their own individuality and were characteristic of the brief period in which they flourished, differing from those of earlier days as well as from those of the seventeenth century and later. Some of these points of difference have been overlooked by succeeding generations of musicians, and certain characteristic features of their method seem to have been misunderstood ever since the first traditions of madrigal-singing in England were broken in the middle of the seventeenth century.

The composers' methods of handling the poetry must be considered in some detail. These Elizabethan musicians seem to have shared with the great poets of their own age that fine instinct of imagination which is essential to the conception of productions of the first rank in all the branches of creative art. When they chose a poem for their purpose, they studied its meaning until the vision of the poet had come to their own eyes. Then they set themselves to interpret that vision through the medium of music.

In contrast to the lutenists' Airs, for which there were often several stanzas of poetry and rarely fewer than two, the madrigalists seldom had use for more than one stanza. A noticeable exception to this rule is to be found in the Ballet, because the more regular measure of that particular form made possible the repetition of the music to further verses of identical metre. In such cases the first stanza was set out with the musical notation, while the rest of the poem was printed in metrical

form at the foot of the page. Byrd's three Sets, which differ
in so many ways from the rest of the madrigal series, differ
from them also in the frequent inclusion of several stanzas
of poetry in addition to those actually set out with the musical
notation. It is more than doubtful whether it was customary
to sing all the verses of these longer poems ; in such bright
numbers as *Though Amaryllis dance in green* (1588 Set, No. 12)
it seems likely that one or two further verses were sung, but
in more elaborate compositions there would have been many
difficulties to surmount, and occasionally the metrical conditions precluded the possibility. *O you that hear this voice*
(Byrd's 1588 Set, No. 16) is a poem by Sidney in nine stanzas,
two of which are used in the musical setting, the remaining
seven being printed at the foot of the page ; in this case four
repetitions would not only be tedious, but there would still
remain an odd stanza with only half the number of lines
required to fit to the music.

The outline of madrigal-construction has been sketched in
a former chapter,[1] but a few details of a more technical nature
may here be added. The musicians' plan was to deal with the
poem line by line, or phrase by phrase, each phrase being
introduced with new musical material woven into imitative
counterpoint. But the madrigalists were striving eagerly to
devise some kind of cohesion and symmetry of design in their
compositions, and they adopted various methods for the purpose ; thus, for instance, some of the more elaborate madrigals
are divided into two, or perhaps three, main sections by the
introduction of a bar or two of homophonic, as contrasted
with polyphonic, texture, the sub-sections being treated in
the ordinary way, phrase by phrase, without any such interruption of style. This method of homophonic punctuation
was a favourite device of Weelkes, and a good example is
provided by that composer's *When Thoralis delights to walk*
(No. 2 of his Madrigals for six voices) ; the poem is eight lines
long and is divided by Weelkes into sections of two, four, and
two lines, each section punctuated at its opening by a homophonic phrase. Wilbye's Oriana madrigal (No. 15 of the
' Triumphs ') shows a somewhat similar use of homophony to

---

[1] See page 52.

mark the opening of fresh sections : for instance, at the words
Then with an olive branch ; and homophonic phrases are used
in this same madrigal for the words : *And thus sang they*, and
again *Then sang the shepherds.* It is noticeable that both the
Cantus and Bassus-parts of these last two passages are almost
identical in repetition, and this illustrates another device of
the madrigalists, namely the repetition of a musical phrase
with the object of linking together two similar ideas. Refer-
ences of this kind are often made with a subtle touch such as
might escape notice without careful scrutiny ; and they were
sometimes disguised by such devices as augmentation, diminution, or inversion. Good examples of this method may be
seen in Weelkes's ' Elegy on Lord Borough ' (1598 Set, No. 24)
or Morley's *Hark! Alleluia* (five and six-voice Canzonets, No. 21).

It must not be supposed, however, that the introduction of
homophonic passages was strictly confined to this purpose ;
some composers, as, for instance, Kirbye, introduced a large
proportion of homophonic writing into their madrigals, and
large sections of Bennet's Oriana madrigal *All creatures now*
are treated homophonically.

The earnest endeavour of these musicians to secure homo-
geneity and symmetry of design for their madrigals is shown
in another direction. There are a few examples which forecast
clearly, if in a very elementary fashion, some of those principles
of form in composition which saw their full development in
the great classical period of the eighteenth and nineteenth
centuries. Some of these early beginnings of the classical
forms will be considered in more detail in later chapters
dealing with the individual style and work of the several
composers, but passing mention may be made of some typical
examples : thus, Morley's *Miraculous love's wounding* (two-
part Canzonets, No. 5) shows some of the principles of ternary
form : and Weelkes's *Ay me, my wonted joys* (No. 9 of his 1597
Set) has in it the elements of Rondo-form. That Wilbye
clearly understood the value of recapitulation as the basis of
form is shown in his *Of joys and pleasing pains* (Set I, Nos. 26
and 27). Farmer's *Take time while time doth last* (No. 16) is built
up on an older principle, with a tenor serving as a *Canto fermo*
in a simple scale passage ; but Farnaby's *Susanna fair* (No. 12)

is a particularly interesting early example of a type of design which was brought to perfection by J. S. Bach in dealing with the Chorale.

It was a common device to repeat the final section of a madrigal, and in such a repeat it was a frequent practice to interchange the parts of the voices of equal compass and range. It was for this reason that the repeated passage was so generally printed out *in extenso*.

The constructive methods of the madrigalists are illustrated from another point of view by the analysis of such examples as Morley's *Ho! who comes here?* (Madrigalls to Foure Voyces, No. 18), or Weelkes's *Take here my heart* (Madrigals of five parts, No. 3), both of which are built up with material designed to illustrate the meaning of the words ; the former vividly reproduces the scene of the Morris dancers making sport in the village to the merry peal of the bells ; Weelkes's madrigal, in a more serious vein, tells of the plighting of a lover's troth with the subtle suggestion of the wedding bells passing through his mind. This latter example is just one of those cases in which the composer was able to add poetry even to the poet's work.

The special method of handling single words or ideas was another characteristic feature of the madrigals. It was the custom of these composers to emphasize their meaning either by the use of some unusual or unexpected chord, or by some suitable musical figure. Countless examples could be cited to illustrate this point. Such words as *joy*, or *sing*, or *fly* were almost invariably set to a phrase of rapid notes ; and not only so, the curve of the notes would in itself illustrate such a thing as the flight of a bird, with the slight fall and rise that is characteristic of many small birds. Similarly in Weelkes's *Thule* (six-part Madrigals, Nos. 7 and 8) it requires but a small effort of imagination in glancing at the vocal score to see *Aetna's flames* shooting up higher and higher ; and even more evident, in the same madrigal, are the *flying fishes*. Dancing was almost always treated in triple rhythm, either with or without the introduction of a fresh time-signature. The word *sigh* was very generally preceded by a rest in order to enhance its realistic effect, but whereas such treatment occasionally led very near

to paths of triviality, there can be no such feeling associated
with the chord used by Gibbons at the word *death* in *The silver
swan* (No. 1 of his Madrigals), or the still more remarkable
chord which Weelkes wrote at the word *dead* in his *Noel
Elegy* (No. 10 of the six-part Madrigals). The chord used by
Gibbons is that with the major third and minor sixth ; it is
not by any means uncommon throughout the works of the
English madrigalists and was used by them without preparation. It is more than lamentable that in a very widely circu-
lated version of *The silver swan* this chord has been destroyed
by the substitution of D for the E flat of the original text.

A very early example of the use of this chord occurs in
Edwards's *O the silly man*, one of the secular pieces in the
Mulliner MS.,[1] the date of which is not later than 1564.

It was also used by Byrd in the first number of his 1588 Set.

These realistic methods of the madrigalists remained in
vogue for a very extended period of musical history ; whatever may be thought of them, it will be readily acknowledged
that many composers in this country a hundred years later
brought these methods into contempt owing to their lack of
the artistic subtlety which almost always saved the madrigalists
from triviality. Familiar examples of realism were of course
superbly handled by Bach, Handel, and Haydn ; and in this
connexion it may be mentioned that the famous passages in
the St. Matthew and St. John Passion of Peter ' weeping
bitterly ' were anticipated by both Byrd and Dowland in their
settings of *If that a sinner's sighs* (Byrd's 1588 Set, No. 30, and
Dowland's ' A Pilgrimes Solace ', No. 13).

Quite apart from the expressive meaning which the madrigalists strove to impart to the words by the use of harmonic
and other devices, they attached great value to correctness of

---

[1] British Museum Add. MSS. 30513, fol. 77 b.

accentuation. This detail is closely associated with the subject of rhythm, which will be fully considered in the following chapter. Meanwhile Morley's comment upon the importance of true syllabic accentuation may be quoted : [1] ' We must also have a care to applie the notes to the words, as in singing there be no barbarisme committed, that is that we cause no syllable which is by nature short, be expressed by manie notes or one long note, nor no long syllable bee expressed with a short note : but in this fault doe the practicioners erre more grossely, then in any other, for you shal find few songs wherein the penult syllables of these words *Dominus, Angelus. filius, miraculum, gloria,* and such like are not expressed with a long note, yea manie times with a whole dossen of notes, & though one should speak of fortie he shuld not say much amisse : which is a grosse barbarisme, & yet might be easily amended.'

Morley was referring chiefly to the music of an age considerably before his own, and he goes on to quote Dunstable as an example of what ' som dunces have not slackt to do ' by way of absurdity ' in the dittying of musick '. Reference to the quotation from Landino's music on p. 51 of the present volume will show the kind of thing which Morley had in his mind.

In the matter of word-bonding, or underlaying the text, as it is technically called, the Elizabethans had a distinctive idiom of their own. A careful study of the part-books cannot fail to reveal the main principles upon which their system was based, but until very recently this feature of Tudor vocal music has been wholly ignored both by editors and by executant musicians. For one thing, a group of four quavers, or crotchets, was scarcely ever divided equally into two pairs of notes as is customary in more modern practice. Such a group was phrased thus :

scorn - ful - ly.   not   scorn - ful - ly.

Slur-marks were scarcely ever printed in the English madrigal part-books, and the evidence to be gleaned from Tomkins's

---

[1] Plain and Easy Introduction, p. 178.

Set on this matter is of some importance, for in his Set there
are some rare and valuable examples of *printed* slur-marks.
A single example will suffice for purposes of illustration :

our   life   a - way doth   post, a   -   way.

There are also some instances of this kind of phrasing in
Youll's canzonet *Slow, slow, fresh fount* (No. 11 of the Set).
It happens that some phrase-marks have been added by a contemporary hand in manuscript to the Bassus-part of the
British Museum copy of this Set ; and these remove any doubt
that might have remained in the absence of further direct
evidence as to the Elizabethan practice in secular music. This
evidence is all the more valuable because the slurs are inserted
in at least two instances at points where the position of the
printed syllables leaves room for ambiguity. The third
among the following examples is the most noticeable and seems
to suggest the use of a kind of *portamento*. Countless examples
of this particular convention of underlaying the words are to be
found in the old Durham Cathedral part-books. The bar-
lines given here do not, of course, appear in the original text :

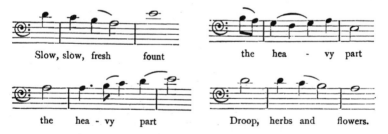

Slow, slow, fresh   fount   the   hea - vy   part

the   hea - vy   part   Droop, herbs and   flowers.

It was a very general rule that when no more than two
syllables were available for a group of three notes, the second
syllable was tied to the last two notes of the group. This
point is well illustrated by the opening bars of Weelkes's *Jockie,
thine hornpipe's dull* ('Ayeres or Phantasticke Spirites', No. 2) :

Jock - ie thine horn - pipe's   dull,   give wind man at   full

These conclusions are strongly supported by the evidence of a contemporary manuscript of certain anthems by Orlando Gibbons in the Christ Church library.[1] Though not actually in the composer's hand the text is authoritative, and the phrase marks indicate the same principles for underlaying the words as those enunciated above.   The following are examples :

and these principles are also amply exemplified in the contemporary manuscript part-books of the Church music of the period.

The absence of slur-marks to indicate the exact underlaying of the words in the madrigal part-books, and the unexpected position of the words in certain instances, must on no account be taken to imply carelessness either on the part of the printers or the composers.   As the special features of this Tudor convention in setting words to music becomes familiar, singers will find a special charm and value revealed in them ; for it will be seen that the true emphasis of the words is greatly enhanced by these methods, and that the bonding of several notes to unimportant syllables or words in certain cases has the direct effect of throwing the accent on to the important words.

As regards harmonic principles, it is very commonly supposed

---

[1] Ch. Ch. Oxford, MS. 21.

that the madrigal-writers were limited by the custom of their time to the use of the common chord and its first inversion and to the most straightforward kinds of suspended discords. This is far from being the case. The special peculiarities of Byrd's harmonic innovations will be more fully discussed in the chapter that is devoted exclusively to that composer ; the two most noticeable of these were the simultaneous use of the major and minor third, and the introduction of the minor third while the fourth was held in suspension to be resolved on to the major third. Byrd made far more use of these particular devices than any of the other madrigalists who succeeded him, but several instances of the conflict of the major and minor third are to be found in the works of Wilbye and Weelkes, and more particularly in Kirbye's Set of madrigals. Morley occasionally wrote the major and minor third simultaneously, but almost always when a fresh phrase opened with a minor third following a full close with the major triad ; in these circumstances the major third was probably not meant to be sustained for its full written value. Similar examples occur throughout the madrigal literature. The sudden contradiction of the major and minor triads, which in later times has also come to be regarded as an elementary form of error and stigmatized as a ' false relation ', was a device which all the madrigalists handled frequently and in most cases with really beautiful effect. Byrd's other device, mentioned above, though not much used by the rest of the school in their secular work, was employed for several generations of English composers, notably by Purcell. Morley throughout his work conformed to the more rigid rules of harmony in which he was trained, and this is the more remarkable because his madrigals, taken as a whole, are quite the gayest of all the series. But Morley's work did not extend beyond the close of the century, and he was not influenced by the harmonic experiments of Weelkes, Dowland, and Kirbye in 1597.

Byrd's anticipation of the free use of the dominant seventh, and especially of the cadence in which the seventh appears as a free passing note, is also dealt with in the chapter on his work. None of his successors made more use of this beautiful cadence than Gibbons, but it was frequently used also by

Weelkes, and never more effectively than in the exquisite close of his *Morley* elegy :

The use of the seventh in this manner is best explained by supposing the sixth to have been eliminated from the chain of consecutive passing-notes. The converse of this idea is to be found in at least two instances in Wilbye's madrigals. Thus in the following phrase he omitted the seventh and retained the sixth as a free passing-note. The passage is from *There where I saw her* (Set II, No. 24) :

Little room was left for further harmonic innovation after the appearance of Weelkes's *Cease, sorrows, now,* and *O care, thou wilt despatch me,* and of Wilbye's *Oft have I vowed,* Farnaby's *Construe my meaning,* and several others ; and the salient features of these is the development of chromatic material of three kinds, namely chromatic scale-passages, unprepared chromatic discords, and chromatic modulation. Among the chromatic discords mention has already been made of the chord of $\begin{smallmatrix}\flat 6\\ \sharp 3\end{smallmatrix}$ as being frequently introduced ; but there are rare examples of other chromatic chords, such as the so-called Italian sixth which occurs in Wilbye's *My throat is sore* (Set I, No. 27) :

Tomkins has a remarkable bar in *Was ever wretch tormented ?* (No. 12) :

and Dowland used a diminished seventh in *Fie on this feigning* (No. 16 of his Third Book) :

while in this same passage attention is directed to the inversion of the dominant eleventh on the subdominant in the cadence. This is a remarkably early instance of such harmony.

Innovations of this character were reflected in most of the Sets of madrigals that appeared after the year 1600; but the only composer in the school who may be said to have introduced further original features after that date was Tomkins. He shared the experience of all artists who attempt to break new ground, in that some of his experiments were not wholly successful. The following bars from a *fa-la* in his fine madrigal *O let me live for true love* (Nos. 7 and 8) are rather curious but by no means ineffective :

On the other hand, there can be no two opinions about the
great beauty of the sequences in the closing passages of *Weep
no more, thou sorry boy* (Nos. 10 and 11) and of the free use of
the $\frac{6}{4}$ chord in *Was ever wretch tormented ?* (No. 12).   These and
other features of Tomkins's work were quite original and are
not to be found before his time in the English madrigals.

One other important technical point to notice is the use by
the English madrigalists of various progressions which are
usually forbidden in the text-books.   The most debatable
detail under this heading is the use of consecutive fifths.
Morley, deploring the growing tendency to ignore the rule
in his time, and referring more particularly to the madrigals
of Croce, in which fifths and octaves frequently occur, states [1]
that such progressions are scarcely ever to be found in the
works of ' Master Alphonso (except in that place which
I cited to you before), Orlando, Striggio, Clemens *non Papa*,
or any of them, nor shal you redily find it in the workes of
anie of those famous Englishmen who have beene nothing
inferior in art to any of the afore named, as Farefax, Taverner,
Shepherde, Mundy, White, Persons, M. Birde, and divers
others, who never thought it greater sacrilidge to spurne
against the Image of a Saint, then to take two perfect cordes
of one kinde together.'   Throughout the whole history of
modern music, as dating from 1600, the use of such a progression has been regarded in academic circles as an error of the
first class, standing on the same level as a false quantity in
Latin verses.

There is no doubt as to the educational value for students of
a training which enforces the strictest observance of definite
and reasonable rules of grammar, nor is there any doubt that
all the greatest music of the Classical Period was composed
with a universal recognition of the rule that consecutive

[1] Morley's Plain and Easy Introduction, p. 151.

fifths and octaves were to be absolutely excluded ; and it
is a fact that scarcely any instances of such progressions can
be quoted from the whole of the works of such composers as
Bach, Handel, Mozart, Haydn, Schubert, Beethoven, and
Brahms. Not only so, but kindred rules, dealing with ' hidden
fifths ' and other such matters, grew to be respected with
almost equal strictness. But in modern days composers are
throwing such rules to the winds, and it cannot be denied that
objection to these forbidden progressions is often based on
no more than academic affectation, and not on purely aesthetic
grounds. But it is sometimes forgotten that the rule about
fifths was being deliberately disregarded by several prominent
musicians in Italy as well as in England at the close of the
sixteenth century ; and the fact that the world's greatest
musicians in the period roughly lying between 1560 and 1900
observed it strictly, does not necessarily establish it for all
time. It is sometimes forgotten also that the earliest kind of
harmonized music took the form of singing a piece of music
right through in consecutive fifths.

In connexion with this subject the practice of the English
madrigalists is full of interest. Direct pairs of fifths seldom
occur in the writings of the majority of these composers, and
practically never in those of Byrd, Morley, Wilbye, and
Weelkes ; but such a composer as Farnaby seems to have felt no
great objection to them, and the large number of such progressions in his canzonets cannot possibly be explained on the
grounds either of negligence or incompetence. It is clear that
he deliberately disregarded the rule.

But as regards ' hidden fifths ', and pairs of consecutive
fifths or octaves on strong beats, the madrigalists appear to
have felt no sort of restriction ; for throughout the madrigal-
literature there are numberless instances of such progressions as:

It cannot for a moment be pretended that these details
amount to blemishes, or that they detract one iota from the
artistic value of music as a whole.

In the matter of the progression of the individual voice-parts the madrigalists did not recognize all the restrictions which have been put upon part-writing by the text-books of more recent times. And yet the intervals which they wrote were in direct defiance of the traditional conventions which had governed composers up to their time. The step from F sharp to B flat was quite a commonplace in such a phrase as :

Isolated examples are even to be found of the use of an augmented second, as in the Cantus-part of Bateson's *Live not, poor bloom* (Set II, No. 7) where its purpose is obvious :

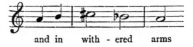

and in the Quintus and Tenor-parts of the same composer's *In depth of grief* (Set II, No. 21) :

The accidentals are actually marked in these instances and leave no room for ambiguity.

Another example occurs in the Altus-part of Ward's *Out from the vale of deep despair* (No. 21) at the words *Daphne's cruelty*. And Weelkes used the same progression in the Quintus-part of *Those spots upon my lady's face* (1597 Set, No. 21) to emphasize the idea of brightness at the words *the other, bright carnation*. Further examples are in the Cantus-part of Farnaby's *Construe my meaning* (No. 20), which is in all respects a most remarkable piece of chromatic writing, and in the Altus-part of Kirbye's *I love, alas* (No. 20). And Kirbye even used an augmented fifth in the Altus-part of *Sound out, my voice* (No. 9):

But quite apart from augmented intervals, the madrigalists did not appear to have recognized any law prohibiting what have since usually been regarded as awkward intervals. Tomkins in *Adieu, ye city-prisoning towers* (No. 22) had no hesitation in writing so bold a phrase as :

trees   are spring-ing.

and even so conservative a theorist as Morley in *Deep lamenting* (three-part Canzonets, No. 9) wrote :

all   too late now, God   wot, all   too late, all too   late.

Bateson in *Sweet, those trammels of your hair* (Set II, No. 6) wrote :

or my thoughts or   I   must die,   or my thoughts or

and the following passage occurs in the same composer's *Ay me, my mistress scorns my love* (Set I, No. 4) :

me,   Ay   me,

There are many other minor points of technique which cannot be touched upon in this brief review, and the reader is invited to study the text of the madrigals themselves for further enlightenment. But enough has been said to show that the rules of Counterpoint as understood by the English madrigalists are by no means in complete agreement with the ordinary modern text-books. These text-books, many of which have great merits of their own and serve the all-important purpose of enforcing a severe discipline upon students, deal with Counterpoint as it was understood by the musicians and theorists of the Continent, rather than the Counterpoint which the great English polyphonic composers wrote, either in their Church music or their madrigals.   English music-students have never been given the chance of receiving a training based upon their national traditions, and one of the first needs in this direction would seem to be a text-book on English Counterpoint dealing courageously with the whole question.

CHAPTER XI

RHYTHM AND BARRING IN TUDOR MUSIC

IF the Elizabethan singers were faced with certain difficulties which modern musical development and contrivances have largely eliminated, yet in the all-important detail of rhythmic interpretation they had an immense advantage over the singers of to-day. For, as the rhythms were not rendered obscure by the ·insertion of bar-lines in the old part-books, they could each phrase their own voice-part independently with small risk of being distracted by the other parts. And, without question, the true rhythmic interpretation of the music could be much more easily and naturally secured under those conditions. But the presence of bar-lines in modern editions of Tudor music must never be allowed to compromise the freedom of accent and phrasing intended by the composers.

The statement that regular barring was first introduced into England by Henry Lawes is not accurate, and it is no doubt founded on a misunderstanding of the practice of the sixteenth-century composers and printers. Tallis's compositions, for instance, were all printed without bars, because none of them were printed in score and it ·was the invariable custom of the time to print single voice-parts without bars ; but there can be little doubt that all the Elizabethan musicians composed in score and that they used some kind of barring in their scores, for it is not possible to suppose that the human eye could have perceived the harmonic connexion of the notes ranged perpendicularly in a manuscript vocal score, say, of six or eight parts, without some such aid as is provided by bar-lines. There is plenty of evidence to prove that the principle both of regular and irregular barring was understood by the Tudor composers, although they did not regard the employment of bar-lines as in any sense indicating a periodic flow of accents to control the rhythm as it did in the music of a later date.

Owing to the fact that for practical use, whether in manuscript or print, the music passed into the performers' hands in single voice-parts, and in that form only, scarcely any contemporary scores have survived. But in all the examples printed in score in Morley's ' Plaine and Easie Introduction to Musicke' regular bar-lines are inserted. Morley called these lines *strokes* and meant to indicate by them where the *tactus*, or periodic beat, came ; but it can be seen at a glance that these strokes or bar-lines do not establish any unit of rhythm, or control any regular flow of accent.

Very interesting evidence as to the prevailing practice in barring at the beginning of the seventeenth century is provided by the full vocal-score of Gibbons's anthems at Christ Church,[1] just as it is in the matter of underlaying the words. This manuscript may be as late as the year 1620, yet we may assume that if any definite system is revealed here it was nothing new, but had been followed in a general way throughout the later polyphonic period in England reaching at least as far back as 1590, if not earlier. This theory is supported by the fact that the same principles of barring were observed by John Amner in his manuscript vocal score of Tudor Church music at Ely Cathedral, and also in the organ-book of Adrian Batten at Tenbury,[2] and in the contemporary organ-books at Durham, Ely, and elsewhere. The leading features of the Christ Church score were as follows : the bar-lines were drawn without a break straight through all the staves in the score ; they were used somewhat sparsely, roughly speaking at a distance of eight minims in duple time and of six minims in triple measure ; the length of the bars was irregular and variable ; the bar-lines frequently cut across the rhythmic outlines of one or more of the voice-parts, and were not designed to control the rhythmic accentuation of the music.

The actual key to this system of barring is lost ; but it should not be impossible to discover the principle upon which the composer varied the size of his bars, sometimes lengthening them to ten or twelve minims, and sometimes shortening them to six or four, while occasionally bar-lengths of five, seven, or nine minims intervene. But by this system the varied and complex rhythms, which will be discussed more fully later in

---

[1] Ch.Ch. Oxford, MS. 21.   [2] Tenbury MS. 791.

this chapter, were certainly not obscured to anything like the same extent as they are by the modern system of short and regular bar-periods. But even so the Tudor composers recognized the danger of misinterpretation and false accent to which the presence of any sort of barring might lead, and for this reason they expunged them in the single voice-parts.

The practice of the lute-song writers in reference to barring has an important bearing upon the subject. It was necessary for the lutenists to retain some kind of barring in order to meet the requirements of lute-tablature. And their system of barring would, without doubt, have been influenced mainly by the predominant importance of a single voice-part, as contrasted with the equality of interest which was the essential feature of the voice-parts of a madrigal. Thus the lutenists recognized the advantages to be obtained by placing their bar-lines at irregular intervals. By this means they not only gave their sanction to the employment of irregular barring, but showed it to be a method of their own for dealing with rhythms of this kind. But the lutenists occasionally barred a song right through with perfect regularity. Thus Dowland's *White as lilies was her face* has four minims in all except the penultimate bar, in which the music prolongs the rhythm of the words with a fine artistic touch.

The two following examples of irregular barring may be quoted from Dowland's *Faction that ever dwells* (Book II, No. 18), and *Stay, Time, awhile thy flying* (Book IV, No. 7) :

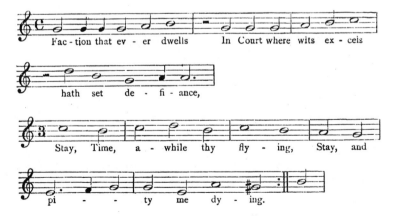

One other point must be mentioned in connexion with the barring of Tudor music. The fine set of part-books at York Minster, known as the Gostling MSS. because they belonged to the son of Purcell's famous bass, afford an example of part-books which are partially barred by the same hand that transcribed the music. They probably belong to the middle of the seventeenth century. The style of barring is similar to that just described as being found in Gibbons's autograph, and no doubt reproduces that of an earlier manuscript from which the transcription was made ; but a remarkable feature of the Gostling part-books is that the barring of the several voice-parts is non-simultaneous and is designed on independent lines, a fact which shows clearly that the music was sung with absolute freedom of phrasing in accordance with the true *ictus* of the words.

As to the actual existence of those irregular and complex rhythms in sixteenth and early seventeenth-century music there is no room whatever for uncertainty, although they are not particularly indicated by the composers. In some instances alternative opinions may reasonably be held as to the best rhythmical interpretation, but the suggestion that the irregular rhythms are no more than the product of modern editorial imagination is manifestly absurd. A careful study of this music cannot fail to reveal the fact that in interpreting it we have to deal, not only with frequent changes of time and rhythm—in determining which the natural accent of the words when well spoken must be the principal guide—but constantly also with complex cross-rhythms between the parts.

On the subject of these rhythms a great deal of misapprehension unfortunately still exists, and some of it is founded upon prejudice of very old standing, reaching back at least as far as the days of Dr. Burney ; and it very probably had its origin in that period of the seventeenth century when madrigal-singing entirely ceased and its traditions were forgotten. Dr. Burney left on record some amazing statements about the Tudor madrigals, especially as regards that feature which he stigmatized as ' false accent '. Writing about two of Morley's canzonets he commented [1] on ' the broken phrases and false accents of the melody, in which there is so total a want of

Burney's History of Music, vol. iii, p. 102.

rhythm as renders the time extremely difficult to keep with accuracy and firmness '. Again, Farmer having stated in the ' Address to the Reader ', with which he prefaced his Set of madrigals, that he had ' fitly link't his Musick to number ', Burney, referring to this, says : [1] ' This boast made me examine his accentuation of the words of his madrigals with some expectation of greater accuracy in that particular than was general at the time ; but on the contrary, his assertion is so far from true that there appears more *false accent* in his songs than in those of his cotemporaries.'

It is evident that Burney's complete misunderstanding of the principles of the madrigal-writers, with their freedom of rhythm, was due to his conception of a rigid rhythmical system moulded by regular accents of four beats in a bar, to which musicians of Burney's day were bound as slaves. Nevertheless it is by Burney's system, more often than not, that Tudor music is still judged to-day ; and that is true of some musicians who should know better than to attempt to impose upon these sixteenth-century compositions rhythmic principles which are not only of later date, but also in every sense unsuitable to them. If its original shape is distorted and its beautiful free pose shackled, Elizabethan music will necessarily be misunderstood and will fail to excite admiration.

At the same time it must be admitted quite frankly that the madrigal-writers were occasionally guilty of extravagance in the complexity of their rhythmic devices. Those craftsmen, not in Music alone, but in all the creative Arts, who gain command of a high degree of facility and ingenious skill, are always subject to the temptation of allowing their cleverness to obtrude itself in excessive proportion to the artistic value of their work. Occasionally this temptation prevails ; and on such occasions the main interest is immediately diverted from its proper subject and becomes focussed upon the technique of the craftsman rather than upon the beauty of the artist's achievement. Contrapuntal device, with its many and varied opportunities for displaying the musician's ingenuity, has led to extravagance in different ways and at different epochs in musical history. The circumstances which led to

[1] Ibid., p. 134.

the Papal decree in reference to Church music at the Council
of Trent need no more than a passing allusion to illustrate
this point.   But the particular temptation of the madrigalists
lay in the simultaneous introduction of a number of cross-
rhythms, overlapping, and combined through the exercise of
extraordinary contrapuntal skill, but appealing to the brain
through the medium of the eye, rather than to the heart
through the ear.   Such complexity was by no means frequently
carried to excess, but it does, for example, seem to mar some
of the work of Giles Farnaby.   Even so smooth a writer as
John Dowland gave way to somewhat undue complexity in
his later work for combined voices, as, for instance, in *Thou
mighty God* (' A Pilgrimes Solace ', No. 14) a serious four-part
Air which is more madrigalian in character than most of this
composer's work.   Byrd himself is not entirely free from
criticism on this score ; for example, in *The match that's made*
(1588 Set, No. 26) ; or in the second section of the simple
Lullaby where the triple time begins (1588 Set, No. 32).   More
complicated still is the closing of his *Christ is risen again*
(1589 Set, No. 47) which is perhaps expressly intended to suggest
the ' first confusion ' of the general Resurrection.   On the other
hand, the rhythmic complexity of Byrd's *Though Amaryllis
dance* (1588 Set, No. 12) is perfectly legitimate and above
criticism, even though it be difficult for modern singers to
interpret it satisfactorily.   It is probably true that complicated
passages of this kind are more difficult to sing when they
occur in triple measure, and certainly it would seem that
greater rhythmic extravagances were committed in triple than
in duple measure.

The bare fact of the existence of varied rhythms, and also
their importance, is becoming more generally recognized, and
this may be due partly to the increasing prevalence of irregular
and varied rhythm in the most modern type of music.   But
the treatment of such rhythms in Tudor music constitutes
the chief difficulty with which an editor of these works has
nowadays to contend, unless he faint-heartedly shirks the whole
problem by putting regular barring throughout the composition
regardless of its rhythmic outlines, and without employing
any kind of method to indicate them.   For it must not be

imagined that all the rhythmic features can possibly be detected by the singers themselves, or even by the conductor, at first sight. This music demands detailed preliminary study before any attempt is made to perform it, and sometimes choice has to be made between alternative readings.

Suggestions for dealing editorially with this difficulty formed the subject of a valuable Paper read before the International Musical Society at its Fourth Congress in the summer of 1911 by Dr. Albert Reinach, who did not hesitate to declare that most of the modern editions which we possess of vocal music of the fifteenth to the seventeenth century fail to pay sufficient attention to the subtleties of rhythm within the individual parts ; and that the original character of the music is often completely destroyed by its division into bars, when these are determined entirely according to a fixed duration of time, whether it be simple or compound. Dr. Reinach went on to say that an attempt had been made to overcome the difficulty by omitting the bar-lines altogether and replacing them by signs, or by the non-simultaneous marking of the bars in the different voice-parts in accordance with their respective rhythms. This method, however, while it undoubtedly succeeds in making the score present a true picture of the rhythmic grouping of the individual voice-parts, does not work out satisfactorily in practice with ordinary choirs.

The present writer in his ' English Madrigal School Series ' has attempted to deal with the problem by a method of his own, which, if not completely satisfactory, has at least the merit of being founded to some extent on the methods of barring used by the Tudor composers themselves, and has also been found workable in actual practice, not only with choirs of trained singers, but also with singers of small musical experience in country villages For, dealing in the first place with passages in which all the parts change the rhythm simultaneously, this method involves the employment of bar-lines at irregular intervals, but at the same point in all the voice-parts. The following example, taken from Morley's *Why sit I here complaining ?* (four-part Madrigals, No. 3), will show how this method is applied, and it will also illustrate the need which it is designed to meet. The small extra bar-lines have been added in this illustration for the purpose of showing where the bars would have fallen if regularity of treatment had been observed :

It is important to add that this principle of irregular barring exactly corresponds with that which the Tudor composers themselves recognized and employed. But since, secondly, it has not been found practicable, as Dr. Reinach also stated, to employ irregular barring to the extent of indicating such cross-rhythms as would involve putting bars at places not coincident in all the parts, a system of accents has been employed in the 'English Madrigal School Series' for such cases. It must be clearly understood that, generally speaking, these accents imply nothing in the nature of *sforzando*, and must be taken only to indicate the beginning of a rhythmic unit, just as a modern bar-line does; for they may sometimes occur on a rest, or during a sustained note (as, for instance, on the third beat of a dotted minim or a semibreve), or even on a weak syllable. In the case of duple rhythm it has been found more helpful as a rule to put an accent mark of this kind on both the strong rhythmical points. The following extract from Morley's *In dew of roses* (four-part Madrigals, No. 7) will serve as an illustration; this madrigal incidentally furnishes also some striking examples of the necessity for indicating the rhythmic outline in some definite manner in a modern edition :

If non-simultaneous irregular barring had been employed instead of this system of accents, the above passage would have read thus, but such a method would obviously be too confusing to the eye for practical purposes :

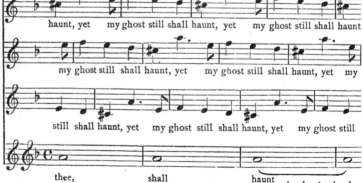

The two alternative methods, which are rendered necessary in dealing with both the simultaneous and non-simultaneous examples of rhythmic variety in this class of music, must not be regarded as conflicting in any way with each other. The bar-lines are to be taken as generally indicating the rhythmic outline except when they are over-ridden by accent-marks, which are then designed to replace them as the means of marking the beginning of the rhythmic unit exactly as a bar-line would have done if printed at that point.

If the system of sparse and irregular barring as found in some of the seventeenth-century manuscripts were adopted in a modern edition of Tudor music, it would be possible further to indicate the irregular and non-simultaneous rhythms by also employing in the individual voice-parts non-simultaneous bars of a less conspicuous character, as contrasted with the main bar-lines drawn more heavily in an unbroken line right through the score. No confusion to the eye need result from this. But it is necessary first to discover the key of the system. And its discovery should carry us much nearer a satisfactory solution of the difficult problem of editing Tudor music, even if it added something further to the difficulty of conducting from such a score.[1]

But in any case more than ordinary attention must be demanded from singers who set themselves the task of performing madrigals, because the constant changes of time and rhythm with which they abound must provide plentiful pitfalls for the inattentive. And certainly the task of conducting such music is no simple one ; it often calls for special, and even novel, methods. Many of these difficulties can be overcome by rehearsing the voice-parts singly, so that the singers may be made familiar with the melodic and rhythmic features of their own individual part, undisturbed by those of the other voice-parts that may appear to conflict with them.

As a good example of simultaneous and non-simultaneous rhythms occurring in a single passage, the following quotation may be cited from Byrd's *I joy not in no earthly bliss* (1588 Set, No. 11) :

The general plan of barring at irregular intervals of six or eight minims has been adopted by the editorial committee of the Tudor Church Music edition, issued under the auspices of the Carnegie United Kingdom Trust.

If this passage were to be barred right through in common time, it may be frankly said that it makes nonsense, and that the true rhythms are unrecognizable. In that form, too, it would justify all that Dr. Burney said about ' false accents ' :

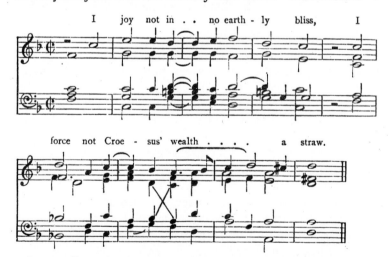

Some editors in the past, having observed the ' false accent ' that seems to result from the insertion of bar-lines at regular intervals, and having failed to perceive the true explanation

of their difficulty, have proceeded to commit the unpardonable error of tampering with the text, rearranging words and
syllables, and sometimes altering the note-values, and acting
under the conviction that they were improving the work of
these great Elizabethans. The unexpected position of a word
in the original text can almost always be explained by the
recognition of some deviation from the normal flow of the
rhythm ; there are, indeed, passages in which the position
of the words has been carelessly printed in the original editions,
and in some few cases a rigid adherence to the text on the
part of an editor might result in the misinterpretation of the
composer's intention ; but such passages are exceptional and
must be treated on their own merits in a conservative spirit.

The extent to which a triple rhythm may be disguised by the
insertion of regular bar-lines four beats apart, is apparent from
the examples quoted above. But rhythms of longer measure
are still more difficult to recognize under such a disguise ; and
many madrigal-singers have probably failed to observe the
rhythmic patterns that are sometimes made up of semibreves
and minims ; interesting designs are often to be discovered
in those sections in which the composers were expressing their
graver thoughts in notes of slow measure. The following is
a phrase taken from the Cantus-part of Byrd's beautiful *Come,
woeful Orpheus* (1611 Set, No. 19) :

The rhythm in this passage runs counter to a similar rhythm in
the other voice-parts, and the passage is one in which accent
marks have been employed in the ' English Madrigal School
Series ' to indicate the rhythm; and the need of some
editorial method of indication will be quickly recognized here,
for it cannot be suggested that the true rhythm easily strikes
the eye in the above form. But the meaning of the passage

is at once simply explained if it is barred in triple measure in spite of the time-signature.

And   tune my voice, and   tune my voice un-to thy skil - ful   wire.

And in numbers of such passages, when looked at, as it were, through glasses properly focussed, each detail of the landscape becomes clear where all was blurred before by the bar-lines.

One or two further rhythmic features of the English madrigals must be briefly noticed here. A good example has just been quoted [1] to show how a triple rhythm was often introduced in three voice-parts each of which entered one beat later than its predecessor. Another pretty instance of this occurs in Wilbye's *Fly aloft to heaven* (Set I, No. 1) at the words *to Carimel see you commend me.* To sing such a passage with complete independence and simplicity is not altogether easy, because any feeling of rivalry between the parts must be scrupulously avoided ; but the effect is delightful if it is skilfully rendered. Sometimes an imitative phrase in duple rhythm was made to follow at the distance of only one beat. Here again it is imperative that the singers should retain absolute independence and yet avoid any feeling of syncopation ; the idea of strong syncopation, which forms such an important feature in the music of Handel and Bach, was almost unknown to the musicians of the period under consideration in these chapters, and the vigorous accent so rightly employed in the interpretation of syncopated passages in eighteenth-century music must never be introduced in the performance of a Madrigal. Singers must interpret the several voice-parts with absolute equality of importance and with exact similarity of rhythmic phrasing and expression ; and it has to be realized that in the separate part-books the music of these imitative passages was precisely identical in appearance, although it looks so different in the modern vocal score with bars inserted. The following is a simple example of a passage of this character from Morley's two-part canzonet *I go before, my darling* (No 4.) :

See p. 129.

There we will to - geth - er   sweet-ly kiss each   ey - ther,   And

There we   will to-geth - er   sweet - ly   kiss each ey - ther, And

The second soprano-part must here be sung exactly as if
the bar-lines occurred one beat later, and as they do in the
first soprano. It is a mistake to suppose that these overlapping
rhythms cannot be sung independently without producing
a confused effect even when such imitations are written in
five or six vocal parts.

And madrigal-singers need to recognize at the outset that
whereas in modern music the first beat of a bar in common
time bears the chief accent while that on the third beat is
subservient to it, the reverse of this rule is very commonly
to be observed in singing Tudor music. This is particularly
the case when a voice-part enters with a point of imitation
two beats after another part ; the phrasing of each part in such
cases should be identical, regardless of the position in the bar.

Music in triple measure gave these composers special opportunities for varied rhythmical treatment. Thus, if the main
rhythm was founded on bars of three minims' length, it was
a simple matter to vary this with a measure twice as long or
twice as short. It is of great importance that singers should
acquire a facility for recognizing and conforming to sudden
alternations of rhythm ; and the key to the phrasing is always
to be sought in the natural accent of the words.

The following table shows some of the ordinary rhythmic
varieties in triple measure :

A good example of the combination of (*a*) and (*b*) in this table is to be found in Byrd's *Though Amaryllis* (see p. 164).

The alternation of (*a*) and (*c*) should constantly be looked for. It always lends great charm to the main outline of the melody. As an illustration we may take a passage in Morley's *Though Philomela lost her love* (three-part Canzonets, No. 23) :

He is a fool that lov - ers prove and leaves to sing to live in pain.

And in the concluding passage of Dowland's familiar *Awake, sweet love* (Book I, No. 19) the accent falls on alternate minims for four consecutive bars.

This point, it must be repeated, is no idle or ingenious fancy of a modern editor ; the device was part of the technique of the Tudor composers and was well understood in their time. As evidence of this fact, reference may be made to Adrian Batten's contemporary manuscript organ-book,[1] in which he has boldly changed the signature in the organ accompaniment of a passage in Gibbons's ' Jubilate in D minor ', and barred it in groups of four minims, although there is no sort of indication in any of the voice-parts of any change from the triple rhythm except the rhythm of the words. The clear inference is that the singers conformed to such changes of rhythm as a matter of ordinary routine.

One favourite device of these composers was to break the rhythm by inserting two bars in $\frac{3}{4}$ time followed by one in $\frac{3}{2}$, thus leading back to the main rhythm. In such cases a new time-signature was seldom introduced, and the variation of rhythm was usually simultaneous in all the voice-parts. The opening passage in Byrd's *I joy not in no earthly bliss* already quoted[2] is an illustration of this. Similarly, in Wilbye's *Long have I made these hills* (Set II, No. 34) the following phrase occurs :

cru - el, if thus my death may please thee, then

<hr />

[1] Tenbury MS. 791.   [2] See p. 132.

Another rhythmic formula was in common use, especially in the final cadences of the madrigals. It is made up of three groups consisting of three, two, and three units before the final note of the cadence is reached. The point will be illustrated by the concluding phrase of Weelkes's *O now weep, now sing* ('Ayeres or Phantasticke Spirites', No. 21) :

to die, to die, and nev - er to   have   end - ing.

Sometimes such a passage can be phrased, if the *ictus* of the words suggests it, in groups of two, three, and three. Thus, the wording of the second stanza of this same composition of Weelkes's necessitates the alternative grouping of the same notes :

to prove, to prove some plea - sure min - gled   with . .   pain.

Byrd made frequent use of this same formula, but more usually in terms of longer notes ; as, for instance, in *As I beheld I saw a herdman* (1588 Set, No. 20) :

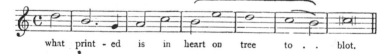

what print - ed is   in heart on tree   to . .   blot.

It is important to remember that the emphasis required for interpreting these rhythms is much lighter and more subtle in character than what is ordinarily employed with good effect in phrasing music of the eighteenth century and later, when the strong four-square rhythms became such an important feature.

In conclusion it must be repeated that the task of performing madrigals with due observance of the complex rhythms together with the other features peculiar to Tudor music is, without doubt, a difficult one. It is sometimes even stated that madrigals can no longer be performed with complete success because the old traditions have been so long forgotten and ignored, and because modern singers are so entirely dominated by regular rhythms designed on the framework of bars of a constant measure. Madrigal-singing postulates, among other things, a faculty for changing from one rhythm to another with perfect independence and precision, unhampered either by the influence of any counter-rhythm in another voice-part or by any feeling based upon the modern convention of regular bar-periods. But these difficulties are not really insuperable. It is true that the conductor in dealing with complex rhythms will find it difficult to employ his customary methods of beating time, but conductors are made for the music and not the music for the conductors, and they must consequently devise new methods, if necessary, so as to adapt their principles to the performance of music which in its own time was interpreted ordinarily without the aid of any conductor. But a madrigal-conductor must make it his first aim to see that, at least, he does not increase the difficulties of the singers by adhering rigidly to the conventional use of the *bâton* with its accepted code of indications which grew up in connexion with music of a later date and style ; remembering always that the technique of the modern conductor's art dates from no earlier than the nineteenth century, whereas the polyphonic music under discussion belongs mainly to the sixteenth. Good madrigal-singing is, without doubt, a very difficult accomplishment for conductors and singers alike ; and, as Mr. Arkwright has pointed out,[1] how few conductors seem to notice that Madrigal-singing is a totally different thing from Part-song-singing. In the Part-song all the voices, as a rule, follow the same rhythmic design, while the expression marks with all their nuances are uniform and coincident in all the parts as representing one whole. But in Madrigals separate accents and effects of expression should be generally aimed at without regard to the accentuation or dynamic force of other parts, so that each group of singers may phrase its own part with absolute independence. It is the conductor's first business to go through the separate parts thoughtfully and carefully, bringing some into prominence, suppressing others, and contriving suitable

---

[1] Accent and Expression, by G. E. P. Arkwright, Old English Edition, Part XXI.

phrasing and emphasis, and that not exclusively in points of imitation. In this lies the secret of successful Madrigal-singing. If, on the other hand, it is ignored, or set aside as being too difficult for attainment, the only reasonable alternative is to leave the Madrigal severely alone. There is no place for a *sors tertia*.

CHAPTER XII

THE MADRIGAL LYRICS

In the selection of words to set to their music the Tudor madrigalists were exceptionally fortunate, since they were able to draw upon an unlimited flow of the purest and best literature that was ever poured forth in the English language. In this matter they had yet another advantage over the continental madrigal-writers. We have already seen that, owing to the late date at which the English Madrigal School arose, and also to the rapid progress of their harmonic development as well as the daring and original methods which they employed, the English madrigalists achieved in this particular Art-form even greater perfection than the composers of the Flemish and Italian Schools, when their work is judged solely as music. But when we look at any of these English compositions from the wider point of view that takes into account the music and the words together as a single entity for criticism, they are raised to a still higher plane, and their supremacy in their own special branch of creative Art stands impregnable.

It has often been suggested that the madrigal-composers wrote many, if not the greater number, of the lyrics themselves. No positive evidence can be cited either to support or to oppose this conjecture, yet the theory cannot be put thoughtlessly aside. The authorship of the words cannot, however, be identified with certainty except in comparatively few instances.

It is known that Thomas Campian wrote most of the words for his books of Airs, if not all of them, and in his ' Address to the Reader ' at the beginning of the third and fourth books, he definitely claimed the authorship of the lyrics as well as of the music. Campian also wrote both the poetry and the music of the first part of the volume of Airs which he published in conjunction with Rosseter. But Campian's claim to authorship has no exact parallel among the other Tudor composers. Another musician, however, who may have written some of

the lyrics for his compositions was John Dowland, and it is
not unlikely that the double accomplishment was more general
among the lutenist-composers than among the actual madrigalists.   Some authorities have conjectured that Dowland was
the author of the lyric which both he and Gibbons set to music,
beginning *Ah, dear heart, why do you rise*—lines which have
often been assigned to the authorship of Dr. John Donne.
There is no direct evidence to support Dowland's authorship.
On the other hand, Weelkes intimated pretty plainly that he
himself wrote none of the words which he set to music, for
he confessed in the dedication to his five-part Madrigals in
1600 that he was unskilled in any art other than music.   In
this same statement, however, he implied that some musicians
were rather proud of their attempts to achieve success also in
other fields than music, no doubt meaning by this that they
wrote at least some of the lyrics themselves.

And it is certainly reasonable, on other grounds also, to
suppose that the madrigal-composers frequently did write
verses for their own setting, although it is probable that in
the great majority of instances the words were either written
or selected by their friends, among whom they could count
' poets who have left a name behind them ', as well as many
more who ' have left no memorial '.   A large number of people
among the educated classes of that day would have been able
to write a lyric or two in the manner of the great poets of the
time, even if they could lay no particular claim to individual
poetical talent.   Thus we frequently encounter among the
madrigals a lyric closely reminiscent of Sidney, or Spenser,
or of some other poet, although not to be found in their
collected works.   To illustrate this point Wilbye's *Wha
needeth all this travail* (Set I, Nos. 7 and 8) may be quoted :

What needeth all this travail and turmoiling,
  Shortening the life's sweet pleasure
  To seek this far-fetched treasure
In those hot climates under Phoebus broiling ?
O fools, can you not see a traffic nearer,
In my sweet lady's face, where Nature showeth
Whatever treasure eye sees or heart knoweth ?
  Rubies and diamonds dainty,
  And orient pearls such plenty,

Coral and ambergris sweeter and dearer
Than which the South Seas or Moluccas send us,
Or either Indies, East or West, do lend us.

This may be compared with Spenser's fifteenth Sonnet, beginning :

Ye tradeful merchants that with weary toil
Do seek most precious things to make your gain,
And both the India's of their treasure spoil ;
What needeth you to seek so far in vain ?
For lo, my Love doth in herself contain
All this world's riches that may far be found.

Again, the first couplet of Weelkes's eighteenth Ballet compares very closely with two lines of Sidney's. Weelkes's version is :

I love and have my love regarded,
And sport with sport as well rewarded.

And in Sidney's ' Arcadia ' (Book I. 5) we read :

We love and have our loves rewarded,
We love and are no wit regarded.

It was not in accordance with the custom of the time to print in the music-books the name of the author of the lyrics. This was not done even in the case of those poems of which we can actually identify the author ; and the presumption is, therefore, that many more of these charming verses were written by the great Elizabethan poets, some of them perhaps by Shakespeare himself. This probability is not inconsistent with the fact that the poems do not happen to have survived apart from the song-books. And the madrigalists would have been on terms of intimacy with most of the leading poets of the time ; indeed Weelkes set to music a quaint skit (No. 6 of his ' Ayeres or Phantasticke Spirites '), which undoubtedly refers to the famous Mermaid Tavern, the favourite resort of Shakespeare, Ben Jonson, Fletcher, Chapman, and many another :

The Ape, the Monkey and Baboon did meet,
And breaking of their fast in Friday Street,
Two of them sware together solemnly
In their three natures was a sympathy.

Nothing could be more probable than that the poets were constantly giving, and being asked for, a few lines of verse suitable for a madrigal, without any thought of perpetuating a claim to authorship. For example : what, in another sphere of life, could have been more natural than that some guest at Rushbrooke Hall, with an amateur's knack of versifying in the prevailing literary style, should have expressed a desire that Kirbye, as the resident musician of the household, should set his lyric to music ? The new madrigal would then perhaps have been sung at sight the same evening, when ' supper being ended, and Musicke bookes (according to the custome) being brought to the tables, the mistresse of the house presented all (the guests) with a part, earnestly requesting them to sing '.[1]

Or, again, it requires little imagination to suppose that, although Sidney died some years before Wilbye came to live at Hengrave Hall, Lady Kytson may have requested Wilbye to set words written by Sidney on one of his visits, words of which the poet may have kept no copy, and which perhaps had subsequently passed out of his memory.[2]

Be all this as it may, authorship is, after all, a secondary consideration in relation to Art. The really important truth remains that in the madrigal-books we possess a wonderful store of lyric poetry, the bulk of which has not otherwise survived for our enjoyment in print ; and almost all of it is worthy of that golden age of English literature to which it belongs.

The English madrigalists by no means confined themselves to the treatment of pastoral subjects, nor yet to words of a light and cheerful nature, although on this latter point madrigal students of all generations have been liable to error. In this matter even so fine a musician as Pearsall went astray, in spite of his admirable enthusiasm for Elizabethan music ; for Pearsall counted cheerfulness among the essential features of a true Madrigal.[3] This erroneous opinion may be easily accounted for by the limited amount of madrigal-literature available for criticism, especially in Pearsall's time. The madrigalists knew how to be grave as well as gay, they treated

---

[1] Morley's Plain and Easy Introduction, p. 1.

[2] Some manuscript letters of Sidney's are still preserved at Hengrave Hall, and it is not unlikely that verses of his were kept at Hengrave in manuscript.

[3] Two chapters on Madrigals, by R. L. Pearsall, printed in Felix Farley's *Bristol Journal* in 1856.

ethical and religious subjects—quite apart from the setting of scriptural words—besides singing of the morris-dance and the May-day revels ; they could express the feelings of passionate emotion, and also the light-hearted conceits of the nymphs and shepherds, or of cruel Amaryllis and her rejected suitor. And in all subjects and moods they succeeded in expressing themselves with amazing perfection.

A good example of religious words may be quoted from Byrd's ' Psalmes, Sonets, and Songs of Sadnes and Pietie ' (No. 31) :

> Care for thy soul as thing of greatest price,
>   Made to the end to taste of power divine,
> Devoid of guilt, abhorring sin and vice,
>   Apt by God's grace to virtue to incline.
> Care for it so as by thy retchless train
> It be not brought to taste eternal pain.

Byrd was not singular in writing such ' songs of piety ', for similar examples are to be found in the works of several other madrigalists ; but he certainly wrote more in this vein than did any of his contemporaries. The finest examples of the ethical madrigal are to be found in the works of Gibbons and Wilbye. It is unnecessary to quote in full Raleigh's splendid lines, set to music by Gibbons (No. 14), and beginning :

> What is our life ?   A play of passion.

but somewhat similar is the following lyric, set by Wilbye (No. 14 of his second volume) ; and both these poems must at once bring into the reader's mind the famous lines of Shakespeare, ' All the world 's a stage . . .'

> Happy, O happy he, who not affecting
>   The endless toils attending worldly cares,
> With mind reposed, all discontents rejecting,
>   In silent peace his way to heaven prepares,
> Deeming his life a Scene, the world a Stage
> Whereon man acts his weary Pilgrimage.

Another type of serious madrigal took the form of an elegy on some departed friend. Weelkes composed as many as three of these, and included them in his madrigal publications, one being entitled ' A remembrance of my friend Mr. Thomas Morley '. Mòrley's *Hark! Alleluia* was a ' reverend memoriall of that honourable true gentleman, Henry Noel, Esquier '.

But the finest poem of this sort in the madrigal-literature is an anonymous elegy in Gibbons's Set (Nos. 17, 18, 19) which may be quoted here in full :

> Nay, let me weep, though others' tears be spent,
>   Though all eyes dried be, let mine be wet.
> Unto thy grave I'll pay this yearly rent ;
>   Thy lifeless corse demands of me this debt.
> I owe more tears than ever corse did crave.
> I'll pay more tears than e'er was paid to grave.
>
> Ne'er let the Sun with his deceiving light
>   Seek to make glad these watery eyes of mine ;
> My sorrow suits with melancholy night,
>   I joy in dole, in languishment I pine.
> My dearest friend is set, he was my Sun,
> With whom my mirth, my joy and all is done.
>
> Yet if that age had frosted o'er his head,
>   Or if his face had furrowed been with years,
> I would not so bemoan that he is dead,
>   I might have been more niggard with my tears.
> But O the Sun, new-rose, is gone to bed,
> And lilies in their Springtime hang their head.

No. 31 of Wilbye's second Set is a characteristic example of the emotional type of madrigal :

> Draw on, sweet Night ! best friend unto those cares
>   That do arise from painful melancholy ;
> My life so ill through want of comfort fares,
>   That unto thee I consecrate it wholly.
> Draw on, sweet Night ! My griefs, when they be told
>   To shades of darkness, find some ease from paining ;
> And while thou all in silence dost enfold,
>   I then shall have best time for my complaining.

Enough has already been said to show that a vast number of madrigals are far removed from being cheerful in character ; yet it must be admitted that the greater part of the madrigal literature is bright and gay, representing every phase of lightsome mood. Numberless examples of delightful words of this kind could be quoted ; the following serenade, selected almost at random, is from Weelkes's five-part Madrigals in his publication of 1600.

> Lady, the birds right fairly
> Are singing ever early,
> The lark, the thrush, the nightingale,
> The make-sport cuckoo, and the quail :
> These sing of love, then why sleep ye ?
> To love your sleep it may not be.

Or again, take No. 11 of Weelkes's Ballets, which may be compared with Herrick's ' Corinna ' :

> In pride of May
> The fields are gay,
> The birds do sweetly sing ;
> So Nature would
> That all things should
> With joy begin the Spring.

> Then, Lady dear,
> Do you appear
> In beauty like the Spring ;
> I well dare say
> The birds that day
> More cheerfully will sing.

In connexion with the Ballet-form of composition it should be stated that the *fa-la* refrain constituted no actual part of the lyric as such, but was added by the composer of the music, who employed it for purposes closely corresponding to an instrumental interlude introduced between clearly defined sections of the words.

This theory, which the present writer believes has never hitherto been enunciated, is amply corroborated by a reference to Youll's *Early before the day doth spring* (No. 22 of his Canzonets). Youll introduced the *fa-la* refrain after the third and fifth lines of this stanza which forms part of Sir John Davies's set of acrostical ' Hymns to Astraea '. The poet's text as published in his own day has no *fa-la*, for of course such a refrain would break up the metre of the verse.

> Early before the day doth spring
> Let us awake, my Muse, and sing,
> It is no time to slumber
> So many joys this time doth bring
> As time will fail to number.

Youll's canzonet is especially interesting, in that it affords the

only example known to the present writer in which the text
of any poem treated by a madrigal-composer with a *fa-la*
refrain was printed in any contemporary volume independent
of the song-books or their influence.

As an example of a curious kind of humour, Robert Jones in
his ' First Set of Madrigals ', No. 12, expanded the usual formula
' Here endeth the songs of four voices ', and solemnly set to
music the following words :

> Here is an end of all the songs,
> Which are in number but four parts,
> And he loves music well we say
> That sings all five before he starts.

The finest individual collection of words to be found in any
one madrigal-Set is perhaps that of the Gibbons volume. The
words were apparently selected for Gibbons by Sir Christopher
Hatton, and it is possible that Hatton himself was the author
of one or more of the lyrics. The four stanzas (Nos. 3 to 6
of the Set), beginning with *I weigh not Fortune's frown nor smile*,
are from Joshua Sylvester's ' Epigrams and Epitaphs '. *Fair
Ladies that to love captived are* (Nos. 10 and 11) are from Spenser's
' Fairy Queen '. *Lais now old* is an imitation of an epigram
of Plato's, though Gibbons's version may have been made
from the translation by Ausonius, which is in many ways
finer than the Greek original. Gibbons's Set includes Sir Walter
Raleigh's fine *What is our life?* (No. 14), and a charming lyric
prefixed to John Donne's poem ' Break of day ', already mentioned as possibly being the work of John Dowland, who also
set it to music. In few other Sets of madrigals can the authorship of so many of the poems be identified as that of Gibbons,
but Ward's Set is also interesting from this point of view.

It would not be possible here to discuss in detail all the sets
of lyrics which these madrigal-books contain ; they provide
sufficient material for a volume dealing exclusively with that
subject. It is enough to say that in addition to the few instances
in which the authorship of the lyrics is known, just a small
proportion are translations. For example, several of Morley's
words were translated from Italian writers ; while classical
authors, such as Horace and Ovid, were occasionally drawn
upon. As an instance of this, Byrd set a hexameter translation

of the opening lines of Ovid's 'First Epistle': *Hanc tua Penelope lento tibi mittit Ulysse.* The translation which Byrd used (1588 Set, No. 23) was not one of any great merit; the first couplet runs thus:

> Constant Penelope sends to thee careless Ulysses;
> Write not again, but come, sweet mate, thyself to revive me.

Wilbye's famous madrigal, *Sweet honey-sucking bees* (Set II, Nos. 17 and 18) is an imitation of one of the *Basia* of Johannes Secundus, the Dutch statesman and poet of the early sixteenth century.

Just as the form of the Tudor Madrigal cannot be defined with any exactness when examined from an exclusively musical point of view, so also the lyric to which the music was wedded was of no fixed design. The favourite type of lyric among the madrigal-composers was certainly that of a stanza of six lines, and a large majority of the madrigal words are in this form. It does not appear, however, that this preference was due to any other reason than that this was a measure extremely popular with all the poets of that period. The poet Surrey was the first to make frequent use of this metre, if he were not actually the originator of it. But the most striking feature of the words of the madrigals is the wonderful variety of metre in which they are written. In this connexion it is an alluring conjecture that the metrical variety which is one of the charms of Herrick's poetry may have been partly owing to that poet's acquaintance with the madrigal-literature of twenty years earlier. Certainly it is easy in reading the 'Hesperides' to imagine that one is listening to the echo of a madrigalist without the music. And here it may be remarked that the excellence of the words, quite apart from the music, has often proved an important factor in securing popularity for particular madrigals, though the true source of such popularity may not have been actually recognized, and the attractive power of the words has exercised its influence unawares. To some extent this statement is true of all kinds of vocal music at all periods, but certainly more than one Tudor madrigal could be mentioned as having become a general favourite, the music of which is not of outstanding merit while the words are first-rate.

It is not a difficult matter, as a rule, to reconstruct the metrical form of the lyrics from the madrigal part-books, in spite of the minor irregularities which are almost inseparable from musical settings of this character. But cases do occur in the writings of some of the madrigalists in which it is evident that small variants, whether intentionally or otherwise, have crept into some of the voice-parts ; and sometimes small extra words are expressly interpolated to suit the needs of the music, these extra words being occasionally printed in brackets in the original part-books. It has been the usual practice of those who have reprinted the words of these songs independently from the music, to include all such extra words, regardless of the rhythm and metre. This does not apply only to recent editions, it was also the course adopted in ' England's Helicon ', a collection of poems printed in 1600. And the practice has undeniably something to be said for it, as representing a sincere intention to give a faithful reproduction of the original text. On the other hand, from the point of view of literature, quite apart from that of music, it is more interesting, if possible, to print lyrics in a form that will scan, and in their original metre, if that can be reconstructed with any degree of probability, as it undoubtedly can be in most instances. An essential feature of madrigal-composition is the use of short musical phrases treated in imitative style by the various voice-parts. More often than not the composer found that a complete line of verse was too lengthy for such a phrase, and it consequently became necessary to divide the line into two or more short sentences. It will be obvious that the task of making such a division would, in many instances, be facilitated by a slight readjustment of the original words, with the object, in the first place, of making sense, and also for purposes of verbal rhythm and balance. This point is borne out in an interesting manner in some of the poems set by the lutenists. The lutenists, it will be remembered, as a general rule set one stanza of a poem with their music and printed the remainder of the poem in metrical form at the foot of the page and apart from the music. This feature is one which especially differentiates the lutenists' Air from the Madrigal. Whether it was the custom to sing the subsequent stanzas by repeating the music set to the first stanza must remain uncertain in the absence of direct evidence; but if they were so sung, metrical difficulties are at once encountered, some of which seem to suggest with a large degree of probability that the composers were in the habit of rearranging the words to suit the requirements of their music. Take, for instance, Dowland's beautiful *Come, heavy sleep, the image of true Death* (Set I, No. 20). The first line of the second stanza, as printed in metrical form in the song-book, runs *Come, shadow of my end, and shape of rest*; but this line must necessarily be altered to *Come, shape of rest, and shadow of my end*, if it is to be sung to the music, and there can be little doubt that if Dowland had set it out with the notes it would have appeared in this form. Similarly, in Dowland's *Toss not, my soul* the first line of the second stanza must inevitably be altered by transposing the word *Assurance* to the beginning of the line if it is to be sung. A curious textual variation occurs between the two stanzas in the refrain : as set to music the first stanza reads, *When once of ill the uttermost is known* and this is changed in the second stanza (set out in metrical form apart from the music) to : *When once the uttermost of ill is known*. It seems unlikely that this variant is due to a printer's error, but as the second version cannot possibly be sung to the music, it would seem that the composer transposed the words as being more suitable for his purpose in that shape, and that, either by an oversight or by deliberate design, the alteration was not made in the second verse when printed in its original metrical form.

Instances of such freedom in the treatment of words might be multiplied indefinitely. These readjustments, which were often of the nature of musical 'poetical licences', occasionally even involved the interchange from line to line of the less essential small words ; the principle was sometimes extended to the addition or elimination of epithets ; and in rare instances to still more drastic treatment of the original poem. Most of the madrigalists treated their words at times with some degree of freedom ; and this is true even of those who as a general rule adhered fairly closely to the text of the lyric. Weelkes, Byrd, and Gibbons seldom indulged in any such freedom. On the other hand, Morley carried this freedom of verbal treatment

to a greater length than any of his contemporaries ; for
whereas a very large proportion of the lyrics set by the other
madrigal-composers can be transcribed with little hesitation
straight into metrical form, such an experience is the exception
rather than the rule in dealing, for instance, with Morley's
1593 Set of Canzonets or his Book of four-part Madrigals.
His Ballets, however, owing to the more regular rhythmical
features of this form of composition, did not admit of, or
indeed render necessary, such freedom of treatment. But
there can be no doubt whatever as to the actual fact of his
altering and varying the words in his other Sets from the form
in which they first came into his hands, and of his making inter-
polations with surprising freedom. Small interjections, such
as ' Alas ' or ' Ay me ', were interpolated very generally
throughout the whole of the madrigal-literature ; but in no
other work do they occur to such an extent as in that of
Morley. This composer was also in the habit of constantly
adding epithets when he needed some further material for
a phrase of music ; and such additions, it is important to
state, do not by any means agree in all the voice-parts. To
illustrate the point we may here examine in detail the first
two lines of Morley's three-part canzonet *What ails my darling ?*
(No. 18). It will be necessary, in the first place, to set out all
the words *in extenso*, just as they appear individually in each
of the three voice-parts :

Cantus. What ails my darling, say what ails my darling,
    what ails my sweet pretty darling, what ails my sweet,
    what ails mine own sweet darling ? What ails my darling
    dear thus sitting all alone, sitting all alone, all alone so
    weary ? Say, why is my dear now not merry ?
Altus. What ails my darling, say what ails my darling,
    what ails my darling dear, what ails mine only sweet,
    mine only sweet darling ? What ails my darling,
    what ails my darling dear, sitting all alone, sitting all
    alone so weary ? Say what grieves my dear that she is not
    merry ?
Bassus. What ails my darling, say what ails my darling,
    what ails my darling, say what ails my dainty, dainty
    darling, what ails mine own sweet dainty darling ? What
    ails my dainty darling, my dainty darling so to sit alone,
    so to sit alone so weary, and is not merry.

In their original form the lines may have run thus :

Say what ails my darling dear to sit alone so weary ?
Say what grieves my dainty sweet that she is now not merry ?

Such a reconstruction must necessarily be of a speculative
nature, and in many cases it is only possible to offer suggestions
in such work.   On the other hand, in a good number of madrigals, besides those of Morley, the result does rest upon grounds
of strong probability.

One of the most remarkable examples of Morley's peculiar
usage in this matter is to be found in his morris-dance madrigal
Ho! who comes here? (No. 18 of his four-part Set of Madrigals).   As the boisterous merriment of the subject works up
to a climax, his freedom in the treatment of the original words
becomes unbounded.   The lines apparently ran in some such
form as this :

Soft awhile, then ! not away so fast ! they melt them !
Piper, see'st thou not the dancers how they swelt them ?

Morley treats this as a sort of dialogue between an excited
spectator and the Piper, who was one of the troupe of morris-
dancers, playing on the bagpipes.   The words ' Soft awhile,
not away so fast, they melt them ' occur alike in all the four
voice-parts, after which the text is as follows :

Cantus.   Piper, piper, piper, be hanged awhile knave, look
    the dancers swelt them.
Altus.   Piper, piper, be hanged awhile then, look, be hanged
    awhile knave, seest not the dancers how they swelt
    them ?
Bassus.   What piper, ho, be hanged awhile knave then, seest
    thou not, seest thou not the dancers how they swelt
    them ?   the dancers swelt them ?

The tenor-part represents the retort of the Piper :

Tenor.   Who calls, who calls ?   be hanged awhile knaves all,
    what care I the dancers though they swelt them ?

It may be objected, however, that Morley wrote the words
himself, and that they were not founded on any original lyric.
But against this it has to be said that Morley's original words
must almost certainly have stood in some kind of metrical form
before a note of the music had been written, and that his freedom

of treatment developed while he composed the music. There is the evidence of the rhyming words ; and so much of the metre is retained as to give a conclusive answer to such an objection.

The 1593 Canzonets and the four-part Madrigals of Morley, and also the work of other madrigalists, provide most interesting material for study from this point of view. It is an aspect of the subject that has not hitherto been discussed by any writer upon English madrigals or madrigal-literature, and is put forward in these pages for the first time. Yet it may deserve consideration, not only from a purely literary aspect, but also because the recognition of the principle at issue might obviate the deplorable and shapeless form in which these words are so frequently served up in concert programmes.

A good example of the compression of the words by a composer is to be found in Ellis Gibbons's *Oriana* madrigal in which the couplet :

I never saw a fairer
I never heard a rarer

appears in some of the voice-parts as one line :

I never heard nor saw a fairer

In this case the full text is only revealed after careful examination of all the part-books. This same poem was also set by Thomas Hunt as another contribution to *The Triumphs of Oriana*, but there is no ambiguity about reconstructing the metrical form of the lines from Hunt's setting. Gibbons's version begins with the words *Long live fair Oriana*, and the words do not occur at all in Hunt's setting ; from this it seems evident that it was Gibbons who conceived the idea of prefacing the poem with the words of the refrain which forms the last line of this entire collection of madrigals ; his device was an artistic one, but the words, of course, should have no place there in the poem ; and this fact is borne out by comparison with Hunt's setting ; yet it illustrates admirably the methods of the madrigalists in handling original words.

Another interesting kind of comparison is to be made between Wilbye's *Lady, when I behold the roses sprouting* and Farnaby's *My lady's coloured cheeks*, which have a common origin as translations of an Italian madrigal.

Suggestions, such as have just been made for attempting to reconstruct the original form of the lyrics as they first reached the hand of the composer, are perfectly justifiable when dealing with the words apart from the music ; but they must not in any sort of way be regarded as marking approval of the practice of altering the words in the musical text itself. No condemnation for such alteration as that can be too strong, and yet this flagrant fault has been widely committed in many of the modern reprints of the English madrigals. Very occasionally, it must be admitted, some slight alteration of the words is necessary, in order to conform to the taste of modern days ; but even in such a case no emendation ought to be made without the addition of a foot-note calling attention to it as being a variant on the original text. Extraordinarily few madrigals call for any such alterations. To suppose that the English madrigals have not been reprinted in modern editions on the ground that the character of the words would not permit it, is a grave error born of lamentable ignorance.

Editors have, in fact, been guilty of unpardonable tampering with the words in two directions. One of these has already been dealt with in connexion with the misinterpretation of the irregular rhythms of the music. The other takes the form of attempting to improve upon the words in combination with the musical text, solely from the point of view of literature. The astounding presumption of such an attempt need not further be commented on. The prime offender in this matter was Thomas Oliphant, who unfortunately did not shrink from attempting to ' improve ' almost every one of the many madrigals which he edited and reprinted in the middle of the nineteenth century. It is difficult to imagine the attitude of mind in which he set to work to produce such alterations, either as a matter of necessity or of expediency. The following are some examples of Oliphant's printed editions, chosen at random.

> Cold winter's ice is fled and gone,
>   And Summer brags on every tree ;
> The Redbreast peeps amidst the throng
>   Of wood-born birds that wanton be.
> Each one forgets what they have been,
> And so doth Phyllis, Summer's Queen.
>   (Weelkes's ' Madrigals of five parts ', No. 1.)

Oliphant's version, as printed with the music, is :

> Cold Winter's ice is fled and gone,
> And Summer blooms on every tree,
> The Redbreast peeps amid the throng
> Of warbling birds that merry be.
> Come let us dance upon the green,
> And crown fair Daphne Summer's Queen.

Moreover, in his edition of this madrigal Oliphant entirely ruined the opening passage of the music by substituting major thirds for minor in the first two chords, though these were expressly designed by the composer to suggest the wintry conditions. It is noteworthy that Oliphant had previously printed the text of this lyric quite correctly in *La Musa Madrigalesca* ; but it is significant that in a note he limited his praise of the poetry to the first four lines, a fact which inevitably suggests that his version of the two final lines, subsequently produced with the music, was, in his opinion, an improvement on the original.

Campian's well-known lyric, which Alison set as a madrigal, was altered in the following manner by Oliphant in his edition of Alison's music :

> There is a garden in her face
> Where roses and white lilies grow.

in Oliphant's version became :

> A garden is my lady's face
> Where roses and white lilies blow.

Again, Farmer's madrigal, beginning :

> A little pretty bonny lass was walking
> In midst of May before the sun 'gan rise.
> I took her by the hand and fell to talking
> Of this and that, as best I could devise.

Oliphant re-edited as follows :

> To take the air a bonny lass was walking
> One morn in May as Phoebus 'gan arise.
> Full soon I greeted her and fell a-talking
> Of this and that, as best I could devise.

Farnaby's ' My lady's coloured cheeks ' became in Oliphant's hands ' A nosegay of spring flowers ' ; while Bennet's ' Weep, O mine eyes ' was transformed into ' Flow, O my tears '.

Oliphant's lamentable efforts in this direction might have been passed by with a mere allusion if it were not for the important fact that so much of his work, printed in separate part-books as well as in vocal score, still forms the basis of the music-libraries belonging to the older madrigal-Societies in this country ; and his text with all its many glaring faults—both as regards words and music—is regularly used and held in great veneration by the members of these Societies. Oliphant, whose great enthusiasm it is impossible not to admire, must not be blamed as an individual so much as a representative of the indifferent taste in such matters that prevailed in the first half of the nineteenth century. And in point of fact we need step back but two generations more to arrive at Dr. Burney, whose history was published in 1789. Burney failed altogether to appreciate either the words or the music of the madrigals, actually saying, ' We should suppose from the words of these madrigals that our Lyric Poetry, which has never been much cultivated by real judges and lovers of music, was in a state of utter barbarism when they were written ; if the sonnets of Spenser and Shakespeare did not bear testimony to the contrary'.[1] And of the madrigals of the ' Triumphs of Oriana ' he says, ' They are inferior in poetry to the present Christmas carols of London bellmen '.

Oliphant in 1838 edited a selection of lyrics from the madrigal-books in the volume just mentioned called *La Musa Madrigalesca*. He added some useful notes upon the author-ship of some of these poems ; but the text is not entirely trustworthy, and the notes are often spoilt by a flippant style utterly out of keeping with the subject. It is a somewhat curious fact that in *La Musa Madrigalesca* Oliphant frequently gave a correct version of the text, and yet saw fit to alter the words ten years later, when he printed them with the music. A reversal of this course of procedure would have protected him from such severe criticism, inasmuch as the reconstruction of the lyrics from the part-books must occasionally be a matter of some uncertainty, and any one is at liberty to print the version which in his opinion most nearly approaches the original text of the poetry.

[1] Burney's History, vol. iii, p. 131.

No complete edition of the madrigal poems has yet been published ;[1] but a certain number have been printed from time to time in various anthologies. Among the earlier publications to include selections from the madrigals were Beloe's ' Anecdotes of Literature ', Brydges's *Censurà Literaria,* and the ' British Biographer'. In the middle of the nineteenth century came Oliphant's *La Musa Madrigalesca* and J. P. Collier's ' Lyrical Poems selected from musical publications, 1589–1600 '. Professor Arber did much more comprehensive work and included in his 'English Garner' the complete Sets of Byrd and Alison among the madrigalists and those of Campian and Dowland among the lutenists, besides Wilbye's first Set, the ' Triumphs of Oriana', Yonge's first Set of *Musica Transalpina.* In later times Mr. A. H. Bullen published his valuable ' Lyrics from Elizabethan Song-books' which include specimens from the works of most of the madrigal-writers. A German volume by Wilhelm Bolle deals very completely with the English song-books up to 1600. A collection by F. A. Cox is marred by his carelessness in verifying the text of several of the poems which he erroneously attributes to well-known authors. Mr. Barclay Squire has edited the lyrics from Robert Jones's 'The Muses Gardin for Delights', and complete editions of Campian's poetical works have been published by Mr. Bullen and Mr. Percival Vivian.

[1] The present writer's ' English Madrigal Verse ', a complete collection of the poems from the music-books of the English madrigal and lutenist schools, has recently been issued by the Clarendon Press.

CHAPTER XIII

WILLIAM BYRD. Born 1543 ; died 1623

WILLIAM BYRD, who, as we have already seen, is to be regarded as the founder of the English Madrigal School, was born in the year 1543, for at the end of 1622 he stated in his Will that he was then in his eightieth year. Neithei the place of his birth nor his parentage are known with any certainty. The earliest authenticated fact of his life is his appointment as organist of Lincoln Cathedral in 1563 at the early age of 20 ; and from this it seems likely that he was a native of Lincolnshire. The name of Byrd was not uncommon in the neighbourhood of Lincoln in the sixteenth century, and an examination of the Wills give some probability to the suggestion that he belonged to a family settled at Epworth ; for the Christian names of that family of Byrds, especially that of Christopher, correspond closely with the names of the composer's children. Unfortunately the Epworth baptismal registers of that date have been tampered with in early times and are partly illegible ; the year 1543 is missing altogether. William Byrd was married at St. Margaret's-in-the-Close, Lincoln, on Sept. 14, 1568.

The statement that he was a chorister at St. Paul's Cathedral and a pupil of Tallis cannot be supported by any actual evidence. After very few years at Lincoln Cathedral Byrd resigned his appointment, having been elected a Gentleman of the Chapel Royal in 1569 ; and soon afterwards he went to live at Harlington, about midway between London and Windsor. It has been thought that he chose this secluded village as his place of residence in order to escape difficulties in connexion with his duties created by the fact that he adhered staunchly to the unreformed Doctrines. The retention by a 'recusant' of a Chapel Royal appointment was by no means unprecedented in Byrd's case. A generation earlier Sebastian Westcote, organist of St. Paul's, enjoyed the same experience on the ground that 'ita charus Elizabethae fuit '.[1] Yet regular

[1] Paper by G. E. P. Arkwright, Musical Association Proceedings, April 1914.

attendance at the Chapel Royal must in these circumstances have taxed Byrd's energies, more particularly because the journey lay across the dangerous Hounslow Heath.

At the close of the century Byrd left Harlington, and he seems to have had an ambition very similar to that which led Shakespeare to acquire a coat-of-Arms and to settle down as a country gentleman. As early as 1595 he had obtained a lease of the property of Stondon Place, near Ongar in Essex, which had been sequestrated from the Shelley family; he duly figures in the Heralds' Visitation of Essex of 1634,[1] with his pedigree among the county families, as being legally entitled to armorial bearings. The composer died eleven years before the Visitation was made, and Stondon Place was then owned by his grandson Thomas, son of his eldest son, Christopher. Meanwhile, Byrd had a good deal of trouble to maintain his title to Stondon Place, which was keenly disputed by the Shelleys; but he had influential support, including that of James I, and successfully resisted all efforts to dislodge him. The feud was kept up until Mrs. Shelley's death in 1609, when Byrd purchased the property. His death took place on July 4, 1623. In his Will [2] he expressed a wish if he should die at Stondon to be buried in Stondon churchyard, where his wife already lay. The parish registers of the date do not survive, but there is every reason to believe that the bones of this great musician, whom many regard as the greatest English composer of all time, lie buried in that churchyard. Our knowledge of most of the details of Byrd's personal history is due to the researches of Mr. Barclay Squire.

Byrd must have been a man of commanding personality in his own time, and he enjoyed to a remarkable degree the esteem and veneration of his contemporaries. Morley said of him that he was ' never without reverence to be named of the musicians '.[3] John Baldwin, of St. George's Chapel, Windsor, who in 1591 transcribed the celebrated virginal book for ' the Lady Nevell ' added at the close of one of the pieces ' Mr. W. Birde. Homo memorabilis '. The entry which records his death in the cheque-book of the Chapel Royal calls him ' a Father of Musicke '.

---

[1] Visitation of Essex, 1634, Harl. Soc. xiii. 365.
[2] P.C.C., 106 Swann.   [3] Morley's Plain and Easy Introduction, p. 115.

Henry Peacham in 1622 wrote of him as follows : [1] ' For Motetts and Musicke of pietie and devotion as well for the honour of our Nation, as the merit of the man, I prefer above all our *Phoenix* M. William Byrd, whom in that kind I know not whether any may equall . . . and being of him selfe naturally disposed to Gravitie and Pietie, his veine is not so much for light Madrigals or Canzonets, yet his *Virginella* and some others of his first Set cannot be mended by the best Italian of them all.'

With Byrd's Church music we are not here primarily concerned; it represents his finest work, and, for example, nothing could be found to approach nearer to perfection in the polyphonic style than his three Masses, especially that for five voices. In instrumental composition Byrd also reached a very high level. He occupies a special place of importance in musical history in connexion with the development of Variation-form, a musical design which has afforded scope for the imaginative skill of all the great composers since his time.

With regard to madrigals, Byrd has been much misunderstood ; it is frequently stated that his work in this department of composition is much inferior to that which he wrote for the Church. One historian has gone so far as to assert that Byrd's contemporaries recognized his inferiority, and that in consequence ' he was not asked ' to contribute to the ' Triumphs of Oriana '. Such an assertion is not worthy of the critical faculties of its author, for not a shred of evidence exists to show whether Byrd was, or was not, invited to write a madrigal for the ' Triumphs '. It so happens that the year 1601 comes in the course of that period from 1589 to 1605 in which none of his music was published. It cannot be supposed that his musical activity ceased entirely during those years but it may possibly mean that he was avoiding publicity. In this connexion the ingenious theory has lately been put forward that, being a ' recusant ', he was forced during this period to live in seclusion, and that he is to be identified with the ' Byrd alias Borne ' who was associated with Henslowe, both as an actor and a dramatist, and who is frequently mentioned by Henslowe and Alleyn. The coincidence of dates is certainly suggestive,

[1] Peacham's The Compleat Gentleman, p. 100.

though further evidence is needed to support the theory. But if, apart from such a theory, we are to speculate as to the reason why Byrd was not a contributor to the ' Triumphs ', it may be suggested that it was due to the fact that he was much preoccupied from 1595 to 1609 by disputes with the Shelleys. The actual reason for Byrd's non-inclusion, whatever it may have been, need not trouble us, but it is important to make his position as a madrigalist perfectly clear.

In the first place, some of his contemporaries did recognize the excellence of his work in the field of secular vocal music. Nicholas Yonge in the preface to his first Set of *Musica Transalpina* in 1588 was undoubtedly referring to Byrd's ' Psalmes, Sonets, and Songs of Sadnes and Pietie ', published a few months earlier, when he used the words ' there be some Englishe songs lately set forth by a great Maister of Musicke which for skill and sweetnes may content the most curious '. Also Thomas Watson described as ' excellent ' the two madrigals of ' Master William Byrds ', composed at his request for his ' First sett of Italian Madrigalls Englished ' in 1590. The origin of the misapprehension as to Byrd's merits as a madrigalist may be ascribed mainly to three causes. Firstly, Peacham's comment in the ' Compleat Gentleman ' lends itself to misunderstanding, and it has been much quoted by historians from the time of Hawkins and Burney to the present day. Yet Peacham's opinion should not be valued at more than its actual worth, for it does not necessarily represent the view of the best musicians of his day. And Peacham does in fact award very high praise to Byrd as a madrigalist, for he mentions ' *La Virginella* and some others ' as comparing favourably with the best Italian work. Also this writer was speaking of the lighter kind of madrigal, and in this sense he was right in saying that Byrd's ' vein ' was not for that type of music, for he did not publish any Ballets or *Fa-las*, and the great majority of his madrigals are of the serious kind. Secondly, Byrd's title to his first published Set has misled many of those who have not examined the volume, both as to its character and its contents. The Set was divided by Byrd himself into four sections : the first was headed ' Psalmes ' and consisted of ten pieces ; the next sixteen compositions were classified as

'Sonets and Pastorales'; then followed seven 'Songes of Sadnes and Pietie'; and the book ended with two 'Funerall Songs of Syr Phillip Sidney'. In making a general title for the Set the mention of Pastorals was no doubt omitted because the word would have disturbed its alliterative character; but the effect of the omission has been to convey the erroneous impression that all the pieces in the Set are either psalms or songs of sadness. Hawkins wrote entirely under this misapprehension;[1] having quoted the title of the Set he added that the compositions contained in it were ' in general as he terms them'. And Hawkins enlarged on this by saying that 'twice in his life' Byrd ' made an essay of his talent for light music' in composing *La Virginella* and *This sweet and merry month of May*. He could not have known such gay examples as *Awake, mine eyes, Come, jolly swains, Though Amaryllis dance in green*, and many others. Byrd never styled *Though Amaryllis* a song of sadness or piety. The third cause of misapprehension about Byrd's merits as a secular composer are due to the fact that these Sets have not been rendered accessible in modern editions, although Mr. Arkwright reprinted the 1589 Set some years ago in his Old English Edition. It is quite impossible to judge of these compositions from the part-books alone, and very little more value is to be attached to criticism founded even upon the score if nothing more than a small selection is rendered available for the purpose.[2] And yet one thing further : the general failure to recognize the freedom and variety of rhythm in all the Tudor music must necessarily be misleading in any endeavour to estimate its true value, inasmuch as such failure results in completely obscuring the spirit in which the music is conceived. This subject has been fully dealt with in a former chapter, so that it is sufficient to add that if such a madrigal as *I joy not in no earthly bliss* (1588 Set, No. 11) is treated ruthlessly with a regular rhythm of four crotchets in a bar, on the ground that it is indicated in the original time-signature, not only will the composer's intention never be realized, but also this false impression that Byrd could not shake himself free from the Church style will unfortunately gain strength.

[1] Hawkins's History, vol. iii, p. 290.

[2] The three complete Sets are now published in the author's English Madrigal School Series, vols. xiv–xvi, Stainer and Bell.

The first publication of this composer with secular work included in it appeared in 1588, the year in which the Armada was defeated. It has already been stated that this was the first published volume to contain English madrigals, and it was the firstfruits of the glorious harvest so shortly afterwards to be garnered. The full title of this Set was ' Psalmes, Sonets, and Songs of Sadnes and pietie, made into Musicke of five parts ', and the circumstances in which it was issued are worthy of some notice. It is clear that some of the compositions had already found their way into the hands of singers, for Byrd mentioned on the title-page, with evident annoyance, that ' some of them going abroade among divers in untrue coppies are heere truely corrected ' ; and he repeated this assertion both in his dedication to Sir Christopher Hatton and in the ' Epistle to the Reader '. In the dedication he recorded that he issued the Set in deference to the wishes of his friends and in ' consideration of many untrue incorrected coppies of divers my songes spread abroade '. From the Epistle to the Reader we gather that some of the pieces were originally designed for solo-voice with instrumental accompaniment, but that they were rearranged ' in all parts for voices to sing the same '. This may also explain the phrase ' The first singing-part ', printed against one of the vocal-parts in several numbers in this Set.

Another special feature which characterizes all three of Byrd's Sets is the inclusion of a certain proportion of sacred compositions, almost all of which are set to words of the Psalms. In the 1588 Set the first ten pieces are settings of English metrical versions of psalms, and the section closes with the quaint sentence : ' Heere endeth the Psalmes, and beginneth the Sonets and Pastorales.' The second section of the Set includes *Though Amaryllis dance in green* (No. 12) ; this is one of the best specimens of Byrd's lighter vein, and a feature of it is the alternative use of the $\frac{3}{2}$ and $\frac{6}{4}$ rhythms, a special characteristic of the *Courante* at a rather later date. In this instance the two rhythms sometimes appear independently, as in the first two bars, the first of which is in $\frac{3}{2}$ and the second in $\frac{6}{4}$, and sometimes simultaneously, as in the sixth bar ; while the fifth bar of the Bassus-part is open to either rhythmical interpretation. In the second section of this madrigal the

$^6_4$ rhythm is employed less and less, until towards the conclusion the $^3_2$ measure becomes finally established ; no doubt the composer was aiming at expressing the idea suggested by the words *Heigh ho ! 'chill*[1] *love no more* and the gradual disappearance of the gayer measure represents the repudiation of love. The following are the opening bars :

Several of the ' Sonnets and Pastorals ' are written in a strong
triple measure, and the vigour of this rhythm in the latter part
of *Who likes to love* (No. 13) almost irresistibly recalls to the
mind of the modern musician the trio in the Brahms B flat
string-sextet. The most notable example of Byrd's treatment
of triple rhythms in this Set is *The match that's made for just
and true respects* (No. 26) ; the refrain which comes at the end
of each stanza is embroidered with rapid notes in a strong
rhythm of $\frac{9}{4}$.

Among the songs of sadness and piety are three pieces
(Nos. 27, 30, and 31) of a semi-religious character, although not
actually set to Scripture words ; and Nos. 28 and 32 belong to
the same serious type that Gibbons treated so nobly a few years
later. *Susanna fair* (No. 29) cannot conveniently be sung to the
original verses, but the great beauty of this madrigal will justify
the substitution of an amended version of the words. One
phrase especially may be quoted from this beautiful composition ; the words given here are from an adaptation of the
original by the present writer.

No. 32 of this Set is the exquisite *Lullaby*, the first section of
which is sometimes sung by itself with the result that its
character as a Carol of the Holy Child is overlooked. The
simplicity and charm of this *Lullaby* almost defy description,
and the tenderness of touch here exhibited amply illustrates
Byrd's capacity for writing in the lighter vein.

Of the two funeral songs, *Come to me, grief, for ever* (No. 34) is
the most attractive. It is quite short, and, unlike many similar
compositions of the madrigalists, it does not name the subject
of the elegy in the text, so that nothing precludes its general use.
It would scarcely be possible to imagine any composition of
this nature inspired with deeper pathos or richer beauty. The

first section is divided into four phrases of five bars each. The following few bars, beginning at bar 6, may be quoted :

In the dedication of the 1588 Set Byrd had hinted at a further publication when he mentioned 'some other things of more depth and skill to folow these, which being not yet finished, are of divers expected and desired '. His second Set followed in the next year under the title of ' Songs of sundrie natures, some of gravitie, and others of myrth, fit for all companies and voyces '. It consists of no fewer than forty-seven numbers, so that within two years Byrd had published over eighty compositions of the kind. Of the forty-seven pieces in the 1589 Set, fourteen are for three voices, eleven for four, twelve for five, and ten for six. The first seven are to metrical versions of the Psalms, and this section concludes with the formula, ' Heere endeth the seaven Psalmes '. No. 8 is another setting of *Susanna fair*, the words being the same as those of No. 29 in the 1588 Set. *The nightin-gale, so pleasant and so gay* (No. 9) affords a good example of Byrd's melodious phrasing and perfect accentuation ; the opening bars of the Superius-part will amply illustrate these features :

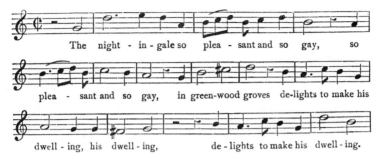

The night - in - gale so plea - sant and so gay, so
plea - sant and so gay, in green-wood groves de-lights to make his
dwell - ing, his dwell - ing, de - lights to make his dwell - ing.

The concluding bars of the above quotation are suggestive of a phrase in Schubert's *Who is Sylvia?*

No. 17, *Wounded I am*, and No. 21, *If Love be just*, both conclude with passages of remarkable beauty. *Whilst that the sun with his beams hot* (No. 23) is a delightful example of the typical madrigal-style dealing with a pastoral subject; it is pervaded throughout with a fresh open-air spirit, much enhanced by the freedom of rhythm. Thus it breaks into a triple rhythm simultaneously in all the parts at the words *Philon the shepherd late forgot*, and the rhythm is broken again with charming effect in the following passage :

played . . he, A - dieu love, a - dieu love, un - true love, un -
song played he, A - dieu love, a - dieu love,

- true love, un - true love, a - dieu love, a - dieu love,
un - true love, a - dieu love, a - dieu love,

This quotation provides a most convincing illustration of the need for irregular barring in printing modern editions of Tudor music ; the whole sense of the phrase would be obscured by adhering strictly to the barring indicated by the original time-signature. This madrigal ends with a pretty touch of pathos.

At this point in the Set there occurs a curious feature in the arrangement of the original edition. Nos. 24 and 25 are the full-choir parts of Christmas carols, of which Nos. 35 and 40, respectively, are the solo-parts. The explanation is that the chorus, being for four voices only, was placed among the four-part compositions, whereas the solo sections, with their full instrumental accompaniment, were included among the five-and six-part pieces. These two carols are in Byrd's finest style and are brimful of Christmas joy ; the two brilliant choruses may quite suitably be sung apart from the sections for solo-voice. It is difficult to conjecture why the two sections of *See, see those sweet eyes* should have been separated in the arrangement of this volume ; for, instead of running consecutively, the first section is No. 29, while the second does not come till No. 34, and a note is printed at the end of No. 29 as follows : ' The second part of this song (Love would discharge) is placed the xxxiiii song.'

Penelope that longed for the sight (No. 27) deals with a favourite subject both among poets and musicians in the latter half of the sixteenth century. Byrd has treated it with great charm and with exactly the right sentiment ; this madrigal is perhaps the finest secular piece in this particular Set. Very few others stand out conspicuously, and the opinion that this Set as a whole does not reach the level of Byrd's best work seems justified. It is possible that he had used up his best available material in the 1588 Set, and that owing to its popularity he was led to publish a second Set sooner than he had anticipated, and for this reason included early work that lay ready to hand, some of which might not otherwise have seen the light.

Twenty-two years elapsed before Byrd issued his remaining volume of this type. It was entitled ' Psalmes, Songs, and Sonnets : some solemne, others joyfull', and was published in 1611. He was then sixty-eight years old ; and whereas in 1589 he had been alone in the field of the English Madrigal School, in 1611 by far the greater part of the English madrigals had already been produced. Such important harmonic developments as are exhibited in the music of Weelkes, Wilbye, and Dowland do not seem to have exercised any influence upon Byrd during this long intervening period, but it is possible to trace something of Morley's influence when we compare Byrd's work in the 1611 Set with that of 1588 and 1589. As an instance of this, *Awake, mine eyes* and *Come, jolly swains* (Nos. 12 and 13 of the 1611 Set) may be cited. The first of these is delightfully gay and has something of the light-hearted spirit that was almost inseparable from Morley's work. And in *Come, jolly swains* it is noteworthy that the latter section is treated in the manner of Morley rather than that of Wilbye. The inclusion in this volume of the four-part setting of *This sweet and merry month of May* (No. 9) suggests the idea that by no means all of these pieces had been newly composed at the date of publication; this particular madrigal had already been printed with Watson's ' First sett of Italian Madrigalls Englished ' as early as 1590.

Retire, my soul (No. 17) is a very notable example of the serious kind of madrigal ; it is written in Byrd's best manner and with great dignity ; but the finest madrigal in the Set is *Come, woeful Orpheus* (No. 19). The words of this poem are more passionate than is usual in Byrd's secular work, and, as a further exception to his ordinary style, it possibly does show traces of the influence of Weelkes and Wilbye. Thus the allusion to *strange chromatic notes* and *sourest sharps and uncouth flats* is treated with methods that are reminiscent of those employed by Wilbye in *Of joys and pleasing pains* (Set I, Nos. 26 and 27), and by Weelkes in *Sweet love, I will no more* (Ballets and Madrigals, No. 3). This madrigal also provides some of the few examples in Byrd's work of the use of an augmented discord taken without preparation. It is brought to a final conclusion by means of a dominant pedal-point with a considerable display of emotion and a final cadence of great beauty :

Of the remaining madrigals in the Set the most interesting are *Crowned with flowers* (No. 22) and *Wedded to Will is Witless* (No. 23), both of which are good specimens of Byrd's vocal writing and thoroughly madrigalian in style. The Set also includes several magnificent pieces of Church music, mostly to words from the Psalms; among these is a superb setting of Psalm li (No. 25), for solo and chorus, and an exceedingly fine *Hodie Christus natus est* to English words (No. 27).

Before concluding this brief review of Byrd's work as a madrigal-writer, some allusion must be made to certain peculiarities of his technique, especially as it is generally stated, and probably with truth, that some of these peculiarities originated with him. In his Epistle to the Reader in the 1588 Set he warned his critics to expect certain effects involving ' jarre or dissonance ', and begged them not to explain away such discords as misprints. The most remarkable of these ' dissonances ' was the simultaneous employment of the major and minor third, a use that has been already discussed in an earlier chapter. Byrd seldom introduced this discord with such severe conflict as that which is sometimes to be found in Weelkes's work, but there are a few instances of direct conflict, as in the following phrase (from No. 32 of the 1588 Set) :

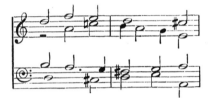

This particular usage certainly did not originate with Byrd ; for at least one example may be quoted from Whythorne's music. Thus in *It doth me good when Zephyrus reigns* (No. 27 of his ' Songes ' published in 1571) the following phrase occurs

Such dissonances are undoubtedly harsh and even intolerable to most modern ears, accustomed to instruments tuned on principles of equal temperament ; but it must be remembered that the effect would have been far less harsh to Tudor musicians to whom the equal temperament was quite unknown. The explanation of these discords is usually to be found by viewing the individual voice-parts horizontally rather than by analysing the chords perpendicularly, and the effect is much softened by

a recognition of the principle of the *terminus acutus* and the
terminus gravis as explained in a former chapter.[1] Occasionally
the simultaneous occurrence of the major and minor third give
an effect that is by no means cacophonous even to modern ears.
Thus, in *Arise, Lord* (No. 18 of the 1611 Set) :

Byrd was also probably the first composer to employ the
minor third simultaneously with the suspended fourth when
resolved on to the major third.   This effect, far from being
harsh, was often beautiful.   A typical example comes from
Care for thy soul (1588 Set, No. 31) :

This idiom remained in common use for more than a hundred
years and is frequently to be found in Purcell's music ; a good
instance occurs in the cadence of the following phrase in
Purcell's *Rejoice in the Lord* :

Byrd combined in one passage both these kinds of dissonance
in the final cadence of his *Lullaby* (1588 Set, No. 32), and the
effect is beautiful.

[1] See p. 99.

The effect of Byrd's influence in this connexion is to be seen in the writings of several of the madrigalists, more particularly in those of Kirbye and Weelkes, and to less extent of Wilbye, Gibbons, and Tomkins.

Another harmonic device characteristic of Byrd was the use of the dominant seventh as a species of free passing-note in a cadence. In this detail he was followed by several of the later English madrigalists. These examples are quoted from Byrd:

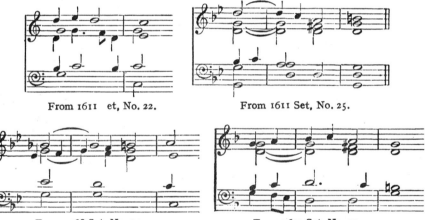

From 1611 et, No. 22.   From 1611 Set, No. 25.

From 1588 Set, No. 35.   From 1611 Set, No. 19.

An expanded form of the second of the above cadences was used by Byrd as early as 1589 in *Penelope, that longed* (No. 27). The chord here employed is a very unusual one for the period at which it was written, and the beauty of the cadence is much increased by following so soon upon the harmonies of B flat major:

The same madrigal ends with another remarkable cadence including a very unusual suspension :

Further examples might be quoted to illustrate the special characteristics of this composer's style ; but enough has been said to show that he is by no means to be regarded as one who was content to work strictly upon conventional lines. It is indeed true that when based upon the purest Italian traditions of the polyphonic style his Art stands unrivalled in this country, and is not inferior even to that of Palestrina himself. But it is still more interesting to dwell upon that aspect of Byrd's genius, so typical of his countrymen in all branches of Art and Literature at the close of the sixteenth century, which led him on to pursue with eagerness the newer methods of expression in the truest and best spirit of progress. It was, perhaps, this feature more than any other which vitalizes Byrd's music.

The Madrigalian Publications of William Byrd

1588. PSALMS, SONNETS, AND SONGS OF SADNESS AND PIETY
made into music of five parts

Psalms

1. O God, give ear and do apply.
2. Mine eyes with fervency of sprite.
3. My soul oppressed with care and grief.
4. How shall a young man prone to ill ?
5. O Lord, how long wilt thou forget ?
6. O Lord, who in thy sacred tent.
7. Help, Lord, for wasted are those men.
8. Blessed is he that fears the Lord.
9. Lord, in thy wrath reprove me not.
10. Even from the depth unto thee, O Lord.

Sonnets and Pastorals

11. I joy not in no earthly bliss.
12. Though Amaryllis dance in green.
13. Who likes to love, let him take heed.
14. My mind to me a kingdom is.
15. Where Fancy fond for Pleasure pleads.
16. O you that hear this voice.
17. If women could be fair and never fond.
18. Ambitious love hath forced me to aspire.
19. What pleasure have great princes ?
20. As I beheld I saw a herdman wild.

1589. SONGS OF SUNDRY NATURES

40. An earthly tree a heavenly fruit it bare.
41. Who made thee, Hob, forsake the plough ?
{ 42. And think ye, nymphs, to scorn at Love ? (*the first part*).
43. Love is a fit of pleasure (*the second part*).

44. If in thine heart thou nourish will.
45. Unto the hills mine eyes I lift.
{ 46. Christ rising again from the dead (*the first part*).
47. Christ is risen again (*the second part*).

1611.   PSALMS, SONGS, AND SONNETS

Songs of three voices

1. The eagle's force subdues each bird.
2. Of flattering speech with sugared words.
{ 3. In Winter cold (*the first part*).
4. Whereat an ant (*the second part*).
5. Who looks may leap.
6. Sing ye to our Lord a new song.
7. I have been young, but now am old.
8. In crystal towers and turrets.

Songs of four voices

9. This sweet and merry month of May.
10. Let not the sluggish sleep.
11. A feigned friend by proof I find.
12. Awake, mine eyes, see Phoebus bright.
13. Come, jolly swains, come let us sit around.
14. What is life or worldly pleasure ?
15. Fantazia (*for strings*).
16. Come, let us rejoice unto our Lord.

Songs of five voices

17. Retire, my soul, consider thine estate.
18. Arise, Lord, into thy rest.
19. Come, woeful Orpheus.
{ 20. Sing we merrily unto God (*the firs part*).
21. Blow up the trumpet in the new moon (*the second part*).
22. Crowned with flowers I saw fair Amaryllis.
23. Wedded to Will is Witless.
24. Make ye joy to God all the earth.

Songs of six voices

25. Have mercy upon me, O God.
26. Fantazia (*for strings*).
27. This day Christ was born.
28. O God, that guides the cheerful sun.
29. Praise our Lord, all ye Gentiles.
30. Turn our captivity, O Lord.
31. Ah ! silly soul, how are thy thoughts confounded ?
32. How vain the toils that mortal men do take.

1588.   TWO MADRIGALS TO FIVE VOICES

included as Nos. 44 and 45 in the first Set of ' Musica Transalpina '

{ The fair young virgin (*the first part*)
But not so soon (*the second part*)

1590.   TWO MADRIGALS

included as Nos. 8 and 28 in Watson's first Set of Italian Madrigals Englished.

This sweet and merry month of May. (*for four voices*), see also 1611 Set, No. 9.
This sweet and merry month of May. (*for six voices*)

CHAPTER XIV

THOMAS MORLEY. Born 1558 ; died 1603

ALTHOUGH Byrd was the actual founder of the English
Madrigal School, his great pupil Thomas Morley was undoubtedly the leading personality, and in a sense the father of the
School. The date of Morley's birth has recently been fixed by the
discovery of a note appended to one of his manuscripts in the
Bodleian Library, which gives his age as 18 in the year 1576.
He took the degree of B.Mus. at Oxford in 1588, at which
date he appears to have been organist of St. Giles, Cripplegate ;
and a baptismal entry in the registers of that church in February
158⅘ undoubtedly refers to one of his sons. Shortly after this
he became organist of St. Paul's Cathedral, and in 1592 he was
appointed to the Chapel Royal. In the latter years of his life
he was living at a house in Little St. Helen's in the parish of
St. Helen's, Bishopsgate, the registers of which church record
the baptism and burial of some of his children. It was while
he was living in Little St. Helen's that he obtained his extraordinary licence to print music ; this was probably through
the influence of Dr. Julius Caesar, a judge of some distinction
who at a later date became Chancellor of the Exchequer and
Master of the Rolls, and was buried in St. Helen's. Caesar at
that time held the office of Master of Requests, and in that
capacity acted as the medium between the Crown and petitioners
desirous of obtaining from the Sovereign occasional extra-
judicial boons.[1]

Morley's health had already begun to fail before 1597, for his
'Plaine and Easie Introduction to Practicall Musicke', published
that year, contains allusions to his poor state of health. The
records of the Chapel Royal show that the vacancy caused by
his resignation was filled in the autumn of 1602, and there can
be little doubt that ill-health was the reason of his retirement.
His death took place in the following year, but the exact place

---

[1] Cox's Annals of St. Helen's, Bishopsgate, p. 290.

of his burial remains unknown. He appears to have died intestate, for the administration of the property of Thomas Morley was granted to his widow in the Prerogative Court on October 25, 1603, and there is every reason to think that this Thomas Morley was identical with the composer. If that is so he was twice married ; his first wife's name is recorded in connexion with the baptism of his children as ' Suzan ' and the widow's name was Margaret. The wording of the dedication of his two-part Canzonets seems to suggest that his first wife had formerly been in the service of Lady Periam.

One very curious episode in Morley's life is revealed in a letter written from Flanders by one Paget, a Roman Catholic intriguer, from which it appears that Morley was employed at one time as a sort of political agent ; and in playing that part he had a narrow escape from very serious consequences. Paget wrote : ' Ther is one Morley that playeth on the organies in poules that was with me in my house. He seemed here to be a good Catholicke and was reconsiled, but notwithstanding, suspecting his behaviour, I intercepted letters that Mr. Nowell [1] wrote to him, whereby I discovered enoughe to have hanged him. Nevertheless he shewing with teares great repentaunce, and asking on his knees forgivenes I was content to let him goe.' [2] It is not easy to estimate the loss that English music would have suffered if Paget had acted otherwise, for the adventure might have cost Morley his life before a single one of his madrigals was published.

Morley's earliest work, entitled ' Canzonets or Little Short Songs to Three Voyces' met with great popularity and ran through three editions in comparatively few years. Published in 1593, it was reprinted in 1606 and again in 1631. It consisted of twenty compositions, to which four more were added in the 1606 Edition. The bright character of his work was in striking contrast to the severity of Byrd's two first Sets, the sole predecessors of this Set of canzonets in the field of English composition of this class. Very nearly all these canzonets reflect the light-hearted spirit of their composer, who excelled all the

---

[1] Perhaps to be identified with Henry Noel, to whose memory Morley wrote *Hark Alleluia* (1597 Canzonets, No. 21), or possibly Dean Nowell of St. Paul's.

[2] G. E. P. Arkwright's account of Thomas Morley in Grove's Dict. of Music (New Ed.).

English madrigalists in this particular vein. His splendid freshness is well illustrated in such pieces as *Good morrow, fair ladies of the May* (No. 6) and *Whither away so fast ?* (No. 7) ; in this latter there is one of those racing passages by means of which Morley was so fond of depicting pursuit. *Arise, get up, my dear* (No. 20) deals with the kind of subject which always appealed to Morley's merry imagination. It represents a scene of wedding festivities ; allusion is made to the feasting ; and the confusion of sound caused by the merry maidens hawking their wares of spice-cake and sops in wine is reproduced by an overlapping rhythm in triple measure. Then follow various details of ritual connected with the bride-lace and gilt rosemary branches, and the piece ends with the boisterous merriment of Kate and Will, Tom and Jill, dancing on the village green in honour of fair Daphne's wedding day. But Morley could also write in a more serious vein, and there is great charm in *Do you not know how Love first lost his seeing ?* (No. 16), the ending of which is especially beautiful and full of passion. The dominant pedal is to be noticed as one of the early examples of this device. The four numbers that were added to this Set of canzonets in the reprint of 1606 belong to the Ballet, or *Fa-la* type of composition ; there is a rare delicacy and finish in the little ballet *Though Philomela lost her love* (No. 23).

Morley's next publication followed in 1594 under the title of the 'First Booke of Madrigalls to Foure Voyces'. This is the very earliest instance of the use of the term Madrigal on the title-page of a volume of English compositions. Here again Morley confined himself almost exclusively to the brighter subjects so well suited to his genius. The Set opens with the well-known *April is in my mistress' face*, a perfect example of the light kind of madrigal. A fine number in this Set is *In dew of roses* (No. 7), which ends with another dominant pedal-point and a mysterious passage in complex rhythm, intended to suggest the fearful prospect of the ghost of the lover perpetually haunting the lady who had cruelly rejected him. *Besides a fountain* (No. 14) is rather similar to this madrigal ; it also ends with a pedal and a complex triple rhythm in the upper parts. *Come, lovers, follow me* (No. 11) is an exceedingly attractive and picturesque bit of work. The treatment of the words *and if he come* is typical of

Morley's methods, and when the Bassus-part enters with an
augmentation of the musical figure just employed all the most
realistic experiences of hide-and-seek, with its sudden surprises,
are vividly depicted.   Two madrigals in the Set, *Hark ! jolly
shepherds* (No. 17) and *Ho ! who comes here ?* (No. 18) deal with
the subject of morris-dancing and show Morley at his best.
Ho ! who comes here ? has been mentioned in a former chapter
as illustrating Morley's extraordinarily free manner of handling
the words of a poem.   This madrigal is treated with such gaiety
and vivid realism that it will be worth while to examine it in
some detail, for the music succeeds in conjuring up the whole
scene of the arrival and performance of the morris-dancers.
The opening bars depict the first announcement of their
approach ; after this passage has been repeated, the townsfolk
can be seen hurrying out to find the dancers already arrived,
and to ' see how trim they dance and trickly '.   Then the
rollicking musical figure at the words *hey there again !* seems to
suggest the horse-play which was an important feature in the
proceedings.   The cry of *Now for our town !* appears to have
been a kind of formula taken up by the crowd, and it was
shouted partly in welcome, and partly in rivalry to encourage
this or that member of the troupe who might belong to their
own town or to some neighbouring place.   The bells refer to the
bells usually hung round the wrists and ankles of the dancers
or jingled in their hands ; but it is possible also that the church-
bells were set ringing, for in this madrigal Morley introduced
a musical figure more suggestive of a peal of five church-bells :

This figure is used in syncopation in a manner that adds
much to the general jangling effect in the gay noisy scene :

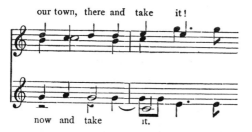

our town, there and take it!

now and take it.

Then follows the dialogue between the Piper and the excited spectators, which is evidently a considerable elaboration of the original theme at the hands of the composer. The madrigal ends with the frolics of the hobby-horse, the buffoon of the troupe. In sharp contrast to this madrigal is *Say, gentle nymphs, that tread these mountains* (No. 20), which is full of quiet charm and is written in a beautiful smooth style.

The volume originally consisted of twenty madrigals, but two more were added in the second edition published in the year 1600. These two additional numbers are below the level of Morley's other work. In No. 21 there occurs a very curious bar which may be regarded as a typical experiment in unconventional harmony. Such experiments were uncommon in this composer, who usually adhered strictly to the older conventionalities :

The chord on the last beat of this bar is virtually that of the dominant thirteenth, of which there are but few examples in the madrigals, though it was used more than once in a similar way by Thomas Tomkins in his 1622 Set. It was also used by Giles Farnaby in his fascinating *Rosa solis* variations in the Fitzwilliam Virginal Book.

With his next volume, published in 1595, Morley struck out a new line, for it consisted of a Set of Ballets. This form of composition was borrowed from the Italians, and Morley admitted that he took Gastoldi for his model, some of the words being translations of Ballets by Gastoldi and other Italian composers. Morley excelled as a Ballet-writer just as he did in all the other light kinds of Madrigal, and he succeeded in infusing a good deal of variety in spite of the much more limited scope offered by the Ballet-form.

The general popularity of this form among singers is due to its well-defined and strong rhythm as well as to its bright character, and Morley's Set has, in consequence, gained wider appreciation than any other of the English madrigal-books. Some of the pieces are especially popular, notably *Now is the month of maying* (No. 3), *My bonny lass she smileth* (No. 7), *Fire! fire!* (No. 14), and several more. One of the finest, but less-known, numbers is *About the maypole new* (No. 11). It is framed upon a more extended design ; each section includes a phrase in triple measure which contrasts effectively with the square rhythm of the opening, and the second *fa-la* has an especially fine and distinctive outline. In spite of the description on the title-page of the book, only the first fifteen numbers are ballets ; the subsequent four have no *fa-la* refrain and are purely madrigalian in style. *Leave, alas, this tormenting* (No. 19) is an excellent example of this composer's sadder mood. The Set closes with a splendid composition for seven voices written in the form of a dialogue. The three upper voice-parts represent ' Phillis Quier ' and should be sung by female voices ; the four lower voices represent Amyntas and should be sung by male voices headed by a counter-tenor. The seven voices are not employed together until the final section, when they combine with a rich and massive effect. A second edition of the Ballets appeared in 1600.

In 1595 Morley also published his ' First booke of Canzonets to Two Voices ', which included nine instrumental fantasies in two parts besides the twelve Canzonets. These canzonets are very remarkable little compositions and unique among the works of the English madrigalists. From many points of view they may be said to display the genius of their composer almost more conspicuously than any of his other works. They are written with consummate skill and with extraordinarily full harmonic effect, while their phrasing and melodic beauty go near perfection. If any two are to be singled out from a Set, all of which are of such excellence, perhaps *Sweet nymph, come to thy lover* (No. 3), and *I go before, my darling* (No. 4) are the most attractive. *Miraculous Love's wounding* (No. 5) is a remarkable composition, not only on account of its inherent beauty, but because it is designed upon lines which forecast what came to be known at a later date as Ternary form. It is the earliest example in English madrigals of an experiment of this nature, although further experiments of a like kind were made very shortly afterwards by Weelkes, Wilbye, and others.

The 'Canzonets or Little Short Aers to five and sixe Voices' which were published in 1597 contain some of Morley's maturest and best work. The first fifteen of the Set are comparatively short, and thus conform to the description on the title-page ; but the last six are on a much bigger scale. Here again Morley showed his preference for the gayer subjects, but two exceptions stand out in sharp relief. One of these is *Hark ! Alleluia cheerly with angels now he singeth* (No. 21), an elegy on the death of Henry Noel, one of Queen Elizabeth's courtiers, who was evidently also a patron of music and a madrigal-lover. This noble piece of music is constructed on a figure which runs through all the voice-parts in the opening sections :

Occasionally this figure is introduced in a rather freely inverted form, and it appears for the last time with splendid strength in the Quintus, or first bass-part, to the words *whose echo heaven ringeth*. This manner of reference to the opening phrase here is, of course, typical of the methods of the madrigalists. At this same point an important full-close occurs and the composition ends with music of massive dignity ; in the last few bars the descending scale passages are in a subtle way reminiscent of the main figure, which welds together the whole structure.

The other serious madrigal in this book is *O grief, even on the bud* (No. 7). It is constructed on much simpler lines, but it is also of entrancing beauty and expresses a passionate emotion.

In the bar's rest which occurs in all the voices together, following the words *the sun hath lowered,* there is a real touch of tragedy which is accentuated with an admirable sense of proportion by the introduction of the major third three bars earlier. The following are the opening bars :

O grief! even on the bud that fair-ly flow - ered, the sun hath low - ered.

The second half of the song is practically a solo for the tenor accompanied by the other voices.

The Set also includes the popular *I follow, lo, the footing* (No. 17), and *Stay, heart, run not so fast* (No. 18). These two are somewhat alike in character, and are examples of Morley's aptitude to express feelings of enthusiastic gaiety. The composer has shown his imaginative power in a subtle little touch of realism in the first of these two madrigals ; the breathless race up and down rapid scale passages in all the voice-parts, sometimes in overlapping rhythms, sometimes in contrary motion, reaches its climax in the penultimate bar, on each beat of which one or other of the voices arrives at the word *caught* and holds it on through the remainder of the bar ; each beat being thus punctuated with the word, the elusive features of the game of 'catch' are wonderfully suggested.

An instance in this same madrigal of the clashing of the major and minor third affords a good example of that kind of convention which is not uncommon in the English madrigals, and has been mentioned in the previous chapter in connexion with Byrd. Another example in Morley's work occurs in *Phyllis, I fain would die now* (Book of Ballets, No. 21) :

The explanation in a case of this kind, which occurs at a full close in the music, is this : in accordance with the laws of *musica ficta* the major third was invariably introduced at every full-close of importance, but when the following phrase was introduced with the minor triad of the same chord, the composer did not trouble to shorten the note and so to avoid overlapping. This was largely for the sake of appearances, for undoubtedly the minim in the above passage gives a better proportion to the appearance of the cadence ; yet the note was probably not held on after the other voices had entered ; or it is possible that a little pause was made in such cases in all the voice-parts before the new phrase began.

These overlapping chords in a cadence were no new thing at the end of the sixteenth century. In *Fond youth is a bubble,* a little part-song by Tallis in the Mulliner MS.,[1] which is not later than 1565 and is possibly fifteen or twenty years older, the following passage occurs :

In this case it may be regarded as quite certain that the F sharp was not sustained after the bass had attacked the B flat. Yet the semibreve has a better ornamental value than a minim at this point.

Morley's ' First book of Aires with little Short Songes to sing

[1] British Museum Add. MS., No. 30513, fol. 29b.

and play to the Lute with Base-Viol' will be mentioned in a subsequent chapter in connexion with the music of the lutenists. But apart from these volumes of original compositions, which include in the aggregate over a hundred pieces, Morley also edited three collections of madrigals. The most important of these was entitled ' The Triumphs of Oriana ', which was published in 1601. This collection was modelled upon a similar Italian Set entitled *Il Trionfo di Dori*. Almost every one of the leading English musicians of the day contributed a madrigal to the Set in honour of Queen Elizabeth. The madrigals numbered twenty-five in all and each of them ends with the same refrain. Michael East's contribution arrived too late for inclusion in the *corpus* of the book, but it was inserted at the back of the title-page ; this arrangement did not affect the numbering of the pieces, which had, no doubt, already been set up by the printer ; thus Norcome's madrigal remained as No. 1, and the Set concluded with Johnson's as No. 24, East's remaining unnumbered. Bateson's contribution arrived later still and could not be included at all, but it eventually appeared with his own first Set. Other posthumous Oriana madrigals are to be found in the Sets of Pilkington and Vautor. Morley himself wrote two fine madrigals for the ' Triumphs '. The whole collection, as befitting the subject, is of course conceived in a joyful strain. Each contributor naturally made a special effort on this occasion, and as a consequence the Set is an extremely fine one. But it may be questioned whether musical historians have not tended to exaggerate the value of the ' Triumphs ' at the expense of much other work produced by these same musicians : and whether, also, the widespread attention which has at all times been directed to this particular Set has not led to some degree of misconception as to the scope and meaning of madrigal-composition as it was understood, for example, by Wilbye, Weelkes, and Orlando Gibbons, among others. Nothing could be more splendid of their kind than these ' Oriana ' madrigals, but it should be clearly recognized that there were also many other types of madrigal written by the Tudor composers, some of which afforded them even greater scope for beauty of expression, for depth of pathos, and for wealth of imagination.

Besides this famous volume, Morley made two collections of the works of Italian composers adapted to English words. The first of these was a Set of Canzonets for four voices and was published in 1597. The other consisted of Madrigals for five voices and came out the next year; Morley himself contributed two original compositions to the Set of Canzonets. These same two four-part canzonets appear among the examples at the end of Morley's 'Plaine and Easie Introduction', where the music is set to Italian words. The examples also include a three-part canzonet to the words *O sleep, fond Fancy*. He was thus responsible altogether for no less than nine volumes of secular Song, containing nearly two hundred pieces in all, while six of these volumes consisted entirely of his own compositions. The nine volumes were published within a period of seven years. During this same short period Morley also edited a volume called 'The First Booke of Consort Lessons, made by divers exquisite Authors for sixe Instruments to play together'; this came out in 1599, two years after he had published his important 'Plaine and Easie Introduction to Practicall Musicke'. When it is remembered that he wrote a considerable amount of Church music, and that he had his duties to perform at the Chapel Royal, it will be readily recognized that he spent a busy life in the pursuit of his Art.

Morley was evidently a man of a very genial and lovable nature, and it is impossible to read his famous treatise without coming under the spell of his personal charm, even at this distance of time. The 'Plaine and Easie Introduction' was in itself a book containing a wonderful amount of sound instruction, and for many generations it had no rival ; it can, moreover, still be studied with no small profit. It is by no means written in the dry style of an ordinary text-book, but is in the form of a dialogue, containing many picturesque little digressions and touches of humour which must fascinate a reader even if he is not especially interested in the theory of music. The opening passage of the book with the description of ' Master *Sophobulus* his banket ', has already been quoted in a former chapter ; but a further extract [1] may be permitted as showing something of the methods

[1] Morley's Plain and Eaşy Introduction, p. 120.

of an Elizabethan musician instructing a pupil during a
country walk :

Master. But I pray you how did you becom so ready in this
kind of singing ?

Polymathes. It would require a long discourse to shew
you all.

Master. I pray you trusse up that long discourse in so fewe
wordes as you may, and let us heare it.

Polymathes. Be then attentive. When I learned descant of
my maister *Bould,* hee seeing mee so toward and willing to
learne, ever had me in his company, and because hee continuallie
carried a plaine-song-booke in his pocket, he caused mee to doe
the like : and so walking in the fields hee would sing the plaine
song, and cause mee sing the descant, and when I sung not
to his contentment hee would shew me wherein I had erred. . . .

> After describing their meeting with a friend of Bould,
> another discanter, and how they ' fell to contention striving
> who should bring the point in soonest ', he tells how they
> ' all parted friendes.' . . .

Yet did none think better of him then hee did of himselfe : for
if one had named and asked his opinion of the best composers
living at this time, he would say in a vaine glory of his owne
sufficiencie ; tush, tush (for these were his usual wordes) hee
is a proper man, but hee is no descanter, hee is no descanter,
there is no stuffe in him, I will not give two pinnes for him
except hee hath descant.

Philomathes. What ? can a composer be without descant ?

Master. No : but it should seeme by his speech that except
a man bee so drownd in descant that hee can doe nothing else in
musicke but wrest and wring in hard points upon a plaine song,
they would not esteem him a descanter.

Among the many original musical examples which Morley
included in his ' Plaine and Easie Introduction ', only one with
English words can properly be classed as madrigalian.

Though Morley died in middle age he lived long enough to see
the success of the great School of composers which he had done
so much to foster, and of which he was the leading spirit. His
genial light-hearted character, unaffected by the strenuous life
which he must have led, is clearly reflected in his music. His
profound learning scarcely ever obtruded itself in his compositions, yet, whenever necessary, he showed rare skill in the
employment of every contrapuntal device. His part-writing
was wonderfully direct and vocal, and he shared with all the

great musicians of his School that faculty for giving exact tone-colour and true emphatic value to words which adds such special distinction to their work.

The Madrigalian Publications of Thomas Morley.

1593. CANZONETS OR LITTLE SHORT SONGS TO THREE VOICES

1. See, mine own sweet jewel.
2. Joy, joy doth so arise and so content me.
3. Cruel, you pull away too soon your lips.
4. Lady, those eyes of yours that shine.
5. Hold out, my heart, with joy's delights accloyed.
6. Good morrow, fair ladies of the May.
7. Whither away so fast ?
8. Blow, shepherds, blow your pipes.
9. Deep lamenting, grief bewraying.
10. Farewell, disdainful, since no love avails me.
11. O fly not ! O take some pity.
12. Thyrsis, let pity move thee.
13. Now must I die recureless.
14. Lady, if I through grief and your disdaining.
15. Cease, mine eyes, cease your lamenting.
16. Do you not know how Love first lost his seeing ?
17. Where art thou, wanton ?
18. What ails my darling ?
19. Say, dear, will you not have me ?
20. Arise, get up, my dear.
21. Love learns by laughing first to speak.
22. This love is but a wanton fit.
23. Though Philomela lost her love.
24. Spring-time mantleth every bough.

1594. FIRST BOOK OF MADRIGALS TO FOUR VOICES

1. April is in my mistress' face.
2. Clorinda false, adieu.
3. Why sit I here complaining ?
4. Since my tears and lamenting.
5. Help ! I fall ! Lady.
6. Lady, why grieve you still me ?
7. In dew of roses steeping.
8. In every place fierce love.
9. Now is the gentle season freshly flowering (the first part).
10. The fields abroad with spangled flowers (the second part).
11. Come, lovers, follow me.
12. O no, thou dost but flout me.
13. I will no more come to thee.
14. Besides a fountain of sweet briar and roses.
15. Sport we, my lovely treasure (the first part).
16. O sweet, alas, what say you ? (the second part).
17. Hark ! jolly shepherds, hark !
18. Ho ! who comes here ?
19. Die now, my heart.
20. Say, gentle nymphs, that tread these mountains.
21. Round, around, as about a wood I walked.
22. On a fair morning.

1595. FIRST BOOK OF BALLETS TO FIVE VOICES

1. Dainty fine sweet nymph delightful.
2. Shoot, false love, I care not.
3. Now is the month of maying.
4. Sing we and chant it.
5. Singing alone sat my sweet Amaryllis.
6. No, no, Nigella !

7. My bonny lass she smileth.
8. I saw my lovely Phyllis.
9. What saith my dainty darling ?
10. Thus saith my Galatea.
11. About the maypole new.
12. My lovely wanton jewel.
13. You that wont to my pipe's sound.
14. Fire ! fire ! my heart.
15. Those dainty daffadillies.

16. Lady, those cherries plenty.
17. I love, alas, I love thee, dainty darling.
18. Lo, she flies when I woo her.
19. Leave, alas, this tormenting.
20. Why weeps, alas, my lady love ?

Dialogue of seven voices

21. Phyllis, I fain would die now.

1595. FIRST BOOK OF CANZONETS TO TWO VOICES

1. Go ye, my canzonets, to my dear darling.
2. When, lo, by break of morning.
3. Sweet nymph, come to thy lover.
4. I go before, my darling.
5. Miraculous Love's wounding !
6. Lo ! here another love from heaven descended.

7. Leave now, mine eyes, lamenting.
8. Fire and lightning from heaven fall !
9. Flora, wilt thou torment me ?
10. In nets of golden wires.
11. O thou that art so cruel.
12. I should for grief and anguish die.

1597. CANZONETS OR LITTLE SHORT AIRS TO FIVE AND SIX VOICES

For five voices

1. Fly, Love, that art so sprightly.
2. False love did me inveigle.
3. Adieu, you kind and cruel.
4. Love's folk in green arraying.
5. Love took his bow and arrow.
6. Lo ! where with flowery head.
7. O grief, even on the bud.
8. Sovereign of my delight.
9. Our Bonny-boots could toot it.
10. Ay me ! the fatal arrow.
11. My nymph, the dear, and her my dear.

12. Cruel, wilt thou persever ?
13. Said I that Amaryllis ?
14. Damon and Phyllis squared.
15. Lady, you think you spite me.
16. You black bright stars that shine.
17. I follow, lo, the footing.

For six voices

18. Stay, heart, run not so fast.
19. Good love, then fly thou to her.
20. Ladies, you see time flieth.
21. Hark ! Alleluia cheerly.

1597. TWO CANZONETS TO FOUR VOICES

included as Nos. 8 and 9 in Morley's collection of Italian canzonets.

My heart, why hast thou taken ? (*Perchè tormi il cor mio ?*)
Still it fryeth. (*Ard' ogn' hora il cor lasso.*)

These same two canzonets, set to Italian words, are among the examples at the end of Morley's Plain and Easy Introduction.

1597. A CANZONET FOR THREE VOICES

included as an example in Morley's Plain and Easy Introduction.

O sleep, fond Fancy.

1601. TWO MADRIGALS

ncluded as Nos. 13 and 23 in the 'Triumphs of Oriana'.

Arise, awake, awake. (*For five voices*)
Hard by a crystal fountain. (*For six voices*)

CHAPTER XV

THOMAS WEELKES. Born *circa* 1575 ; died 1623

In 1596 no important madrigalian work was published ; but 1597 and the four years that followed it represent the richest period in the history of the English School. In 1597 Thomas Weelkes produced his first volume. Byrd, Morley, and John Mundy were the only Englishmen who up to that date had published work of this kind, and they were each of them men of mature years and tried capacity. This being so, it is not surprising that Weelkes should have shown some diffidence in venturing into the lists.

The date and place of Weelkes's birth are not known, though the date may be fixed with a good deal of probability at 1575 or 1576. The surname with that particular spelling is exceedingly uncommon, but a family of the name, so spelt, was living at Sawley, near Ripon, in the sixteenth century. There is, however, no evidence to connect the composer with that locality. Certain indications seem to point to some connexion with the county of Cheshire ; but the name cannot be found in any of the archives of Chester Cathedral. It has also been suggested that Weelkes was a native of Hampshire, and the first known fact about his life is that he was organist of Winchester College in the closing years of the sixteenth century. It is not unreasonable to conjecture that he may have been formerly a chorister either at the cathedral or college. He took the degree of B.Mus. at Oxford on leaving Winchester College for Chichester Cathedral in the year 1602 ; and he held the position of cathedral organist until his death. This took place in London on November 30, 1623, at the house of his Chester friend Henry Drinkwater in the parish of St. Bride's. Weelkes was on a visit to Drinkwater at the time. He was buried on the following day at St. Bride's, Fleet Street, and the record of his burial may still be seen in the parish registers of that church. It is very remarkable that although this interesting fact was quite unknown [1] to John Immyns when he founded the London Madrigal Society in 1741, the first meetings of that Society were held at the ' Twelve Bells ' in Bride Lane, almost over the very bones of Thomas Weelkes.   He had married before leaving Winchester and left descendants ; his wife died a year before him and was buried at Chichester Cathedral.   His will was proved in' the Dean's Peculiar Court at Chichester (vol. iii, fol. 174) and has been reprinted in full by Mr. Arkwright.[2]

Weelkes was perhaps twenty-one or twenty-two years of age when he published his First Set of ' Madrigals to 3. 4. 5. and 6. voyces ' ; and, as just stated, he was full of apology for putting forth such a work while still of ' unripened years ', for so he described himself in the dedication of this volume. This was only the second Set of English works to which the title of Madrigal was actually given.   Yet Weelkes's precocity, if such it was, was more than amply justified by the result, for almost all of the twenty-four madrigals which the Set includes are mature work of the highest class.   The most notable number in the Set is *Cease, sorrows, now* (No. 6) which is probably the finest English madrigal for three voices in existence.   The surprisingly keen sense of imagination and the inventive power of the composer are illustrated in this work by the dramatic effect produced in the *knolling of the bell*, as well as by the wonderful chromatic passage which follows at the words *I'll sing my faint farewell* ; this phrase is taken up in imitation by each of the voices and brings the piece to its conclusion.   And all this is the more noteworthy when we realize that nothing whatever of the kind had been written before this youthful genius produced this remarkable piece of music in all its novelty.   We can hardly imagine the effect of Weelkes's daring harmonic experiments upon the older musicians of his day, nor the astonishment of the singers who experienced for the first time these new musical sensations.   In the final cadence of this madrigal there is an instance of the major and minor third being used simultaneously in the manner already

[1] His burial-place remained unknown until the present Author had the good fortune to discover it.   See the Author's paper in the Musical Association Proceedings, 1915–16 ; and The English Madrigal School Series, vol. ix, p. 2.

[2] Old English Edition, Part XIII, preface.

described as peculiar to the English composers. Another such a clash is to be found in Weelkes's *Those sweet delightful lilies* (No. 18 of this Set) and it is not unfrequently to be met with throughout his madrigals. In the madrigal under consideration, if this discord is handled carefully it can be made to sound very beautiful. The whole of the concluding section may be quoted here :

Another interesting madrigal in this Set is *Ay me ! my wonted joys* (No. 9). This composition represents one of the early experiments in constructive form as founded upon the principles of repetition ; and it illustrates further the inventive genius of Weelkes as displayed in his very first publication. In the matter of design this madrigal may be regarded as a primitive forerunner of Rondo-form. The first section is repeated in its entirety in the ordinary way, but the music of the latter part of it, which is set to the words *and deep despair doth overtake me*, reappears a third time at the conclusion of the madrigal to the words *for love hath wrought my misery*.

In *Three virgin nymphs* (No. 10) we have a good example of the realistic effects at which the madrigalists so often aimed. The madrigal is written for three equal soprano voices, with a bass voice, as the fourth, to represent Silvanus. He makes his entry first of all from the distance in a manner that may be truly described as terrifying; the demure walk of the nymphs, as expressed in steady crotchets, becomes more and more disturbed, and the climax is reached in the grotesque musical figures in which Silvanus snatches at them. *Our country swains* and *Lo! country sports* (Nos. 11 and 12) are two delightful numbers dealing with morris-dancing; the compass of the voices makes them available for female voices. *Those spots upon my lady's face* (No. 21) has a very beautiful ending and belongs to that class of serious madrigal in which Wilbye so greatly excelled. Being in six parts it is written for a somewhat unusual combination of voices; the five top parts all lie easily within the range of female voices, while the lowest part ranges with the octave D to D and is suitable either to bass or tenor voices. In the Quintus-part of this madrigal there occurs an early example of the progression of an augmented second, from B flat to C sharp. This interval must have been startling to the more conservative musicians of that day.

The   o - ther   bright   car - na - tion

It may be noted that Kirbye used a similar progression in *I love alas*, No. 20 of his Set, which was also published in 1597.

Encouraged by his early success, but still apologizing for his immaturity, Weelkes published a second volume in 1598 entitled 'Balletts and Madrigals to five voyces'. Of the twenty-four compositions in this book seventeen are Ballets, six are Madrigals, and the last is an Elegy for six voices upon the death of Lord Borough. A few of these Ballets are very similar in style and rhythmic design to those which Morley published three years earlier ; notably *All at once well met* (No. 1), the opening rhythm of which is exactly similar to *Dainty fine sweet nymph*, the first Ballet in Morley's book. But to many of them Weelkes gave a decided stamp of individuality : for instance, *On the plains, fairy trains* (No. 5) with its unusual rhythm in the opening bars, and the triple measure introduced at the words *Now they dance, now they prance* : or again, *Hark ! all ye lovely saints above* (No. 9), or *Now is my Cloris fresh as May* (No. 22) in which the *Fa-las* are set in strong triple rhythms running counter to each other in the different voice-parts.

It has not been generally realized how few Ballets, comparatively speaking, were written by the English madrigalists outside the Sets of Morley, Weelkes, and Hilton. Several composers included a small number of Ballets in their Madrigal Sets without distinctive mention on their title-pages, and by far the most important of these was Tomkins, whose *Fa-las* are of first-rate merit ; but none of them wrote anything like so many as Morley and Weelkes, while in the published Sets of such composers as Byrd, Wilbye, Gibbons, Bateson, Ward, Kirbye, and Bennet, among others, no Ballets were included. The younger Hilton's set of *Fa-las* did not appear until so late a date as 1627, by which time scope for originality in this special class had become much narrowed, and his work is very inferior when placed beside that of Morley, Weelkes, and Tomkins. There is no necessity for the comparisons that have been made between the Ballets of Morley and Weelkes, each of whose work may be said to reach the highest possible excellence in this branch of their Art.

In this Set of Ballets there are few characteristic examples of Weelkes's chromatic harmonization, but a remarkable suspension occurs in *Phyllis, go take thy pleasure* (No. 10) which is a Madrigal and not a Ballet. This suspension comes at the words *my heart now thou hast broken*, and in some respects it resembles one of the famous discords used by Sebastian Wesley more than two and a half centuries later in his beautiful anthem, *Cast me not away*.

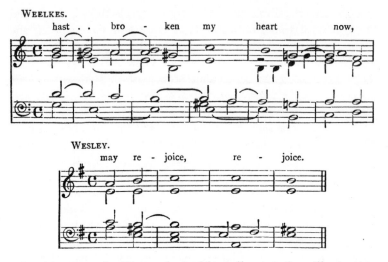

In this connexion it may be incidentally stated, as illustrating
further how marvellously Weelkes anticipated the future, that
another of Wesley's beautiful discords in this same anthem is
foreshadowed in a striking manner in the opening of the second
part of Weelkes's *O Care, thou wilt despatch me,* quoted more
fully on p. 200.

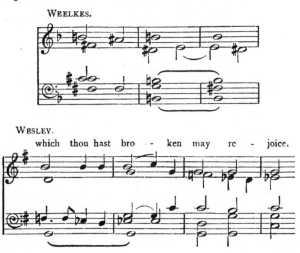

Returning to Weelkes's 1598 Set, an example of the simultaneous use of the major and minor third may be noted in the

elegy on Lord Borough at the words *give Sorrow leave to speak.*
G sharp and G natural at that point come together at the
same pitch, producing a very harsh effect upon modern ears
accustomed to equal temperament. In this elegy is also to be
noticed a further illustration of Weelkes's tendency to seek in
repetition the basis of structural form in music ; for the final
passage is constructed upon material already used in the
earlier sections. Thus the music set to the words *live still on
earth* recalls the phrase used for *Borough is dead* ; and the last
twelve bars are almost identical with a passage near the
beginning, where the words *whose timeless death a stony heart
would break* occur. Repetition of a somewhat different type,
but also illustrating this composer's feeling after form, is to be
observed in the charming passage *Phyllis my choice of choice
shall be,* which occurs at the end of both parts of the madrigal
Come clap thy hands (Nos. 19 and 20 of this Set) ; the same
device was employed by Weelkes in a later Set in *Thule, the
period of cosmography* (Madrigals of six parts, Nos. 7 and 8) ;
and once again in *What, have the gods their comfort sent ?* (Nos. 3
and 4 of the six-part Set).

Weelkes's finest work is to be seen in his magnificent
' Madrigals of 5. and 6. parts ' which were published in
1600, having almost certainly been composed in Winchester
College, where, as organist of the College, he is known to have
been living at the time. It was apparently his original intention
to bring out these twenty madrigals in one volume, but he
divided them into two Sets, with independent dedications,
title-pages, and numeration ; thus each Set contains ten
madrigals, the five-part and six-part compositions being kept
separate.

One small point of interest attaches to these two Sets in
that they were the first to bear on the title-page the description
' Apt for the Viols and voices ', a formula that became so common
in the publications of all the later English madrigalists, and
the exact meaning of which has led to much discussion.

It would be difficult to praise these two Sets of madrigals
too highly, especially those in the five-part volume. In
character they are somewhat more massive than similar
compositions of Wilbye, and, partly for this very reason, they

seem to lack something of the graceful delicacy of finish which Wilbye achieved with such perfection in his best work. Yet from the point of view of dramatic treatment and force of emotional expression Weelkes's work in these two Sets stands alone in English madrigal-literature. There is also a remarkable variety of style to be observed in these twenty compositions viewed as a whole. It will be necessary here to examine some of these madrigals in considerable detail.

The composer's imagination shows itself in the very first phrase of the opening number, *Cold winter's ice is fled and gone,* for the ice may be said to melt before our eyes, and yet not too suddenly, for the minor triad reappears in the repetition of the phrase by the lower voices before we feel the gaiety of summer which ' brags on every tree ' to the bright music of the chirping birds. In *Take here my heart* (No. 3) there is a simple and tender beauty that can scarcely be matched in the entire realm of Part-song. The words *I give it thee for ever* are set to a charming phrase suggesting the wedding-bells in anticipation ; there is splendid conviction, yet tender feeling, in the music to the words *For Hope and Love command my heart to stay,* and it is followed again by the wedding-bells. The madrigal closes with extraordinarily suitable music to the words *Love but my heart, my heart will never change.* The whole song is handled with a perfect sense of proportion and with a subtlety of emotional expression absolutely suited to the subject, yet entirely free from any taint of sentimentalism.

The next in the Set, *O Care, thou wilt despatch me,* is one of the finest madrigals in existence and is very characteristic of Weelkes's work. The story is that of a person distracted with care and seeking relief in music, yet failing to find more than partial comfort. The opening passage is treated with chromatic harmonies that must have amazed contemporary musicians, and perhaps they will equally amaze those modern musicians who suppose that Tudor madrigals are built up entirely upon academic counterpoint :

The next section, *if music do not match thee*, is followed by
a half-hearted *Fa-la* set to the simple harmonies of G major;
after this comes another chromatic passage, typical of this
composer, and dealing with Care's 'deadly sting', which is
finally expressed in a realistic way by a clash between F sharp
and F natural. The first half of the madrigal closes with an
effort to replace Care with Mirth by means of a gay musical
figure, which is clothed in harmonies that occasionally suggest
the triumph of Mirth, but which finally confess failure in the
F natural of the penultimate bar in the Cantus and Tenor-
parts. The second half opens to the words *Hence Care! thou
art too cruel* with a chromatic passage even more remarkable
than the first. In the course of this passage the modulations
carry the composer so far afield as to involve the employment
of the note A sharp. This is one of the very rare instances of
the occurrence of this note in the Tudor madrigals; perhaps
the only other example in an English madrigal is to be found

in Bateson's *Come, sorrow, help me to lament* (Set II, No. 24),
which, however, was published eighteen years later than this
madrigal of Weelkes.   Dowland, too, used an A sharp in *From
silent night* ('A Pilgrimes Solace', No. 10), and Dowland
appears to go one degree further in *Sweet, stay awhile* (No. 2
of the same Set), where he uses E sharp ; but that note is used
as a passing chromatic rather than as belonging to the harmonic
structure of the passage.   Returning to Weelkes's madrigal, it
will be noticed with what telling effect he repeatedly dis-
appoints expectations of a full-close in these wonderful bars :

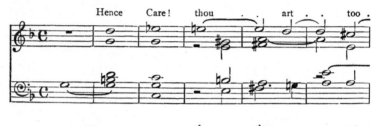

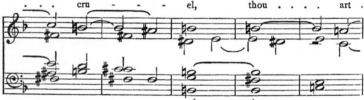

The words *Come, music, sick man's jewel* are made to anticipate the *Fa-la* by the device of augmentation, yet the phrase is so subtly treated that the point might easily escape notice.

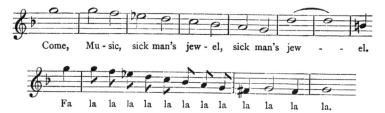

Come, Mu - sic, sick man's jew - el, sick man's jew - - el.

Fa la la la la la la la la la la la la.

Here again a gay musical figure is employed for the *Fa-la*, but the harmonies are wonderfully designed to suggest a sad and almost tragic sense of colour. The following bar will suffice to illustrate this point :

Among many other interesting features, attention may be drawn to the pedal-point on the words *but thou dost now sustain me* by means of which the idea of sustaining was no doubt intended to be suggested ; and an additional touch of realism is added by the descending musical phrase, bearing, as it were, heavily upon the support of the pedal in the Bass-part. The harmonies upon this pedal-point are certainly remarkable when it is recalled that the madrigal was composed in the year 1600 :

The composition ends with a sad-toned *Fa-la* that represents final failure.

This madrigal has been dealt with here in considerable detail, partly with the object of illustrating the principles of analysis to which such imaginative work as that of Weelkes especially lends itself, and at the same time to serve as a suggestion that the writings of all the great madrigalists contain much material of interest, as well as constructive features, that do not meet the eye except after something more than a cursory examination. But, further, this madrigal takes a place among the most remarkable of all the compositions of the Tudor period, whether it be valued on account of its pure beauty, or for its constructive ingenuity, or for the wealth of imagination displayed in it by a composer whose power of invention and careless disregard of convention enabled him to peer so far into the distant future of musical development.

The rest of the madrigals in these two Sets of 1600 must be passed over with brief comment, but mention should be made of the delightful *Lady, the birds right fairly* (No. 9 of the five-part Set) with its charming cuckoo phrase ; and of the fine massive writing in *Like two proud armies* (No. 1 of the six-part Set) with its great quaver run for the two bass voice-parts in the ' thundering fight '. This madrigal is similar in style to *Mars in a fury* (No. 6). *When Thoralis delights to walk* (No. 2) is teeming with fresh and simple beauty. In *Methinks I hear Amphion's warbling strings* (No. 4) the composer again shows his originality in the use of a pedal-point extending over six bars for the words *Whilst that old Phemius softly plays the ground* :

Thule, the period of cosmography (No. 7 and 8 of the six-part Set) is another splendid madrigal, the quaint words of which gave Weelkes ample scope for his brilliant power of invention. Space will not allow of an analysis of this madrigal here in such detail as *O Care, thou wilt despatch me,* but it provides almost as much interesting material for examination. It is full of realistic effects : thus among things we see the ' sulphureous ' fire of Hecla and the flames of Etna ascending higher and higher, while such a little touch as the introduction of triple measure to give point to the meaning of Trinacria must not be overlooked. In the second half of the madrigal a mere glance at the score in itself provides a perfect picture of the flying fishes ; and in the marvellous chromatic passage in which the composer depicts ' how strangely Fogo burns ', the mysterious scene of the distant volcano in remote Terra del Fuego, as viewed from the sea, is brought before our eyes with a dramatic effect that could scarcely be surpassed by any modern musician, in spite of the largely increased resources which the intervening 300 years have placed at his disposal.

The volume closes with a fine Elegy on the death of Henry Noel, already mentioned as a favourite at the Court of Queen Elizabeth and an amateur of music, to whose memory Morley wrote his *Hark ! Alleluia* (Canzonets to five and six Voices, No. 21). Queen Elizabeth is said to have made the following rebus on his name :

> The word of negation, and letter of fifty
> Make that gentleman's name who will never be thrifty.

In this elegy Weelkes three times within nine bars used the major and minor third of the chord simultaneously; this effect thus repeated is necessarily cacophonous to modern ears ; but a very beautiful chord is introduced on the last word of the phrase *now thou art dead* :

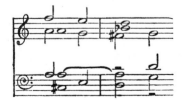

Weelkes was still a young man, probably not more than twenty-five years old, in 1600 ; yet his publications in that year were his last of any importance in the field of madrigal-composition.   His remaining volume, published in 1608, was quaintly entitled, 'Ayeres or Phantasticke Spirites for three voices'.   This consists almost entirely of small pieces of a light type, and several are of the nature of political or personal skits, as, for example, *The Ape, the Monkey, and Baboon* (No. 10), which apparently was intended to satirize certain *habitués* of the famous Mermaid Tavern.   But there are several delightful little pieces in this Set ; among these is the well-known and ingeniously written *The Nightingale* (No. 25) ; but the only one in which may be recognized the touch of the great composer who had revealed his splendid genius in the 1600 madrigal-Sets is the massive dirge (No. 26) written in remembrance of his friend Thomas Morley, whose death had taken place in 1603.   In this dirge one very curious piece of realism is intro-duced ; after a long-sustained chord of D major in a very low register, representing the silent sleep in the grave, a few dis-jointed bars follow, and then comes a moment of complete silence in all the voice-parts.   This silence is broken in an astonishing fashion by all the six voices entering suddenly and in rapid succession with a short phrase to the words *until the world shall end,* and no doubt the composer intended thus to represent the crack of doom.

Although Weelkes employed these realistic methods with perhaps greater frequency than the other English madri-galists, and certainly with more fertile imagination and invention, it must not be forgotten that all the composers of that date used these methods to a considerable extent. If it be urged that such methods were grotesque and even trivial, it must be admitted that occasionally they were both ; but we have also to remember that they were part of the conven-tion of the time, and it speaks volumes in praise of the general sense of fitness shown by these composers, that they so rarely allowed their attempts at realistic expression to savour of the grotesque, or to interfere with the beauty or the broad outline of their music.   These methods of realistic expression were not confined to the Tudor musicians, for they are abundantly evident in the music of the Restoration period, notably in that of Henry Purcell. Two examples from Purcell's work will illustrate this statement : his anthem *They that go down to the sea in ships* opens with a descending scale of two whole octaves for the solo bass voice : and in a vocal trio in his setting of the fifty-sixth Psalm, at the words *they hold altogether and keep themselves close*, the three voices have to sing simultaneously three consecutive notes of the scale :

keep them-selves close

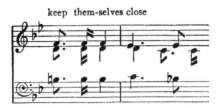

Well-known examples of a similar kind of realism are also to be found in Handel's *Israel in Egypt*, Bach's *St. Matthew Passion*, Haydn's *Creation*, and elsewhere.

It remains to mention Weelkes's contribution to the 'Triumphs of Oriana', *As Vesta was from Latmos hill descending* (No. 17). This is probably his best-known and most popular work ; it is full of spirit and splendidly fresh and pure, but it is modelled upon much more conventional lines than most of the great madrigals of his 1600 Sets, and for this reason, fine as it certainly is, it lacks something of the characteristic distinction of this composer's best work.

To sum up, Weelkes must be regarded as one of the greatest, if not the greatest, of the Tudor madrigalists with the sole possible exception of Wilbye. Wilbye, no doubt, wrote with a more highly polished style and a greater delicacy of expression, and also with a deeper sense of beauty than Weelkes. In the latter's work there is nothing quite so beautiful as Wilbye's *Oft have I vowed* (Set II, No. 20), or, on a smaller scale, so graceful as *Adieu, sweet Amaryllis* (Set I, No. 12) ; and Wilbye was unrivalled in the kind of madrigal of which *Happy, oh happy he!* (Set II, No. 16) is an example. On the other hand, Weelkes certainly surpassed all his contemporaries in wealth of imagination, and he earns special recognition on account of his originality ; for he was something much more than an innovator, in that he achieved remarkable success in the fields which he explored as a pioneer. And as a musical prophet we can only contemplate him with amazement, although he shares this distinction with another very great innovator, the lutenist-composer John Dowland, whose ' First Booke of Songes or Ayres of fowre partes' was also published in 1597 ; for some of the harmonies which these two composers were the first to use were not again commonly employed until many generations had intervened in the history of musical development.

Weelkes's work seems to have had but little influence over those older madrigalists who had already published volumes before his first Set appeared; for instance, scarcely any trace of his chromatic innovations is to be seen in the subsequent work of Byrd or Morley. The ' jarre and dissonance ' for which Byrd prepared his critics in the ' Epistle to the Reader ' of his 1588 Set, and which is occasionally to be met with in his work, is of a totally different nature from the novel harmonies which Weelkes wrote. But his influence upon those who succeeded him, even though their style differed in many respects from his, was considerable, and it is particularly to be observed in the work of Wilbye, Gibbons, and Tomkins, the three greatest madrigalists to make their first appearance subsequent to the year 1597.

Weelkes wrote a fair quantity of Church music, all of which is allowed to remain in oblivion at the present time. Not a note of his manuscript survives in the library of Chichester Cathedral.

The Madrigalian Publications of Thomas Weelkes

1597. MADRIGALS TO 3. 4. 5. AND 6. VOICES

Songs of three parts

1. Sit down and sing.
2. My flocks feed not (*the first part*).
3. In black mourn I (*the second part*).
4. Clear wells spring not (*the third part*).
5. A country pair were walking all alone,
6. Cease, sorrows, now.

Songs of four parts

7. Now every tree renews his summer green.
8. Young Cupid hath proclaimed.
9. Ay me ! my wonted joys forsake me.
10. Three virgin nymphs were walking.
11. Our country swains in the morris-dance.
12. Lo ! country sports that seldom fades.

Songs of five parts

13. Your beauty it allureth.
14. If thy deceitful looks have chained my heart.
15. Those sweet delightful lilies.
16. Lady, your spotless feature.
17. Make haste, ye lovers, plaining.
18. What haste, fair lady ? leave me not.

Songs of six parts

19. Retire, my thoughts, unto your rest.
20. Say, dear, when will your frowning leave ?
21. Those spots upon my lady's face.
22. If beauty be a treasure.
23. My tears do not avail me.
24. My Phyllis bids me pack away.

1598. BALLETS AND MADRIGALS TO FIVE VOICES

1. All at once well met, fair ladies.
2. To shorten Winter's sadness.
3. Sweet love, I will no more abuse thee.
4. Whilst youthful sports are lasting.
5. On the plains, fairy trains.
6. Sweet heart, arise, why do you sleep ?
7. Give me my heart and I will go.
8. Hark ! all ye lovely saints above.
9. Say, dainty dames, shall we go play ?
10. Phyllis, go take thy pleasure !
11. In pride of May the fields are gay.
12. Sing we at pleasure.
13. Now is the bridals of fair Choralis.
14. Sing, shepherds, after me.
15. Welcome, sweet pleasure.
16. Lady, your eye my love enforced.
17. We shepherds sing, we pipe, we play.
18. I love and have my love regarded.
19. Come clap thy hands, thou shepherd swain (*the first part*).
20. Phyllis hath sworn she loves the man (*the second part*).
21. Farewell my joy.
22. Now is my Cloris fresh as May.
23. Unto our flocks, sweet Corolus.

To six voices

24. Cease now, Delight.

1600. MADRIGALS OF FIVE PARTS

1. Cold winter's ice is fled and gone.
2. Now let us make a merry greeting.
3. Take here my heart.
4. O Care, thou wilt despatch me (*the first part*).
5. Hence Care ! thou art too cruel (*the second part*).
6. See where the maids are singing.
7. Why are you ladies staying ? (*the first part*).
8. Hark ! I hear some dancing (*the second part*).
9. Lady, the birds right fairly.
10. As wanton birds, when day begins.

1600. MADRIGALS OF SIX PARTS

1. Like two proud armies.
2. When Thoralis delights to walk.
3. What, have the gods their comfort sent (*the first part*).
4. Methinks I hear Amphion's warbling strings (*the second part*).
5. Three times a day my prayer is.
6. Mars in a fury.
7. Thule, the period of Cosmography (*the first part*).
8. The Andalusian merchant (*the second part*).
9. A Sparrow-hawk proud.
10. Noel, adieu, thou Court's delight.

1608. AIRS OR FANTASTIC SPIRITS FOR THREE VOICES

 1. Come, lets begin to revel't out.
 2. Jockie, thine horn-pipe's dull.
 3. Some men desire spouses.
 4. To-morrow is the marriage day.
 5. Upon a hill the bonny boy.
 6. Come, sirrah Jack, ho !
 7. Tan ta ra, cries Mars on bloody rapier.
 8. The gods have heard my vows.
 9. Though my carriage be but careless.
10. The Ape, the Monkey, and Baboon did meet.
11. No, no, though I shrink still.
12. Ay me ! alas ! heigh ho.
13. Late is my rash accounting.
14. Four arms, two necks, one wreathing.
15. Lord ! when I think what a paltry thing.
16. Say, wanton, will you love me ?
17. I bei ligustri e rose.
18. Strike it up, Tabor.
19. Ha ha ! this world doth pass.
20. Since Robin Hood, Maid Marian.
21. O now weep, now sing !
22. Alas, tarry but one half hour.
23. As deadly serpents lurking.
24. Donna il vostro bel viso.
25. The nightingale, the organ of delight.

For six voices

26. Death hath deprived me of my dearest friend.

1601.   A MADRIGAL TO SIX VOICES

included as No. 17 in the ' Triumphs of Oriana '.

As Vesta was from Latmos hill descending.

CHAPTER XVI

JOHN WILBYE.   Born 1574 ; died 1638

UNTIL recently the personal history of John Wilbye, who by common consent is regarded as the greatest of the English madrigal-composers, remained buried in oblivion.   The discovery of his Will [1] made it possible to reconstruct the story of his life, for it provided clues which led to information that surpassed all expectation.[2]

Wilbye was born at Diss in Norfolk early in the year 1574, and his baptism is recorded in the registers of the parish church on March 7 of that year.   He was the third son of Matthew Wilbye, a tanner living in prosperous circumstances at Diss and owning landed property in the neighbourhood.   Matthew was evidently an amateur of music, for we learn from his Will [3] that he bequeathed his lute to his son John, who may have owed something to his father's musical influence in his childhood.   Within a few miles of Diss was Brome Hall, the seat of Sir Thomas Cornwallis ; and it would appear that John Wilbye's musical abilities attracted the notice of the Cornwallis family while he was still a child.   Cornwallis's daughter Elizabeth was married to Sir Thomas Kytson of Hengrave Hall, a few miles distant across the Suffolk border, and the circumstance led to the appointment of Wilbye about the year 1593 to the office of household musician to the Kytsons, and for over thirty years he lived in the service of that family.

Hengrave Hall is a magnificent Tudor house situated not far from Bury St. Edmunds.   The house has undergone very little alteration since it was built by the father of Wilbye's patron, and it has even been possible to determine with great probability the actual room which was set apart for the composer's use.   The original inventories, still preserved at Hengrave as

---

[1] P.C.C., 145 Lee.
[2] See the author's paper on John Wilbye, Musical Association Proceedings, 1914–15.   [3] Proved at Norwich, July 6, 1605.

part of a collection of records of remarkable value, also give in detail the items of furniture, and even the colour and texture of the curtains and other hangings in ' Wilbee's Chamber ', so that it is possible to picture, with an unusual degree of exactness, the surroundings of this composer, as well as the room at Hengrave Hall in which many of his famous madrigals were written. The Hengrave inventories furnish a complete list [1] of all the musical instruments and music-books belonging to the establishment, and these would in consequence have been under Wilbye's control. Sir Thomas Kytson also tenanted a London house in Austin Friars during the last decade of the sixteenth century, and Wilbye would have frequently accompanied the family to London. Thus his first Set of Madrigals, published in 1598, was dated from the Austin Friars. The publication was dedicated to Sir Charles Cavendish of Welbeck, who had married Elizabeth, the eldest daughter of Sir Thomas Kytson. Wilbye's second Set of Madrigals, published in 1609, was dedicated to the unfortunate Lady Arabella Stuart, whose mother, Lady Lennox, was sister of Sir Charles Cavendish. Lady Arabella was an occasional visitor at Hengrave, and this explains how Wilbye became acquainted with her.

Sir Thomas died in 1602, but Lady Kytson continued to live at Hengrave Hall and to maintain the establishment in the same degree of state as formerly until her death in 1626. Meanwhile in 1613 Lady Kytson granted Wilbye a lease of Sexten's Farm,[2] which was reputed the best sheep-farm in the entire district. The lease was drawn upon specially favourable terms in recognition of his faithful services. But Wilbye still continued to live at the Hall and to superintend the music there, and it must be supposed that he employed a bailiff to manage his farm. But incidentally this new interest seems, strangely enough, to have dried up his fount of composition, for in the following year, 1614, were published the two motets which he contributed to Leighton's ' Teares or Lamentacions ', and these are positively the last compositions of his that we know ; yet he lived for another twenty-five years. The lease of this prosperous farm undoubtedly formed the foundation of

[1] See Musical Association Proceedings, 1914–15.
[2] Hengrave MSS. at Hengrave Hall.

the considerable fortune which he owned at the time of his death.

After Lady Kytson's death in 1628 the splendid establishment was broken up. The letters and other documents preserved among the Hengrave MSS. tell many amusing details of domestic squabbles and jealousies connected with that crisis, and Wilbye seems to have had his share of troubles in the household. An autograph letter written by the composer at this date is still to be seen at Hengrave.[1] On leaving the Hall Wilbye went to live at the house of Lady Rivers at Colchester. Lady Rivers was the younger daughter of Sir Thomas Kytson, and she seems to have been Wilbye's special patroness throughout his life, being a few years his senior. Her marriage to Lord Rivers was not a happy one ; his family seat was at St. Osyth, and it was when she left him that she went to live at Colchester, some nine miles distant. The house is still standing and was described by Morant[2] as the ' great brickhouse opposite the west end of ' Holy Trinity Church. Here, too, Wilbye lived for the last twelve years of his life, and it is interesting that the two houses in which he spent the greater part of his life are still in existence. He died in the late summer of 1638 and was buried at Holy Trinity, Colchester.

The Will of John Wilbye was proved in the Prerogative Court of Canterbury in the following November.[3] He died possessed of a comparatively important estate, and as he died unmarried his principal legatees were his nephews and nieces. He owned a good deal of land in and around the town of Bury St. Edmunds and also in the neighbourhood of Diss. A deed dated 1622 shows that in that year he had bought some land near his native place and jointly owned by his brother Matthew and his nephew John Wilbye. The money legacies mentioned in his Will, apart from the residue, amounted to more than £400, a large sum judged by the standard of that time. He left a small legacy to his life-long friend Lady Rivers, who survived

---

[1] This letter is reproduced in facsimile as a frontispiece to the author's edition of Wilbye's works. The English Madrigal School, vol. vi. Stainer and Bell.

[2] Morant's History of Colchester, part iii, p. 9.

[3] The Will is printed in full in the Author's paper on Wilbye. Musical Association Proceedings, 1914–15.

him a few years, and his best viol to Charles, Prince of Wales, afterwards Charles II.

Wilbye published two Sets of Madrigals, in 1598 and 1609 respectively. They contain together sixty-four madrigals, and to these must be added his contribution to the ' Triumphs of Oriana '. Viewed as a whole they reach a uniformly high standard, while certain individual compositions stand out to defy comparison with anything in the whole range of madrigal-literature. Wilbye showed a predilection for sad and sombre words, though he wrote in all styles and excelled in them all. It was, however, in the serious and emotional type of madrigal that he reached heights that were not quite attained even by Weelkes at his best. He may not have written anything quite so original and unconventional as Weelkes's *Hence Care ! thou wilt despatch me* ; but the consummate style and finish of his work, together with the restraint with which he handled the more emotional subjects, impart a dignity to his greatest madrigals which sets them apart as the finest of their kind.

It is in his gayer mood that Wilbye is best known to the majority of modern madrigal-singers ; and, in fact, *Sweet honeysucking bees* (Set II, Nos. 17 and 18) and *Flora gave me fairest flowers* (Set I, No. 22) are perhaps two of the most widely-. known of all the English madrigals ; but *The Lady Oriana*, from the ' Triumphs ', the six-voice setting of *Lady, when I behold* (Set I, No. 24), *Stay, Corydon* (Set II, No. 32), and *Adieu, sweet Amaryllis* (Set I, No. 12) are also very general favourites. Other less-known examples of Wilbye's brighter style are *As fair as morn* (Set II, No. 5), *What needeth all this travail ?* (Set I, Nos. 7 and 8), *Thus saith my Cloris bright* (Set I, No. 11), and *Ye that do live in pleasures plenty* (Set II, No. 25). On the other hand, the serious class of madrigal, in which Wilbye more especially excelled, has for some reason been almost entirely ignored. It was this type of subject which afforded him scope, not only for the various ingenious devices by which he gave dramatic colour to his words, but also for more freedom and sometimes even complexity of rhythm, and further for the varied emotional sentiment which he expressed with great depth of feeling, although with such true artistic reserve that his work was never tainted with anything approaching sentimentalism. He showed his pre-eminence by the power of his imagination, and by the subtle delicacy of touch which enabled him to colour with exact truth each varying shade of emotion expressed in the words that he so happily wedded to his music. A careful study of Wilbye's madrigals cannot fail to open a new door for those who may be disposed to regard a Madrigal as no more than an academic essay in counterpoint. Perhaps the madrigal of this composer that makes the most direct impression in this kind of treatment is *Unkind, O stay thy flying* (Set I, No. 20) ; the opening bars, with the suspended F natural, giving point to the word *unkind*, have their obvious meaning ; and the handling of the phrase *Stay for me*, reiterated as it is with increasing insistence, could not fail deeply to move a listener by its pathetic appeal. The following are some other fine examples of Wilbye's work, to mention but a few, which seem, each in their different way, to reach the highest possible level of emotional treatment : *I always beg* (Set I, Nos. 16 and 17), *All pleasure is of this condition* (Set II, No. 19), *Of joys and pleasing pains* (Set I, Nos. 26 and 27), *Ah ! cannot sighs ?* (Set II, No. 30), *Oft have I vowed* (Set II, No. 20), *Happy, O happy he !* (Set II, No. 16). and *Alas ! what a wretched life* (Set I, No. 19).

It will not be possible within the short limits of this chapter to consider more than three or four of these madrigals in detail. *Oft have I vowed* (Set II, No. 20) is certainly one of the most beautiful of all Wilbye's madrigals. It opens with a straight-forward rhythmical figure which at first sight suggests gaiety of treatment ; but the composer's intention was to awaken memories of happy hopes which had since proved baseless during the bitter days in which the despairing lover wasted away in grief. It is important that the opening bars should be sung with a proper appreciation of the spirit of the latter part of the madrigal and of its meaning as a whole. The rhythm of the opening bars is again introduced at the words *still hoping to remove thee*, thus connecting the idea of the two passages. The line *Millions of tears I tendered to thy beauty*, is treated in a striking manner : the whole section in which these words occur is constructed on a dominant-pedal of unusual length for music of this period. The passage is rendered all the more noticeable by the fact that the harmonies built upon the pedal-point are of a chromatic nature, and the whole effect is surprisingly modern when the date of the composition is borne in mind :

A sustained *crescendo* will add much to the effect in this place.   Then follows the device used by all the madrigalists in setting the word *sighs*, which consisted of delaying the word by a crochet rest ; but more subtle is the little forced laugh a bar or so later on the words *silly tears*.   After a full close in B flat there follows another wonderful passage on a descending chromatic scale to the words *suff'rest my feeble heart to pine with anguish*.   This passage inevitably recalls the concluding section of Weelkes's *Cease, sorrows, now* (1597 Set, No. 6), but it is of even finer quality.   The Bassus-part passes right down the scale from B flat to G, a tenth below, and ends in a dominant-pedal upon which chromatic scales appear in the upper voice-

parts. This effect, too, is extraordinarily modern and exceedingly beautiful :

suf - f'rest my fee - ble heart, my fee - ble

heart to pine with an - -

guish to . . . . pine . . . .

A few bars later, with another characteristic little touch, the
feeling of bitterness is intensified by the avoidance of the leading
note, and the phrase is repeated a little further on :

my bit - ter days

do waste and I do lan - - guish.

The madrigal closes with a passage full of emotion and
constructed upon the same material that was used for the
words *suff'rest my feeble heart to pine* ; yet Wilbye achieved
his purpose of recalling the former phrase to mind by more
subtle means than the mere repetition of the music, and the
allusion would remain unnoticed except to a careful observer.
It provides an excellent illustration of the maxim *Summa ars
est celare artem.*

Another very fine madrigal, full of imaginative interest, is
Of joys and pleasing pains (Set I, Nos. 26 and 27). This madrigal
provides some typical examples of Wilbye's method of treating
his words with the object of giving them special colour and
emphasis.   The tendency which he showed, in common with
Morley and Weelkes, to anticipate one of the leading principles
upon which Form in musical structure was founded in later
times, is also strikingly exemplified in this madrigal.   This is
one of those longer compositions which is divided into two
separate sections ; and the opening passage of the music, the
words of which are *Of joys and pleasing pains I late went singing,* is recapitulated in its entirety right at the end, thus most
appropriately linking up the ideas, the concluding couplet of
the words being :

> Yet still and still I sing, yet ne'er am linning [1]
> For still the close points to my first beginning.

---

[1] An obsolete word meaning *ending* or *ceasing.*

As if to press the point home, this recapitulation is made twice over. The device has an excellent effect in rounding off the whole composition.

A noticeable feature in the first section is a great outburst of emotion at the words *the baleful notes . . . are ruth and moan, frights, sobs, and loud lamenting.* The value of the octave interval in the Bassus, although a small detail in itself, will not be passed unnoticed :

In the second section is an instance of the simultaneous use of the major and minor third, and the effect in this case is peculiarly harsh as the notes are brought into conflict at the same pitch. But it cannot be doubted that Wilbye wrote this discord deliberately to enforce the meaning of the words *my voice is hoarse with shrieking,* and it stands as an example, whether we approve of it or not, of those experiments which the madrigalists at least had the courage to make, although not all of them can be regarded as completely successful. The introduction of the so-called Italian sixth in this madrigal has been mentioned in a former chapter. It occurs in the line *my song runs all on sharps,* and here the composer has contrived to write for each voice on the word *sharps* a note that necessitated the employment of the sharp sign in the notation of the period. A similar example of this form of realism may be seen in Byrd's *Come, woeful Orpheus* (1611 Set, No. 19). Another noticeable piece of realistic writing in this madrigal occurs at the words

Striking time on my breast ; each voice strikes in upon independent beats with the word *time,* and finally the Bassus booms
out the whole phrase in single slow notes.

  Of the brighter type of madrigal there are no finer specimens
in Wilbye than the popular *Flora gave me fairest flowers* (Set I,
No. 22) and *Sweet honey-sucking bees* (Set II, Nos. 17 and 18),
and these owe their popularity very rightly to the splendid
strength of their rhythm. Nothing could possibly be finer in
its way than the passage in *Flora,* first given in C minor and
then repeated in B flat major, to the words *Come, ye wantons, here
to play.* Nevertheless it should be noticed that although so
much of the rhythm of these two madrigals is cast in a regular
and simple mould, the composer, with the hand of a genuine
artist, has occasionally varied it with an irregular rhythm in
triple measure. In *Sweet honey-sucking bees* the monotony of
rhythmic texture is broken at the words *Keeping their spring-
tide graces* by the introduction of a triple rhythm which imparts
an extraordinary flexibility to the composition as a whole :

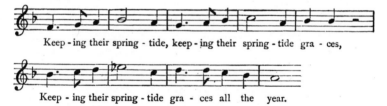

Keep - ing their spring - tide, keep - ing their spring - tide gra - ces,

Keep - ing their spring - tide gra - ces all the year.

  As a result of this interruption, too, the vigour of the passage
For if one flaming dart seems to have been increased twofold.

  This composition is exceedingly effective when played upon
strings, the volume in which it is printed being one of those
described on the title-page as containing music apt both for
voices and viols. It is especially well designed for strings for
the further reason that the Altus and Tenor-parts are written
for equal compass and are admirably suited to the viola.

  One other feature of Wilbye's methods is exemplified in
Sweet honey-sucking bees ; and it illustrates his originality of
design in yet another direction as well as his evident desire to
throw off the yoke of convention. It was customary at all the
principal cadences of a composition to use the major, and not
the minor, triad, this being one of the old laws of *musica ficta* ;

it was also an invariable rule that the final chord of all should never be the minor triad, although it was permissible to end without a third of either sort, as in the case just quoted from *Oft have I vowed*. In other words, to use the terms somewhat loosely, a composition written in a minor key would conclude with the chord of the tonic major. In *Sweet honey-sucking bees* Wilbye developed this principle by modulating to the key of the tonic major several bars before the end, instead of waiting for the final chord. He passes into G major at the first appearance of the words *Ah then you die*, and the effect of the first B natural at that point is very striking, almost more so on strings than on voices. The same device was introduced in the charming little *Adieu, sweet Amaryllis* (Set I, No. 12).

Wilbye hardly ever employed the seventh as a free passing-note in his cadences after the manner of Byrd, Gibbons, and Weelkes: on the other hand, he made occasional use of passing notes that formed no actual part of the harmony, but which were either approached or quitted by a skip instead of diatonically. A good instance of this occurs in *Flora gave me fairest flowers*. The G in the Altus-part on the second syllable of the word *Phyllis* has been mistaken by most editors of this madrigal for a misprint and altered to F. It is certainly not a misprint, but, rather, a remarkably original experiment on the part of Wilbye. It will be noticed that when the G is retained, as it undoubtedly should be, the phrase forms an exact imitation of what has just been sung in the Quintus-part ; and it contains also a reminiscence of the three crotchets sung by the Tenor and Bassus-parts to the words *I placed on* in each of these two phrases. The resulting discord is one which was frequently used by the eighteenth-century composers and was figured by them $^6_5$.

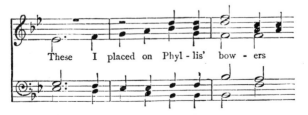

Another example of a somewhat similar character occurs in

There, where I saw her lovely beauty (Set II, No. 24). This is perhaps rather the more remarkable of the two, because the passing-note, which is again approached by the skip of a third, is C natural against the chord of E major ; and, moreover, it forms the point of a temporary modulation, being the first of a series of C naturals following several C sharps. If this note had been C sharp it would have been precisely in line with the chord in *Flora* :

Another noticeable characteristic of Wilbye's madrigals is the lightness of his scoring, especially when writing for five or six voices. Other composers commonly employed all their voices throughout the greater part of a madrigal, but it is almost an exception to find all the parts in simultaneous use in Wilbye. This feature is in marked contrast to Weelkes's style, for his scoring is, generally speaking, very full. It is this characteristic more, perhaps, than any other which imparts such a wonderful sense of style and finish to Wilbye's madrigals. He clearly realized the wide scope for variety which was opened out in so many directions as a result of this reserved method in the utilization of his resources.

Something has already been said about the use of pedal-points in the writings of the madrigalists. Wilbye utilized this device frequently and sometimes with very modern effect, as may be seen in the examples quoted above. One other interesting example is to be found in *Ye that do live in pleasures plenty* (Set II, No. 25), an extremely fine madrigal of a gay character.

It has been said of Wilbye, with truth, that he is one of the
greatest figures in English music. It is the directness and
purity of his style, his strong sense of beauty, and the admirably
vocal nature of his part-writing—in a word, the perfection of
his workmanship—that impress themselves irresistibly on the
mind of any one who studies his music. It may even be said
that Wilbye has had few equals in the whole range of secular
Part-song, whether in his own country or on the Continent.

The Madrigalian Publications of John Wilbye.

1598. THE FIRST SET OF MADRIGALS TO 3. 4. 5. AND 6. VOICES

Songs of three voices

1. Fly, Love, aloft to heaven and look out Fortune.
2. Away ! thou shalt not love me.
3. Ay me ! can every rumour ?
4. Weep, O mine eyes, and cease not.
5. Dear Pity, how ? oh how ?
6. Ye restless thoughts that harbour discontent.

Songs of four voices

7. What needeth all this travail ? (*the first part*).
8. O fools, can you not see a traffic nearer ? (*the second part*).
9. Alas, what hope of speeding ?
10. Lady, when I behold the roses sprouting.
11. Thus saith my Cloris bright.
12. Adieu, sweet Amaryllis.

Songs of five voices

13. Die, hapless man, since she denies.
14. I fall, I fall, O stay me! (*the first part*).
15. And though my love abounding (*the second part*).
16. I always beg, yet never am relieved (*the first part*).
17. Thus Love commands (*the second part*).
18. Lady, your words do spite me.
19. Alas, what a wretched life is this!
20. Unkind, O stay thy flying.
21. I sung sometimes my thoughts.
22. Flora gave me fairest flowers.

Songs of six voices

23. Sweet Love, if thou wilt gain a monarch's glory.
24. Lady, when I behold the roses sprouting.
25. When shall my wretched life give place?
26. Of joys and pleasing pains (*the first part*).
27. My throat is sore, my voice is hoarse (*the second part*).
28. Cruel, behold my heavy ending.
29. Thou art but young, thou sayest.
30. Why dost thou shoot?

1609. THE SECOND SET OF MADRIGALS TO 3. 4. 5. AND 6. PARTS

Songs to three voices

1. Come, shepherd swains, that wont to hear me sing.
2. Flourish, ye hillocks, set with fragrant flowers
3. Ah, cruel Amaryllis, since thou tak'st delight.
4. So light is Love in matchless beauty shining.
5. As fair as morn, as fresh as May.
6. O what shall I do?
7. I live, and yet methinks I do not breathe.
8. There is a jewel which no Indian mines.

Songs to four voices

9. When Cloris heard of her Amyntas dying.
10. Happy streams, whose trembling fall.
11. Change me, O heavens, into the ruby stone.
12. Love me not for comely grace.
13. Fly not so swift, my dear, behold me dying.
14. I love, alas, yet am not loved.
15. As matchless beauty thee a Phoenix proves.
16. Happy, O happy he, who not affecting.

Songs to five voices

17. Sweet honey-sucking bees (*the first part*).
18. Yet, sweet, take heed (*the second part*).
19. All pleasure is of this condition.
20. Oft have I vowed how dearly I did love thee.
21. Down in a valley as Alexis trips (*the first part*).
22. Hard destinies are Love and Beauty parted (*the second part*).
23. Weep, weep, mine eyes, my heart can take no rest.
24. There, where I saw her lovely beauty.
25. Ye that do live in pleasures plenty.
26. A silly sylvan, kissing heaven-born fire.

Songs to six voices

27. O wretched man! why lov'st thou earthly life?
28. Where most my thoughts there least my eye (*the first part*).
29. Despiteful thus unto myself I languish (*the second part*).
30. Ah, cannot sighs, nor tears.
31. Draw on, sweet night.
32. Stay, Corydon, thou swain.
33. Softly, O softly drop, my eyes.
34. Long have I made these hills and valleys weary.

1601. A MADRIGAL FOR SIX VOICES
included as No. 15 in the 'Triumphs of Oriana'.
The Lady Oriana.

CHAPTER XVII

JOHN MUNDY—GEORGE KIRBYE—NATHANIEL PATTRICK—WIL-
LIAM HOLBORNE—GILES FARNABY—MICHAEL CAVENDISH—
JOHN FARMER—JOHN BENNET—THE ORIANA COMPOSERS.

THE four preceding chapters have dealt in considerable
detail with the life and works of Byrd, Morley, Weelkes, and
Wilbye, as having claim to special notice on the ground that
they were, for different reasons, the four most important and
influential personalities in the history of the English Madrigal
School. For it must be borne in mind that Orlando Gibbons,
by comparison with these four, wrote but a small number of
madrigals, and that, although these were exceptionally fine,
his great reputation as a composer is founded mainly upon his
noble Church music.

These four leading madrigalists were discussed in the
chronological order of their first entry into the field with
published Sets of this class of music. It is now proposed
to consider in much briefer detail the rest of the Tudor madrigalists, and the same plan will be followed as regards chronological order. With reference to this, two points may be
observed. Firstly, by far the greater portion of the work of
these four composers belongs to the closing years of the sixteenth century ; only three of their Sets were later than 1600,
namely Weelkes's 'Ayeres or Phantasticke Spirites' (1608), a
publication of comparatively small importance, Wilbye's second
Set (1609), and Byrd's last volume (1611). Secondly, the selection of these four composers for separate and fuller consideration but slightly interferes with this principle of chronological
arrangement ; thus, Mundy should have come next after Morley
and before Weelkes, while Kirbye and William Holborne
should be placed between Weelkes and Wilbye. The relative
position of all the madrigalists to each other, especially from
a chronological point of view, is a matter of great importance·
in estimating, with a true sense of perspective, the actual
artistic value of the English Madrigal School as a whole, as
well as the individual merits of the composers.

JOHN MUNDY. Born *circa* 1560 ; died 1630

John Mundy was a son of William Mundy, a vicar-choral of
St. Paul's Cathedral and a gentleman of the Chapel Royal.
The elder Mundy was also a composer of note. The son was
appointed organist of Eton College in 1585, and it may be
inferred that he was not more than twenty-five years old at
the time. He took the degree of B.Mus. at Oxford in the
following year and proceeded to that of D.Mus. in 1624.
Meanwhile he had succeeded the famous John Merbecke, after
a brief interval, as organist of St. George's Chapel in Windsor
Castle. He died at Windsor on June 29, 1630, and was buried
in the Cloisters.

John Mundy's volume was published in 1594 with the title
' Songs and Psalmes composed into 3. 4. and 5. parts for the
use and delight of all such as either love or learne Musicke '. He
evidently modelled his style to some extent upon that of Byrd,
and the title, as well as the design of this volume, is reminiscent
of his publications. This was perhaps to be expected, for
apart from Byrd's two Sets, Morley's three-part Canzonets
were, up to that date, the only English works of the kind that
had been previously published. Out of the thirty compositions
in Mundy's Set sixteen were psalms, and several more were
written to serious words of the ethical type. But there are
five or six characteristic Madrigals among them, even though
they are of a somewhat conventional type. The most attractive
of these is *Heigh ho ! 'chill go to plough no more* (No. 22) ; it
contains one especially madrigalian passage at the words :

> But I love, I love ; and who, thinks you ?
> The finest lass that e'er you knew.

Without altering the time-signature the composer introduced
a triple rhythm which amply expressed the whole-hearted joy
of the declaration :

Another good madrigal in the Set is *Of all the birds that I have heard* (No. 10). *The Shepherd Strephon* (Nos. 20 and 21) is for solo-voice and string accompaniment.

Mundy was also a contributor to the ' Triumphs of Oriana '. He also wrote some Church music besides that contained in this Set and several instrumental pieces by him were included in the ' Fitzwilliam Virginal Book '.

The Madrigalian Publications of John Mundy

1594. SONGS AND PSALMS COMPOSED INTO 3. 4. AND 5. PARTS

Songs of three parts

1. Praise the Lord, O my soul.
2. Save me, O God, and that with speed.
3. O all ye nations of the Lord.
4. Blessed art thou that fearest God (*the first part*).
5. Thus art thou blest (*the second part*).
6. Hear my prayer, O Lord.
7. Ye people all with one accord.
8. O Lord, turn not away thy face.
9. O come, let us lift up our voice.
10. Of all the birds that I have heard.
11. As I went a walking.
12. Turn about and see me.

Songs of four parts

13. Lord, to thee I make my moan.
14. O Lord, of whom I do depend.
15. Sing ye unto the Lord our God.
16. I lift my heart to thee.
17. My prime of youth is but a frost of cares.

18. In deep distress to live without delight.
19. The longer that I live.
20. The shepherd Strephon loved fair Dorida (*the first part*).
21. Witness, ye heavens, the palace of the gods (*the second part*).
22. Heigh ho ! 'chill go to plough no more.

Songs of five parts

23. Lord, arise and help thy servant.
24. Have mercy on me, O Lord.
25. Unto thee lift I up mine eyes.
26. Were I a king I might command content.
27. In midst of woods or pleasant grove (*the first part*).
28. The blackbird made the sweetest sound (*the second part*).
29. Penelope, that longed for the sight.
30. Who loves a life devoid of quiet rest ?

1601. A MADRIGAL FOR FIVE VOICES
included as No. 2 in the ' Triumphs of Oriana '.
Lightly she whipped o'er the dales.

GEORGE KIRBYE. Born *circa* 1565 ; died 1634

Of the early life of Kirbye nothing is known, but it may be conjectured that he was born about the year 1565, for he was a contributor to East's ' The Whole Booke of Psalmes ', printed in 1592, and he could not have been wholly unknown before that date. Later he occupied a position in the household of

Sir Robert Jermyn at Rushbrooke Hall in Suffolk similar to that held by Wilbye at Hengrave. As the two houses are situated within a few miles of each other, it is to be supposed that Kirbye and Wilbye were constantly in touch, and it is to be noted that the lyric *Alas, what hope of speeding* was set to music by them both. The words of Kirbye's *I love, alas, yet am I not beloved* are not identical with Wilbye's *I love, alas, yet am not loved* though they are sometimes said to be. Kirbye was a few years older than Wilbye. The latter part of his life was spent at Bury St. Edmunds, where he had a house in Whiting Street ; and for some years he held office as church-warden in the parish of St. Mary's. He died in 1634 and was buried at St. Mary's Church ; his wife predeceased him in 1626. His Will was proved at Bury.[1] Our knowledge of these biographical details is the outcome of Mr. Arkwright's researches.

Kirbye's only publication was issued in 1597. It was entitled ' The first set of English Madrigalls to 4. 5. and 6. voyces ', and was dedicated to Jermyn's daughters. Although at one time he seems to have enjoyed a considerable reputation as a madrigal-writer, and was praised by Burney as one of the best of the Elizabethan composers,[2] yet his name is probably less known among English madrigal-singers of the present day than that of almost any of his contemporaries. Not one of Kirbye's madrigals had been reprinted until Mr. Arkwright published the entire Set.[3] But some of them may be ranked among the best English work of this class, and they are marked by a certain individuality both as regards style and technique.

Kirbye stands very much on the same level as Bateson as a madrigalist ; he does not seem to have had the imaginative power of Wilbye or Weelkes in handling such a passage as *the fearful dreams effects that trouble me* in *Sorrow consumes me* (No. 12) or the *grisly ghosts* in Spenser's *Up then, Melpomene !* (Nos. 22 and 23) though this latter is a very fine madrigal, full of poetic suggestion. On the other hand, the tender treatment of such subjects as *Ah, sweet, alas, when first I saw* (No. 7) or *Sleep now, my Muse* (No. 24) reveals a poetic feeling of a very

---

[1] Arkwright's Old English Edition, Part V, preface.
[2] Burney's History, vol. iii, p. 123.
[3] Arkwright's Old English Edition, Parts III–V.

high order. This last is for six voices, but the madrigal was also arranged, with much of the same thematic material, for four voices and included as No. 6 of the Set. The six-part version has a very beautiful ending :

The harmonies employed here are very remarkable for so early a date as 1597, and this passage alone would be enough to entitle Kirbye to a place among the great pioneers of the English Madrigal School.

Kirbye followed Byrd's example in the use of certain harmonic peculiarities, notably in the simultaneous employment of the major and minor third. Several instances could be quoted from this Set, but none illustrate the point better than the following phrase from *Why wail we thus ?* (No. 23). In this passage a pair of consecutive fifths will be noticed between the Cantus secundus and the Altus-parts ; such progressions, as mentioned in a former chapter, are not altogether uncommon in the secular music of this date :

Kirbye usually had some point to illustrate when he introduced these dissonances. Thus, at the words *crossed are my joys* in *Mourn now, my soul* (No. 8) the voices not only cross with a group of four quavers but bring the major and minor third into conflict ; the effect is repeated to the same words a few bars later. In *O heavens, what shall I do ?* (No. 13) the major third appears simultaneously with the suspended fourth with a harsh effect to match the words *be murderer of myself.* Similarly the words *hard are my torments* in *Mourn now, my soul* (No. 8) are set with the major and minor third simultaneously.

On the other hand, the effect produced in *Sound out, my voice* (No. 9) at the words *that love to me inspireth* is of a different character ; the introduction of the G sharp in the Altus-part gives the sustained G natural in the Cantus primus the effect of suspended discord requiring resolution and being duly resolved. The phrase may be quoted :

In *Ah, cruel hateful fortune!* a form of cadence occurs which seems to be peculiar to this composer ; it involves the simultaneous presence of the major and minor third and the temporary crossing of the tenor part below the dominant. It will be noticed that this cadence occurs here in connexion with the word *death* :

A precisely similar example of this cadence is to be found in *Up then, Melpomene!* at the words *such cause of mourning never hadst afore.*

Another somewhat distinctive feature of Kirbye's writing is his use of discordant harmonies either in the form of passing notes or in scale-passages in contrary motion. Three very good examples of this may be seen in *Woe am I ! my heart dies* (No. 4) at the words *pleased and contented.* No harshness is produced in such passages ; on the contrary a peculiar beauty and strength of effect is often to be found in them. The following beautiful phrase from *Ah sweet, alas, when first I saw* (No. 7) is characteristic of Kirbye :

One other detail should be mentioned.   Kirbye showed
something of Wilbye's feeling for colour-contrast in his method
of employing three or four voices in groups in a composition
of five or six parts, and particularly when repeating a section
of the music.   Thus in *Ah, cruel, hateful fortune!* (No. 19) his
treatment of the repeat of the final section is something much
more elaborate than the conventional interchange of the
voices of equal range.   This passage is in fact a very suggestive
forecast of the principles of varied orchestral colouring.

Interesting madrigals in this Set besides those already men-
tioned are *Alas! what hope of speeding?* (No. 2), *What can
I do, my dearest?* (No. 3), *Sound out, my voice* (Nos. 9 and 10),
Why should I love? (No. 14), and *See what a maze of error*
(No. 17).

The Madrigalian Publications of George Kirbye

1597. THE FIRST SET OF ENGLISH MADRIGALS
TO 4. 5. AND 6. VOICES

Songs to four voices

1. Lo! here my heart I leave with her.
2. Alas! what hope of speeding?
3. What can I do, my dearest.
4. Woe am I! when my heart dies.
5. Farewell, my love, I part contented.
6. Sleep now, my Muse.

Songs to five voices

7. Ah sweet, alas, when first I saw those eyes.
8. Mourn now, my soul, with anguish.
{ 9. Sound out, my voice, with pleasant tunes (*the first part*).
10. She that my plaints with rigour (*the second part*).
11. What? shall I part thus unregarded?

{ 12. Sorrow consumes me, and instead of rest (*the first part*).
13. O heavens, what shall I do? (*the second part*).
14. Why should I love since she doth prove.
15. Sweet love, O cease thy flying.
16. That Muse, which sung the beauty.
17. See what a maze of error.
18. If Pity reign with Beauty.

Songs to six voices

19. Ah, cruel hateful fortune!
20. I love, alas, yet am I not beloved.
21. Must I part, O my jewel?
{ 22. Up then, Melpomene! (*the first part*).
23. Why wail we thus? (*the second part*).
24. Sleep now, my Muse.

1601. A MADRIGAL FOR SIX VOICES
included (with alternative words[1]) as No. 20 in the 'Triumphs of Oriana'.

Bright Phoebus greets most clearly. (*First Edition*)

or

With angel's face and brightness. (*Second Edition*)

[1] See p. 247.

NATHANIEL PATTRICK. Born *circa* 1560–70 (?) ; died 1595

Nathaniel Pattrick was a composer of some importance of whom no notice appears either in Grove's ' Dictionary of Music ' or in the ' Dictionary of National Biography ', or in other similar books of reference. He was organist of Worcester Cathedral from 1590–4, and is best known to-day in cathedral circles as the composer of a complete Church service in G minor. Pattrick also wrote some secular vocal music, although very little of it has survived. The British Museum Additional MSS. 17786–91 include three of his compositions, namely : *Climb not too high*, *Prepare to die*, and *Send forth thy sighs* ; and in the Additional MSS. 18936–9 is his *Sacred Pan*. But this composer claims a place among the English madrigalists in virtue of a volume licensed to Thomas East, the printer, in 1597. No copy of this volume is known to exist ; it is possible that it was never actually published, and in any case it would have been a posthumous work, because Pattrick died two years previously. The title of this volume was as follows : ' Songes of Sundrye Natures whereof some ar Divine, some are Madrigalles and the rest Psalmes and Hymnes in Latin composed for 5. and 6. voyces and one for 8. voyces by Nathanaell Pattrick sometyme Master of the children of the Cathedrall Churche of Worcester and organist of the same.' [1]

Nathaniel Pattrick no doubt belonged to the Worcestershire family of that name, and may have been nearly related to Dr. Giles Pattrick, a physician who was granted an annuity by the Dean and Chapter of Worcester in 1594[2] and died in 1598. Nathaniel first appears in the Cathedral treasurer's accounts at Michaelmas 1590 and his last payment was at Michaelmas 1594. His retirement was in all probability due to ill health, and it may be conjectured that he was a young man at the time of his death in March 1595, for he had been but recently married to Alice Hassard at St. Michael's, Worcester, on September 23, 1593. He was buried on March 23, 1595, at St. Michael's, where his son, probably his only child, Francis

---

[1] Staf. Reg. iii, 93.
[2] Worcester Cathedral records, A vii, 5, fol. 95.

was buried in the previous August. His Will, dated March 12, 1595, was proved in the following May.[1]

It seems more than probable that the Alice Hassard who married Thomas Tomkins the composer, and Pattrick's successor at Worcester Cathedral, is to be identified with Pattrick's widow, and the conjecture gains support from the fact that Tomkins's son received the name of Nathaniel.

WILLIAM HOLBORNE. Born *circa* 1575 ; date of death unknown

In 1597 Anthony Holborne published a book called ' The Cittharn Schoole' at the end of which he included ' sixe short Aers Neapolitan like to three voyces, without the Instrument ' by his brother William. These were published, according to his own statement, because ' incorrect and unauthorized coppies are got about '. Allusion is also made to the composer's youth, from which we may infer that he was born about the year 1575. Nothing further is known about him.

The Madrigalian Publications of William Holborne

1597. SIX SHORT AIRS OR CANZONETS TO THREE VOICES
included by Anthony Holborne in ' The Cithern School'

1. Change then, for lo she changeth.
2. Since Bonny-boots was dead.
3. Here rest, my thoughts.
4. Sweet, I grant that I am as black.
5. Gush forth, my tears, and stay the burning.
6. Sit still and stir not, lady.

GILES FARNABY. Born *circa* 1560 ; died probably *circa* 1600

Giles Farnaby was born, most probably, about the year 1560. The statement that he was nearly related to Thomas Farnaby, an eminent philologist and schoolmaster who sailed with Drake and Hawkins, cannot be supported by definite evidence. He was married at St. Helen's Bishopsgate on March 28, 1587, to Katharine Roane, and one of his sons was baptized at St. Mary-

---

[1] Worcester Wills, vol. vii, fol. 83.

[2] For the biographical details of this composer the author is indebted to Sir Ivor Atkins, the present organist of Worcester Cathedral.

le-Bow in 1598. He took the degree of B.Mus. at Oxford in 1592, and was one of the contributors to East's 'Whole Booke of Psalmes' in the same year. The absence of Farnaby's name from the contributors to the 'Triumphs of Oriana', coupled with the fact that no second Set of madrigals was published by him, suggests with great probability that his death had occurred before 1601. The inclusion of some of his tunes in Ravenscroft's 'Psalter' in 1621 constitutes no evidence that he was alive at that date, and the same statement applies to his work in the 'Fitzwilliam Virginal Book'. It is an error to regard this latter book as a collection of pieces specially contributed by contemporary composers ; it was a MS. collection made by a private individual, probably about the year 1620, and it represents that individual's personal choice, the source of his text being unknown. Farnaby's pieces in the Fitzwilliam book rank next to those of Byrd in importance and interest. The same book also includes a few compositions by Richard Farnaby, son of Giles, who may have been about thirty years old in 1620.

As a madrigal-writer Farnaby's work was unfortunately limited to a single volume published in 1598 and entitled 'Canzonets to Fowre Voyces with a Song of eight parts'. These canzonets for the most part are quite unpretentious in design, but they frequently reveal the masterly hand of their composer. For instance, *Construe my meaning* (No. 20) is a magnificent bit of work, very forceful and beautiful, and written in a chromatic style of remarkable originality. Nothing else in the book quite reaches the standard of this composition, but there are many other good things in the Set. Among these is the realistic representation of Vulcan's hammer-strokes towards the close of *Some time she would, and some time not* (No. 16). This is one of those cases in which the composer could add something to the work of the poet, thus widening his range of vision ; the poet naturally makes no allusion to the hammer and the anvil, but the musician sees in the mention of Vulcan's name the opportunity for painting in a background that recalls leading ideas associated with that deity, yet without distracting attention from the poet's main theme. Thus for several bars each of the two strong.

beats is punctuated in one voice-part or another with the word *Vulcan,* while the anvil rings again on the ear. There is moreover a subtle little touch in the consecutive tenths with which the stroke falls in one place. Yet these devices are so skilfully handled and so unobtrusively introduced that many an eye might fail to detect in the score this secondary thread of interest so cleverly woven into the texture of the poet's design.

Farnaby's methods of underlaying the words are often very far removed from those which govern the regularly-barred music of a later period, and the performance of some of these canzonets demands unusual care and forethought in order to secure the right *ictus* of the words. Unless absolute freedom and independence of rhythm are secured much of Farnaby's work will be exposed to the criticism of false accenting. There are indeed some few passages that are difficult to explain as regards accent, and possibly he sacrificed something in this department in order to develop imitative points that occasionally are almost unduly intricate. Indeed, there can be little doubt that Farnaby's work is sometimes marred by the undue complexity of his rhythmic designs. Yet he often used overlapping rhythms with beautiful effect, and a favourite device was to introduce triple rhythms in measures of six crotchets whereas the rhythm indicated by the time-signature was duple. As an illustration of this the Cantus-part of No. 3 opens with a beautiful phrase in this triple rhythm :

Phil - li - da be - wailed the want of Co - ry - don,

while the Altus enters a semibreve later than the Cantus thus :

Phil - li - da be - wailed the want of

Co - ry - don, and Her - pu - lus,

Another feature of Farnaby's writing is his somewhat free disregard for convention as to the use of consecutive fifths. There are certainly more examples of this ' forbidden ' progression in this Set than in any other volume of English madrigals. But it is ridiculous to suppose that the composer of *Construe my meaning* was devoid of taste, and still more that he was the victim either of negligence or incompetence.

Ay me ! poor heart (No. 15), transcribed for the virginal, is among Farnaby's pieces in the Fitzwilliam book. Comparison of the two versions is very instructive. Several more of his virginal pieces appear to be similar transcriptions, but no other example has survived both in its vocal and instrumental setting.

The Madrigalian Publications of Giles Farnaby

1598. CANZONETS TO FOUR VOICES

1. My lady's coloured cheeks were like the roses.
2. Carters, now cast down your whips.
3. Phillida bewailed the want of Corydon.
4. Daphne, on the rainbow riding.
5. Blind Love was shooting.
6. Pearce did love fair Petronel.
7. Pearce did dance with Petronella.
8. The wavering planet most unstable.
9. Lady, the silly flea of all disdained.
10. Thrice blessed be the giver.
11. The curtain drawn, I saw my love.
12. Susanna fair, sometime.

13. Love, shooting among many (*the first part*).
14. Love, shooting at another (*the second part*).
15. Ay me ! poor heart.
16. Some time she would, and some time not.
17. Among the daffadillies.
18. Simkin said that Sis was fair.
19. Lady, when I behold your passions.
20. Construe my meaning, wrest not my method.

A song of eight parts

21. Witness, ye heavens, I vow to love the fairest.

MICHAEL CAVENDISH.   Born *circa* 1565 ; died 1628

Michael Cavendish was the composer of one of the madrigals in the ' Triumphs of Oriana ' ; he was also a contributor to East's ' Whole Booke of Psalmes ', and he published a volume of Airs mentioned in East's catalogue in 1609. Beyond these facts nothing whatever was known about him until recently. East's record of Cavendish's book of Airs was quoted by subsequent bibliographers such as Clavel, Rimbault, Hazlitt, and Steele, but no exemplar of this volume was known until 1918, when a copy appeared in a London sale-room and was acquired by the authorities of the British Museum. The title-page is damaged and the exact title remains unknown, but, although the date of publication is 1598, it cannot be doubted that this book is to be identified with the work of Cavendish recorded by East as having been issued in 1599.

The music of the volume is not of outstanding excellence,

although it is well up to the average high standard of the English Madrigal School ; but its chief interest lies in other directions. The only other volume in the whole range of the Tudor School which resembles it in including orthodox Madrigals together with Airs with lute accompaniment, is Greaves's ' Songes of sundrie kindes ', which came out six years later. Like that of Greaves, Cavendish's book consists mainly of lutenists' Airs, and both are printed in folio as contrasted with the quarto part-books of the madrigalists. Before 1598, when Cavendish's volume was issued, Dowland alone had published work of this novel character and class, and no further Set of Airs for voice and lute saw the light before the year 1600.

A noticeable feature in Cavendish's book is the inclusion of the madrigal *Come, gentle swains* (No. 24) ; the words are the same as those of his madrigal in the ' Triumphs ', but the music, although similar in material, was extensively rewritten before it appeared under Morley's editorship in 1601. But it is remarkable that this is the only Oriana madrigal which was printed before the publication of the celebrated collection, and Cavendish composed his first version of it no more than a year after the appearance of the Italian *Il Trionfo di Dori*, on which the ' Triumphs of Oriana ' are admittedly modelled, so that it seems likely that the idea of an English Oriana madrigal, with its refrain, *Then sang the shepherds,* &c., originated in the mind of Michael Cavendish.

The book opens with twenty Airs and ends with eight Madrigals, each of which is for five voices. Two of the Madrigals are alternative settings of the Airs, namely *Every bush new springing* (Nos. 13 and 27) and *Wandering in this place* (Nos. 12 and 28) while *Fair are those eyes* figures both as a two-part and a four-part Air (Nos. 11 and 17). The Madrigals are for the most part gay in style and are written with that command of technique which is so characteristic of these English com- posers. Cavendish was evidently influenced by the bright nature of Morley's work. *Every bush new springing* (No. 27) is a good example of the gayer sort ; it opens somewhat in the ballet-style, with a strong clear-cut rhythm treated homo- phonically ; but it has no *Fa-la*. By contrast, *Wandering in this place* (No. 28) is set in a more serious vein and has some

features of plaintive beauty ; as, for instance, at the words
desolate of joy :

and the final cadence is treated with some harmonic originality
and much beauty :

The discovery of Cavendish's song-book has thrown some light upon his personal history. The book is dated ' from Cavendish ' and on the page giving the Table of Contents there is a woodcut of the coat-of-Arms of the Cavendishes. These facts prove with certainty that the composer was a member of the family now represented by the Duke of Devonshire. In all the printed pedigrees and family histories the descendants of this elder branch of the Cavendish family have been ignored, but a more complete record is to be found in Davy's ' Suffolk Collections '.[1] In this manuscript Michael's place in the pedigree is clearly stated as one of the grandsons of George Cavendish of the Manor of Cavendish Overhall in Suffolk, the faithful adherent of Cardinal Wolsey. George had but one son William, who inherited the Manor, and who, by Ann his wife, daughter of John Cocks of Beamonds, had three sons : William, Ralph, and Michael, the composer. Of the three brothers Ralph alone seems to have had children, and the baptism of his son William is recorded in the Cavendish parish register in 1612. The parish registers begin in the year 1594, but earlier transcripts, dating from 1564, are preserved in the Archdeaconry Registry at Bury St. Edmunds ; they do not, however, record the baptism of Michael, the date of whose birth may be conjectured at *circa* 1565.

Michael Cavendish was a second cousin of Lady Arabella Stuart, to whom he dedicated his volume ; and Sir Charles Cavendish, Lady Lennox, and Lady Pierpoint, the wife of Greaves's patron, were his father's first cousins. These details provide an interesting link too between Michael Cavendish and that other great East-Anglian musician, John Wilbye.

The nuncupative Will of Michael Cavendish was proved July 11, 1628,[2] and there need be no hesitation in identifying the testator with the composer, for the surname was very uncommon and the combination of names removes all reasonable doubt ; moreover the date fits the circumstances. This Will gives no information of consequence beyond the fact that the written statement was made on July 5 ; and this was presumably the date of death. The death took place in the

---

[1] Davy's Suff. Coll., xlvi, fol. 348, 377 (Brit. Mus. Add. MSS. 19122).

[2] P.C.C., 72 Barrington.

parish of St. Mary Aldermanbury, London, but the place of burial remains unknown.

The Madrigalian Publications of Michael Cavendish

1598. MADRIGALS FOR FIVE VOICES
included in a volume the title of which is unknown.

21. In flower of April springing.
22. Zephyrus brings the time.
23. Much it delighted to see Phyllis smiling.
24. Come, gentle swains and shepherds' dainty daughters
25. To former joy now turns the grove.
26. Faustina hath the fairer face.
27. Every bush new springing.
28. Wandering in this place.

1601. A MADRIGAL FOR FIVE VOICES
included as No. 11 in the 'Triumphs of Oriana'.
Come, gentle swains.

JOHN FARMER.   Born *circa* 1565 ;   died *circa* 1605

John Farmer's 'Set of English Madrigals : To Foure Voices' made its appearance in 1599. This collection contains seventeen pieces, the last of which, as in Farnaby's Set, is for eight voices. This eight-part madrigal is the least satisfactory thing in the Set, and the part-writing shows a decided weakness in certain sections. On the other hand, most of the remaining madrigals, if modest in their aims, are nevertheless delightfully melodious and attractive. Especially charming are *You pretty flowers* (No. 1) and *Cease now thy mourning* (No. 13) ; while, in another style, *A little pretty bonny lass* (No. 14) and *Fair Phyllis I saw* (No. 15) are each full of buoyant gaiety that cannot fail to fascinate. No. 14 has come into general use in the old Madrigal Societies with Oliphant's lamentable alterations *To take the air*. The concluding passage of *You pretty flowers* may be quoted here as being typical of Farmer's writing ;. the *tempo* should be rather slow, and the effect of the C major chord three bars from the end adds a beautiful touch of pathos to the Altus-part :

which dou - bles tear for tear, which dou - bles

tear for tear, which dou - bles tear for . . tear.

Take time while Time doth last (No. 16) is constructed on a *canto fermo* in the Tenor-part, consisting of six notes of the scale up and down, and repeated four times ; but there is not much spontaneity about the music.

Farmer wrote a fine six-part madrigal for the ' Triumphs of Oriana ' ; and he was also a contributor to East's ' Whole Booke of Psalmes ' in 1592. In 1591 he published a short musical treatise entitled ' Divers and sundry waies of two parts in one '.

The date of this composer's birth can only be approximately conjectured. He must have been at least twenty-five years of age in 1591, and his appointment as organist of Christ Church Cathedral, Dublin, dates from 1595. It seems probable, therefore, that he was born about the year 1565. In 1597 the cathedral records show that he had deserted his post and that a Chapter order was issued in July that year calling upon him to return before August 1 on pain of forfeiting his appointment. This order was obeyed and Farmer remained in Dublin until the spring of 1599, when he left for London. In the meantime he had been presented to the Vicarage of Kilsheelan in November 1598 ; but not being in Holy Orders he seems to have appointed a deputy to minister in that parish. On leaving Dublin in 1599 he was permitted to appoint a deputy to perform his cathedral duties, but at the end of that year his vicarchoralship was declared vacant and his successor appointed. Farmer is believed to have died in London about the year 1605.

The Madrigalian Publications of John Farmer

1599. FIRST SET OF ENGLISH MADRIGALS TO FOUR VOICES

1. You pretty flowers that smile.
2. Now each creature joys the other.
3. You'll never leave still tossing to and fro.
4. Lady, my flame still burning (*the first part*).
5. Sweet Lord, your flame still burning (*the second part*).
6. Soon as the hungry lion seeks his prey.
7. O stay, sweet love, see here the place (*the first part*).
8. I thought, my love, that I should overtake you (*the second part*).
9. Compare me to the child that plays with fire.
10. Who would have thought that face of thine ?
11. Sweet friend, thy absence grieves.
12. The flattering words, sharp glosses.
13. Cease now thy mourning.
14. A little pretty bonny lass was walking.
15. Fair Phyllis I saw sitting all alone.
16. Take time while Time doth last.

Song of eight voices

17. You blessed bowers, whose green leaves.

1601.   A MADRIGAL FOR SIX VOICES

included as No. 14 in the 'Triumphs of Oriana'.

Fair nymph, I heard one telling.

JOHN BENNET.   Dates of birth and death unknown

John Bennet's only volume of madrigals, containing seventeen pieces for four voices, was published in 1599.   He also composed six songs for Ravenscroft's 'Briefe Discourse', which appeared in 1614, but, among these, the delightful little *Elves' Dance* alone can be classed as madrigalian, although *Lure, falconers !* is also for four unaccompanied voices ; the rest are solo-songs or duets with chorus.   In the preface to the 'Briefe Discourse' Ravenscroft praised Bennet warmly, speaking of his 'natural instinct or better inspiration by which in all his works the very life of that passion which the ditty sounded is so truly expressed as if he had measured it alone by his own soul'. At all times musicians have agreed in assigning to Bennet a high place among the English madrigalists ; but he owes his popularity among modern madrigal-singers almost exclusively to his sparkling *All creatures now are merry minded* (No. 4 of the 'Triumphs of Oriana') and *Weep, O mine eyes* (No. 13 of his Set).   Both of these are quite first-class in their own line, but the Oriana madrigal is much more homophonic in construction than was usual in this kind of work.

In estimating Bennet's relative position among his contemporaries it must be borne in mind that, with the exception
of the Oriana madrigal, his work was quite unpretentious in
design, while his output of composition was comparatively small.
Several of these little madrigals are of first-rate value, notably
Weep, O mine eyes (No. 13), *Let go! why do you stay me?*
(No. 4), *Come, shepherds, follow me* (No. 5), *Sing out, ye nymphs*
(No. 7) and *Thyrsis, sleepest thou?* (No. 8). But Bennet's
work exposes itself to criticism on the ground of lack of variety.
This will be very apparent if the first twelve madrigals in the
Set are read through consecutively; and Bennet's case is
rather singular in this particular. Every one of these twelve
ends with the chord of G major. From the point of view of technique Bennet's work was distinctly conservative in character;
he makes use of the madrigalists' favourite augmented chord
once only, namely towards the end of *O sweet grief* (No. 16);
this is the most chromatic of his madrigals, but it cannot be
regarded as a great success, especially when placed beside
subjects of similar character as treated by Wilbye and Weelkes.

There are some interesting constructive features in *Let go!
why do you stay me?* the recapitulation of the opening phrase
was clearly indicated by the form of the poem, the first
couplet of which is repeated at the conclusion of the stanza
with the order of the lines reversed.

An allusion to the cuckoo in *Thyrsis, sleepest thou?* is
treated after the manner which so many of these composers
affected, but which they never made cheap or vulgar. Bennet's
phrase here is very fascinating and the melody of the Cantus-
part is turned to perfection:

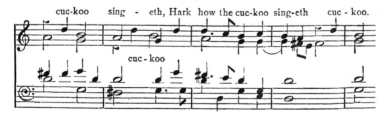

A few bars later the *sigh* is represented by the device so
commonly used by the madrigalists, and it is emphasized here

by the homophonic entry of the voices on the principle discussed in a former chapter.[1]

Bennet was essentially a refined and tuneful musician, with a sound technique as far as it went ; but it would seem that, fine composer as he was, his importance in the great English school of madrigalists has usually been somewhat over-estimated. He was certainly at his best in the gayer moods, and his quaver passages are admirably vocal and brilliant ; but for the graver subjects, in spite of the excellence of *Weep, O mine eyes*, he appears to have lacked the requisite amount of imagination for first-rate success. This statement is borne out by the evidence of the three last madrigals in the Set : the greater composers would not have been content with so quiet a setting of the couplet :

> Our concords have some discords mixed among ;
> Discording concords makes the sweetest song.

Nothing whatever is known of Bennet's personal history.

The Madrigalian Publications of John Bennet

1599. MADRIGALS TO FOUR VOICES

1. I wander up and down.
2. Weep, silly soul disdained.
3. So gracious is thy sweet self.
4. Let go, let go ! why do you stay me?
5. Come, shepherds, follow me.
6. I languish to complain me.
7. Sing out, ye nymphs and shepherds.
8. Thyrsis, sleepest thou ? Holla !
9. Ye restless thoughts that harbour discontent.
10. Whenas I glance upon my lovely Phyllis.
11. Cruel, unkind, my heart thou hast bereft me.
12. O sleep, fond Fancy, sleep.
13. Weep, O mine eyes, and cease not.
14. Since neither tunes of joy nor notes of sadness.
15. O grief ! where shall poor grief find patient hearing ? (*the first part*).
16. O sweet grief ! O sweet sighs ! (*the second part*).
17. Rest now, Amphion, rest thy charming lyre.

1601.   A MADRIGAL TO FIVE VOICES
included as No. 4 in the ' Triumphs of Oriana '.

All creatures now are merry-minded.

1614.   TWO SONGS TO FOUR VOICES
included in Thomas Ravenscroft's ' A Brief Discourse '.

No. 5. Lure, falconers ! (*for the heron and duck*).
No. 9. Round about in a fair ring. (*The Elves' dance*).

[1] See p. 106.

THE LESS-KNOWN CONTRIBUTORS TO
THE ' TRIUMPHS OF ORIANA '

Those composers must here be briefly noticed who contributed madrigals to the ' Triumphs of Oriana ' but who did not publish separate Sets. It is rather remarkable that out of the twenty-three contributors as many as eleven come under this heading. Ellis Gibbons is the only contributor who shared with Morley the honour of having two madrigals included in this famous Set.

DANIEL NORCOME, or NURCOMBE, was a Minor Canon of St. George's Chapel, Windsor. He appears to have been the son of John Nurcombe, a lay-clerk of the same chapel, and was born in 1576. He died before 1626, in which year the chapel registers record the burial of his widow. ELLIS GIBBONS was an elder brother of the more famous Orlando, and son of William Gibbons, one of the Waits of the town of Cambridge. He was born at Cambridge in 1573 and died there in May 1603. Little is known about him. The statement that he became organist of Salisbury Cathedral has proved untrue. He wrote two madrigals for the ' Triumphs '. JOHN HILTON has until lately been confused with his son of the same name. In 1584 his name has been found as a lay-clerk of Lincoln Cathedral. In 1594 he was appointed organist of Trinity College, Cambridge. He died in 1608 at Cambridge, as shown by an inventory on his property. The proof of the existence of two John Hiltons disposes of the only real obstacle in assigning to the elder Hilton, organist of Trinity, the authorship of the anthem *Lord, for thy tender mercies' sake*, at one time ascribed to Farrant but in seventeenth-century part-books described as the composition of Hilton. Oliphant printed two four-part madrigals by Hilton ' from a manuscript ' the source of which he unfortunately did not record. GEORGE MARSON was born *circa* 1565. He became organist and master of the choristers of Canterbury some time before 1597 and held this position until his death in 1622. He was also a Minor Canon of the cathedral. He must not be confused with George Mason, who with John Earsden composed some Airs for a performance at Brougham Castle in 1618. Some Church music by Marson is in existence. JOHN HOLMES was Master of the choristers at

Salisbury Cathedral from 1621 until 1629, having for some years previously held office as organist of Winchester Cathedral. Among his pupils was Adrian Batten as a chorister at Winchester. He died at Salisbury on March 25, 1638. A good deal of his Church music is included in Batten's autograph MS., now at St. Michael's College, Tenbury.[1] RICHARD NICOLSON became organist of Magdalen College, Oxford, in 1595 and held the post until his death in 1639. He was the first to hold a lectureship at Oxford on Musical Praxis, which was founded in 1626 by Dr. Heather. A set of nine canzonets of a light kind by this composer, dealing consecutively with the courtship of John and Joan, are to be found in an incomplete set of manuscript part-books dating *circa* 1630 and recently belonging to the library of Carlisle Cathedral. One of these canzonets is also to be found in the British Museum Add. MSS. 17786–91. In the Barnard MS.[2] THOMAS HUNT is called Organist of Wells. WILLIAM COBBOLD became organist of Norwich Cathedral in 1599. He was born in the parish of St. Andrew's, Norwich, on January 5, 1560. He resigned the organistship in 1608, when he was succeeded by William Inglott. From 1608 till 1639 he held office in the cathedral as a lay-clerk. In his Will, dated August 4, 1637, he expressed a desire to be buried in Norwich Cathedral, where his wife Alice, who died in 1630, and his son Francis already lay; but he was in fact buried at Beccles, where he died on November 7, 1639. A monumental inscription to his memory still remains in Beccles Parish Church. Cobbold was another of the contributors to East's ' Whole Booke of Psalmes '; some ' London cries ' and other light forms of composition by him survive in manuscript at the British Museum, and an incomplete manuscript of a madrigal by Cobbold is in the library of the Royal College of Music. JOHN MILTON was father of the poet and had a romantic career. He belonged to an old Roman Catholic family, but was disinherited by his father for joining the Protestant branch of the Church. Consequently, although he had been educated at Christ Church, Oxford, he was at one time working as a scrivener in Bread Street, Cheapside, adopting for his shop-sign a spread-eagle, that being the charge on his family coat-of-Arms. He contributed four

---

[1] Tenbury MSS. 791.   [2] R.C.M. MSS. 1045–51.

motets to Leighton's 'Teares or Lamentacions' and his skill as a musician was celebrated by his more famous son in a Latin poem *Ad patrem*. He died in March 164⅚ and was buried at St. Giles's, Cripplegate. Of JOHN LISLEY nothing is known. EDWARD JOHNSON took the degree of B.Mus. at Cambridge in 1594. He was at one time in the service of Sir Thomas Kytson at Hengrave Hall, where Wilbye subsequently spent so many years. Recent research in the Hengrave manuscripts shows that it was Edward, and not Robert, Johnson who was in the service of the Kytsons. Edward Johnson and Milton were contributors to East's 'Whole Booke of Psalmes'.

1601. THE 'TRIUMPHS OF ORIANA'

For five voices

Hence stars! too dim of light. *Michael East.*
1. With angel's face and brightness. *Daniel Norcome.*
2. Lightly she whipped o'er the dales. *John Mundy.*
3. Long live fair Oriana! *Ellis Gibbons.*
    (Hark! did you ever hear?)
4. All creatures now are merry-minded. *John Bennet.*
5. Fair Oriana, Beauty's Queen. *John Hilton* (senior).
6. The nymphs and shepherds danced. *George Marson.*
7. Calm was the air and clear the sky. *Richard Carlton.*
8. Thus Bonny-boots the birthday celebrated. *John Holmes.*
9. Sing, shepherds all, and in your roundelays. *Richard Nicolson.*
10. The fauns and satyrs tripping. *Thomas Tomkins.*
11. Come, gentle swains, and shepherds' dainty daughters. *Michael Cavendish.*
12. With wreaths of rose and laurel. *William Cobbold.*
13. Arise, awake, awake! *Thomas Morley.*

For six voices

14. Fair nymph, I heard one telling. *John Farmer.*
15. The lady Oriana. *John Wilbye.*
16. Hark! did ye ever hear? *Thomas Hunt.*
17. As Vesta was from Latmos hill descending. *Thomas Weelkes.*
18. Fair Orian in the morn. *John Milton.*
19. Round about her chariot. *Ellis Gibbons.*
20 [1] { Bright Phoebus greets most clearly. } *George Kirbye.*
     { With angel's face and brightness. }
21. Fair Oriana, seeming to wink at folly. *Robert Jones.*
22. Fair Cytherea presents her doves. *John Lisley.*
23. Hard by a crystal fountain. *Thomas Morley.*
24. Come, blessed bird, and with thy sugared relish. *Edward Johnson.*

Attention was first directed in a general way by Mr. Arkwright [2] to the fact that alternative words to Kirbye's madrigal

---

[1] The two editions of 1601 vary in giving alternate words to the music of this number.   [2] Old English Edition, Part III, p. 4.

(No. 20) are to be found in the various known copies of the
' Triumphs ', all of which bear the date 1601, but the point
was not followed up at the time.

A close comparison of the copies shows that the contents of
the book as a whole are identical, with the sole exception of the
words of No. 20, the music of this composition being the same
in both cases. Yet every page in the volume is differently
set up, and this fact points without any doubt to two distinct
editions. The further question then arises as to which is the
earlier edition ; and three reasons may be given to support
the opinion that the first edition is that which has the words
Bright Phoebus for the Kirbye madrigal.

1. On the signature $C_4{}^b$ of the Cantus, Altus, Tenor, Quintus,
and Bassus part-books there is in the *Angel's face* copies the
formula ' Heere endeth the songs of five parts '. In the
Bright Phoebus copies this formula occurs only in the Altus
and Bassus part-books. It is obvious, from their almost
identical typographical appearance, that the one edition must
have been reprinted from the other, and it would seem unlikely
that this formula should have been omitted in the Cantus,
Tenor, and Quintus books after having been printed in an
earlier edition.

2. The word *her* in ' her Maiesties honorable Chappell ' is
so spelt on the title-pages of all the parts in the *Angel's face*
copies, whereas it is spelt *hir* in the *Bright Phoebus* copies.
In spite of the vagaries of Elizabethan spelling the presumption
is that *her* was substituted for *hir* rather than the reverse.

3. In one of the voice-parts of the *Bright Phoebus* copies the
signature of sheet B is misprinted D ; but in the *Angel's face*
copies it is correct.

On the other hand, there can be no doubt whatever, on
internal evidence, that Kirbye composed the music to the
words of *With angel's face* in the first instance. The setting
of such passages as *With nimble feet she tripped, at last in dale
she rested,* and especially *the fauns and satyrs, dancing did show
their nimble lightness,* prove this point conclusively. It would
seem then that Kirbye sent his contribution in this form, but
that either Morley, or East, the printer, substituted the words
of *Bright Phoebus,* which follow the detail and metre of the

other lyric with praiseworthy exactness, the object, presumably, being to distinguish the madrigal from that of Daniel Norcome (No. 1). We may suppose that Kirbye protested, and that in the second edition, which appeared immediately, the original words were restored.

The British Museum copy and that in the Christ Church library are examples of the *Bright Phoebus* edition, whereas the *Angel's face* edition is represented by the three copies in the Bodleian Library, also by that in the Royal College of Music, by the copy formerly in the Huth Library and sold in July 1916, and by the copies owned by Mr. Christie-Miller and Miss Willmott.

CHAPTER XVIII

RICHARD CARLTON — MICHAEL EAST — THOMAS BATESON — THOMAS GREAVES — RICHARD ALISON — ROBERT JONES — HENRY YOULL — THOMAS RAVENSCROFT — ORLANDO GIBBONS.

RICHARD CARLTON. Born *circa* 1558; date of death unknown

RICHARD CARLTON, who published a Set of madrigals to five voices in 1601, was also a contributor to the ' Triumphs of Oriana '. He took his B.A. degree at Clare College, Cambridge, in 1577 and was subsequently ordained. He became Vicar of St. Stephen's, Norwich, in 1597 and at the same time held the position of Minor Canon and Master of the choristers in Norwich Cathedral. In 1612 he was presented to the living of Bawsey and Glosthorp in Norfolk, but the date of his death is unknown. There is no evidence to show that he was the son of Nicholas Carlton, as has been stated. Carlton's volume contains no madrigal of outstanding interest, nor is his work marked by any especially distinctive individuality. The theme of the second madrigal in the Set was clearly beyond the range of his imaginative skill. It begins with the couplet :

> Content thyself with thy estate .
> Seek not to climb above the skies.

Nevertheless several of the madrigals reach a very good average level ; the best is, perhaps, *The witless boy, that blind is to behold* (No. 16). The volume also includes a somewhat ponderous elegy to Sir John Shelton, a member of an old Norfolk family, who was ' slain with the fatal sword '.

The Madrigalian Publications of Richard Carlton

1601. MADRIGALS TO FIVE VOICES

1. The love of change hath changed the world.
2. Content thyself with thy estate.
3. The self-same things that gives me cause.

{ 4. When Flora fair the pleasant tidings bringeth (*the first part*).
{ 5. All creatures then with summer are delighted (*the second part*).
{ 6. From stately tower King David (*the first part*).
{ 7. With her sweet looks (*the second part*).
  8. Like as the gentle heart itself bewrays.
{ 9. Nought under heaven so strongly doth allure (*the first part*).
{ 10. So whilom learned that mighty Jewish swain (*the second part*).
{ 11. Sound, saddest notes, with rueful moaning (*the first part*).
{ 12. Let every sharp in sharp tune figure (*the second part*).
  13. If women can be courteous when they list.
  14. Nought is on earth more sacred.
  15. Ye gentle ladies, in whose sovereign power.
  16. The witless boy, that blind is to behold.
  17. Who seeks to captivate the freest minds.
  18. Who vows devotion to fair Beauty's shrine.
  19. The heathen gods for love forsook their state.
  20. O vain desire, wherewith the world bewitches.
  21. Even as the flowers do wither.

1601. A MADRIGAL TO FIVE VOICES
included as No. 7 in the ' Triumphs of Oriana '.
Calm was the air and clear the sky.

MICHAEL EAST. Born *circa* 1580 ; died *circa* 1640

Michael East, or Este, or Est, as his name is variously spelt,
is believed to have been the son of Thomas East, who as the
printer of the bulk of their works played such an important
part in connexion with the English madrigalists. Little is
known of the personal history of Michael East beyond the
fact that he was at one time organist of Lichfield Cathedral
and that he held the degree of B.Mus. He was a voluminous
composer. His first Set appeared in 1604 and was entitled,
' Madrigales to 3. 4. and 5. parts '. His second Set, also written
for 3. 4. and 5. parts, was published two years later. His
third volume, published in 1610, was of a somewhat different
character and was described on the title-page as ' The Third
Set of Bookes : Wherein are Pastorals, Anthemes, Neopolitanes,
Fancies, and Madrigales to 5. and 6. parts : Apt both for Viols
and Voyces '. There are twenty-two pieces in this book, eight
of which are Fancies for instruments only, four are Anthems,
and the remaining ten are Madrigals, Neapolitans, and Pastorals.
The Neapolitans and Pastorals are indistinguishable from the
Madrigals both as regards the style and design of the music ;
but the words of *Dainty white pearl* (No. 18) described as

a Neapolitan, are in a very unusual metre. East's 'Fourth Set of Bookes' consisted of anthems for versus and chorus, madrigals, and songs of other kinds to 4. 5. and 6. parts. This fourth book appeared in 1619, but, curiously enough, 1618 is the date given on the title-page of his 'Fift Set of Bookes, Wherein are Songs full of Spirit and delight, so Composed in 3. Parts, that they are as apt for Vyols as Voyces'. In spite of the statement on the title-page it is difficult to conjecture how this fifth book was intended to be used for singers, because it is one of those Sets in which no more than the opening words are given in any of the part-books, and the lyrics have completely perished with the exception of these few which were used elsewhere by East or other madrigalists. The same thing occurs again in East's 'Seventh Set of Bookes', the final section of which is described as 'ayerie fancies of 4. parts that may be as well sung as plaid '. The sixth and seventh books were published in 1624 and 1638 respectively, but contain no further contributions to the madrigal-literature ; the 1624 book consists solely of anthems with one secular song printed on the fly-leaf ; and the 1638 book is devoted to instrumental music, although, as just stated, the composer's original intention was that the last fourteen numbers might be either sung or played. The title-page of the 1638 book shows that East still held the position of organist of Lichfield Cathedral at that date.

The madrigal *Hence stars!* East's contribution to the 'Triumphs of Oriana', was his first madrigal publication. The late arrival of this madrigal and its consequent insertion before No. 1 in the volume have already been mentioned. As Thomas East, the assignee of Morley, was the printer of this Set, we may conjecture that the invitation to Michael was an afterthought, extended as a compliment by Morley to the elder East while his son was still quite a youth. Apart from this Oriana madrigal the only madrigal of East's reprinted since his time is *How merrily we live* (Set II, No. 4). This is all the more extraordinary because, without reaching the greatest heights, East succeeded in producing work that was for the most part well up to the average, and much of it is bright and attractive. *How merrily we live* may be taken as a typical example of his work. He wrote throughout with an easy style, and not without some appreciation of the words which he set, but on the other hand without showing any great depth of feeling. He was wise enough to know his own limitations, for he never attempted anything in the way of the ethical madrigal, or chose words that called for deep emotional expression.

From East's large store of madrigals the following few examples may be quoted, besides those already mentioned, as representing his best style of work : *In the merry month of May* (Set I, No. 2) ; *Joy of my life* (Set I, No. 16) ; and *All ye that joy in wailing* (Set I, No. 17). This five-part madrigal, without expressing that degree of emotion which is found in the work of his great contemporaries, is very pretty, especially in the concluding section set to the words :

> And after my death do this in my behove
> Tell Cressid Troilus is dead for love.

Very similar comment applies to *Now must I part, my darling* (Set III, No. 22). East knew the value of contrast, and, although a little conventional, the following quotation provides a typical example of his method of dealing with his words. The passage is from the six-part madrigal *Lo! here I leave my heart* (Set III, No. 20) :

see, ... to see me weep - ing.

Young Cupid hath proclaimed (Set I, No. 4) is a three-part setting of words used by Weelkes (1597 Set, No. 8). East's treatment of the phrase *a thousand Cupids may not Cloris touch* in this madrigal is strongly reminiscent of Weelkes's setting.

The Madrigalian Publications of Michael East

1604. MADRIGALS TO 3. 4. AND 5. PARTS

Songs to three voices

1. O come again, my lovely jewel.
2. In the merry month of May (*the first part*).
3. Corydon would kiss her then (*the second part*).
4. Young Cupid hath proclaimed.
5. To bed, to bed ! she calls.
6. O do not run away from me, my jewel.
7. In an evening late as I was walking.
8. Alas ! must I run away from her that loves me ?

Songs to four voices

9. O stay, fair cruel, do not still torment me.
10. My Hope a counsel with my Love.
11. Pity, dear love, my pity-moving words.
12. Mopsie, leave off to love.
13. Sweet love, I err, and do my error know.
14. In vain, my tongue, thou begg'st.
15. When on my dear I do demand the due.
16. Joy of my life, that hath my love in hold.

Songs to five voices

17. All ye that joy in wailing.
18. My prime of youth is but a frost of cares (*the first part*).
19. The Spring is past and yet it hath not sprung (*the second part*).
20. Fair is my love, my dear and only jewel.
21. Sly thief, if so you will believe (*the first part*).
22. What thing more cruel can you do ? (*the second part*).
23. Ye restless cares, companions of the night.
24. You mournful gods and goddesses descend.

1606. THE SECOND SET OF MADRIGALS TO 3. 4. AND 5. PARTS

Songs to three voices

1. I do not love my Phyllis for her beauty.
2. See Amaryllis shamed.
3. Why smilest thou, sweet jewel ?
4. How merrily we live that shepherds be.
5. Follow me, sweet love and soul's delight,
6. Round about I follow thee.

Songs of four voices

7. In dolorous complaining (*the first part*).
8. Since tears could not obtain (*the second part*).

9. Why runs away my love from me
   (*the first part*).
10. Why do you seek by flight?
    (*the second part*).
11. Farewell, false love, for so I find.
12. So much to give, and be so small
    regarded.
13. Sound out, my voice, with
    pleasant tunes (*the first part*).
14. She that my plaints with rigour
    (*the second part*).

Songs of five voices

15. Why smilest thou, sweet jewel?
16. Dear, why do you joy and take
    such pleasure?
17. Now Cloris laughs and swears
    (*the first part*).
18. Forsaken Thyrsis sighing sings
    (*the second part*).
19. I fall and then I rise again aloft.
20. What doth my pretty darling?
21. Hence stars! too dim of light.
22. O metaphysical tobacco.

1610. THE THIRD SET OF BOOKS

wherein are Pastorals, Anthems, Fancies, and Madrigals to 5. and 6. parts.

Songs of five parts

PASTORALS

1. Sweet muses, nymphs and shepherds sporting (*the first part*).
2. Ay me! wherefore sighs fair
   Sylvia? (*the second part*).
3. My peace and my pleasure (*the
   third part*).

ANTHEM

4. When Israel came out of Egypt
   (*the first part*).
5. What aileth thee, O thou sea?
   (*the second part*).

NEAPOLITAN

6. Come life, come death, I care not.
Nos. 7–14 are FANCIES for instruments.

Songs of six parts

NEAPOLITAN

15. Poor is the life that misses.

ANTHEM

16. Turn thy face from my wicked-
    ness (*the first part*).
17. O give me the comfort of thy
    help again (*the second part*).

NEAPOLITAN

18. Dainty white pearl, and you
    fresh-smiling roses.

MADRIGALS

19. Say, dear, when will your frown-
    ing leave?
20. Lo! here I leave my heart in
    keeping.
21. Life, tell me what is the cause.
22. Now must I part, my darling.

1619. THE FOURTH SET OF BOOKS

wherein are Anthems for Versus and Chorus, Madrigals and Songs of
other kinds to 4. 5. and 6. parts.

N.B. This Book bears the date 1619 although the Fifth Book is dated 1618.

Songs of four voices

1. Thyrsis, sleepest thou? Holla!
2. I did woo her with my looks.
3. Why are our summer sports so
   brittle?
4. Dear love, be not unkind to thy
   beloved.

5. Whenas I glance on my sweet
   lovely Phyllis.
6. Your shining eyes and golden
   hair.
7. When I lament my light o' love.
8. Farewell, sweet woods and
   mountains.

Songs of five voices

9. To hear men sing I care not.
10. O clap your hands together (*the first part*).
11. God is gone up with a merry noise (*the second part*).
12. I heard three virgins sweetly singing (*the first part*).
13. What heart such doubled force resisteth (*the second part*).
14. Fair Daphne, gentle shepherdess, sat weeping.
15. O Lord, of whom I do depend.
16. Come, shepherd swains, and on this cypress tree.

Songs of six voices

17. Be nimble! quick! dispatch! away! (*the first part*).
18. No haste but good, yet stay! (*the second part*).
19. Fly away, Care, for Venus goes a maying.
20. When David heard that Absalom was slain.
21. Haste thee, O God, to deliver me (*the first part*).
22. But let all those that seek thee (*the second part*).
23. Weep not, dear love, but joy.
24. Your shining eyes and golden hair.

1618. THE FIFTH SET OF BOOKS

wherein are songs full of spirit and delight composed in 3 parts.

1. Trip it lightly.
2. Turn round about.
3. Fly not away.
4. Softly for falling.
5. My lovely Phyllis.
6. And I as well as thou.
7. Love is a toy.
8. Sweet Lady, stay.
9. What art thou?
10. No haste but good.
11. White as lilies was her face.
12. Do what you can.
13. Mourning I die.
14. Stay yet awhile.
15. Come let's be gone.
16. I cannot stay.
17. Fear not the end.
18. Lively my heart.
19. My time is spent.
20. Smooth and soft.

N.B. Only the opening words are printed in these part-books, the music is therefore not available for voices.

1601. A MADRIGAL TO FIVE VOICES

included, unnumbered, at the beginning of the ' Triumphs of Oriana '.
Hence stars! too dim of light.

THOMAS BATESON. Born *circa* 1570; died 1630

Bateson is certainly to be reckoned one of the more important madrigalists of the English School. His two Sets, published in 1604 and 1618, contain, respectively, twenty-eight and thirty numbers. In addition to these his madrigal *When Oriana walked to take the air* was printed on the back of the dedication page in the 1604 Set as an extra number, and a note was added by Thomas East, the printer, explaining that it had arrived too late for inclusion in the ·' Triumphs of Oriana '. This gives a total of fifty-nine madrigals from Bateson's pen. It is curious that the insertion of the Oriana madrigal was made by the printer and not by the composer. Bateson wrote one other Oriana

madrigal which he called 'Orianaes farewell' (Set I, No. 22);
it seems likely that he wrote this because of the non-inclusion
of his original contribution to the famous Set, and regarding
that as being out of date after the death of Queen Elizabeth.

Bateson wrote many fine madrigals; but his work, when
viewed as a whole, falls just a little short of that of Wilbye,
Weelkes, or Morley. This becomes apparent if we compare
his setting of such lines as, *Life is a death where sorrow cannot
die* in No. 16 of Set II, or, *My grieved ghost with shrieks and
dreadful crying* in No. 18 of Set I, or, *O break asunder, heart,
to satisfy her* in No. 14 of Set I, with similar work of Wilbye :
or again, when the chromatic opening of his *Come, Sorrow,
help me to lament* (Set II, No. 24), remarkable though it be,
is placed beside Weelkes's *O Care, thou wilt despatch me.*
Nor are such technical flaws to be found in Morley's writing
as the consecutive fifths and octaves which Bateson not
infrequently wrote, and very bald examples of which are to be
found, for instance, in *The nightingale in silent night* (Set II,
No. 8) which is otherwise a charming madrigal, and in *Pleasure
is a wanton thing* (Set II, No. 5), to quote no others. Moreover
an occasional poverty in his part-writing betrays itself in
the inner voice-parts : for example, in *Why do I, dying, live?*
(Set II, No. 20) and *I heard a noise* (Set II, No. 18) ; also
there is a good deal of conventionality in his style, more
particularly in his first Set.

Yet these criticisms must not be pressed too far ; they serve
to emphasize the greatness of the above-mentioned composers
rather than to detract from the undoubtedly high merit of
Bateson himself.

Bateson laid a splendid foundation for success as a madrigal-
composer in the selection of his lyrics. The poetry throughout
is of a uniformly high standard. *Sister, awake* (Set I, No. 21)
is a good example ; this madrigal is deservedly among the
most popular, and it could hardly be surpassed in genuine
gaiety of spirit both as regards words and music. But only
in one instance has the authorship of any of Bateson's charming
lyrics been identified, namely : *The Nightingale, so soon as
April bringeth* (Set I, No. 3) which is by Sir Philip Sidney ;
Bateson's music is admirably wedded to it.

Among so large a number of madrigals by this composer only a few can be noticed here in detail. In the first Set *Come follow me, fair nymphs* (No. 5) is an attractive example of bright imaginative writing for three voices, introducing plenty of telling contrast. *Adieu, sweet love!* (No. 10) belongs to the best type of the madrigalian style and has a very pretty ending. In *Those sweet delightful lilies* (No. 13) Bateson followed the free rhythmic outline employed by Weelkes in his setting of the same words. *Sweet Gemma* (Nos. 15 and 16) is a fine madrigal, designed in two separate sections ; the first section ends effectively, and there are some noticeable contrapuntal features in the opening of the second section. *Strange were the life* (No. 17) contains much that is interesting ; it is one of the few madrigals of a serious character in the Set. Another fine five-part number is *Alas, where is my love?* (No. 18). Bateson's treatment of the words *till heartless, I die* is not to be compared with that of Wilbye in expressing similar emotions, but it is very effective and pathetic. *Sister, awake* (No. 21) has already been mentioned. *Hark! hear you not?* (No. 22) is widely known and is a great favourite ; the double suspension in this madrigal has been noticed and commented upon by various musicians, but it is by no means a unique example of such a chord in the English madrigals even if it cannot be matched in this exact position :

Bateson himself used an equally remarkable chord in the
closing bars of *With bitter sighs* (Set II, No. 19) :

and the double suspension in *Sweet Gemma* (Set I, Nos. 15
and 16) at the words *O tiger cruel,* is practically identical with
the one in *Orianaes farewell.*

In this connexion reference may be made to Ward's use of
double suspensions and suspensions in general ; [1] while a beautiful phrase containing a double suspension may be quoted from
John Dowland's *Time's eldest son, Old Age* (Set II, No. 6)
published four years earlier than Bateson's First Set.   (The
quotation is here made from the composer's version as a solo-
song with lute accompaniment.)

Dowland, too, employed a very remarkable triple suspension
of a somewhat different character in *I must complain* (Book III,
No. 17) :

---

[1] See p. 280.

In fact, from Dowland's works instances of almost every harmonic novelty of the period can be quoted, and the subject of his harmonies provides material for special study. But Dowland, it must be remembered, was not in the stricter sense a madrigal-composer, and his work, being of a somewhat different scope and character, lends itself more easily perhaps to free harmonic treatment than that of the stricter madrigal-style ; and it lies, in a sense, outside the main subject of this volume.

The six-part works in the first Set are somewhat conventional.

In the years that intervened between the publication of the two Sets Bateson seems to have gained much experience, for his second Set is far the more interesting of the two. It includes a larger proportion of serious and emotional subjects ; and the style as a whole is less conventional. Yet even here there is evidence of inability to work out ideas which are themselves conceived sometimes in the finest spirit. Thus, the exquisite opening of *Sadness, sit down* (No. 16) leads to disappointment as the madrigal develops. The first five bars are profoundly moving :

Sad - ness sit   down,   sad - ness sit   down

Sweet, those trammels of your hair (No. 6) is a charming madrigal for three voices ; it should be sung at a slowish *tempo* to secure the best effect. *Live not, poor bloom* (No. 7) is an admirable number with just the right touch of pathos ; the progression of·an augmented second on the word *withered* should be noticed. The phrase at the words *thus with loathed burden choked* curiously foreshadows a passage in Mendelssohn's anthem ' Judge me, O God '. *Have I found her ? O rich finding !* (No. 13) is another admirable bit of work in a cheerful mood ; the irregular rhythm of the opening bars catches the spirit of the words to perfection. And *Down the hills Corinna trips* is also an attractive example of the gay type. *Cupid in a bed of roses* (Nos. 25 and 26) is one of the best things in the Set ;

it is constructed on important lines and the interest is well sustained. There is an entrancing phrase near the beginning. where a tenor or baritone, singing *sotto voce*, has an opportunity of producing a lovely dreamy effect on the word *sleeping* :

Bateson made a few experiments in harmony which are worth noticing as being characteristic of the spirit of this group of composers. Naturally they are not all equally successful, but the following selected examples may be cited and judged on their own merits :

From Set I, No. 7.

From Set I, No. 22.

From Set II, No. 17.

From Set II, No. 18.

From Set II, No. 18.

From Set II, No. 20.

As far as can be judged from such evidence as exists, Bateson was born about the year 1570. He became organist of Chester Cathedral in 1599 and held that office for nine years, after which he left to take a similar appointment at Christ Church Cathedral, Dublin. In 1615 he took the degree of B.Mus., and he is believed to have been the first musical graduate of Trinity College, Dublin. His death took place in Dublin early in the year 1630.

The Madrigalian Publications of Thomas Bateson

1604. THE FIRST SET OF ENGLISH MADRIGALS
TO 3. 4. 5. AND 6. VOICES

When Oriana walked to take the air (*for six voices*).

Songs to three voices

1. Beauty is a lovely sweet.
2. Love would discharge the duty.
3. The Nightingale, so soon as April bringeth.
4. Ay me! my mistress scorns my love.
5. Come, follow me, fair nymphs.
6. Your shining eyes and golden hair.

Songs to four voices

7. Whither so fast? See how the kindly flowers.
8. Dame Venus, hence to Paphos go.
9. Down from above falls Jove in rain.
10. Adieu, sweet love! O thus to part.
11. If Love be blind, how hath he then the sight?
12. Phyllis, farewell, I may no longer live.

Songs to five voices

13. Those sweet delightful lilies.
14. And must I needs depart then?

15. Sweet Gemma, when I first beheld (*the first part*).
16. Yet stay, alway be chained to my heart (*the second part*).
17. Strange were the life that every man would like.
18. Alas, where is my love?
19. O fly not, love, O fly not me.
20. Who prostrate lies at women's feet.
21. Sister, awake, close not your eyes.
22. Hark! hear you not a heavenly harmony (*Orianaes farewell*).

Songs to six voices

23. Dear, if you wish my dying.
24. Fair Hebe when dame Flora meets.
25. Phyllis, farewell, I may no longer live.
26. Thyrsis on his fair Phyllis' breast reposing.
27. Merrily my love and I.
28. Music some thinks no music is.

1618. ·THE SECOND SET OF MADRIGALS
TO 3. 4. 5. AND 6. PARTS

Songs of three voices

1. Love is the fire that burns me.
2. My mistress after service due.
3. One woman scarce of twenty.
4. If I seek to enjoy the fruits of my pain.
5. Pleasure is a wanton thing.
6. Sweet, those trammels of your hair.

Songs of four voices

7. Live not, poor bloom, but perish.
8. The nightingale in silent night.
9. O what is she, whose looks like lightnings pierce (*the first part*).
10. See, forth her eyes her startled spirit peeps (*the second part*).

11. When to the gloomy woods.
12. If floods of tears could cleanse my follies past.

Songs of five voices

13. Have I found her? O rich finding.
14. Down the hills Corinna trips.
15. Camilla fair tripped o'er the plain.
16. Sadness, sit down, on my soul feed.
17. Life of my life, how should I live?
18. I heard a noise and wished for a sight.

THOMAS GREAVES.　Date of birth and death unknown.

In 1604 Thomas Greaves, lutenist to Sir Henry Pierpoint of Holm in Nottinghamshire, published a volume which he described as ' Songes of sundrie kindes '. It contained twenty-one compositions, of which the first nine were Airs to be sung to the lute and bass viol ; the next six were ' Songes of sadnesse ' for the viols and voice, and the last six were Madrigals for five voices. *Come away, sweet love, and play thee* (No. 21) is a Ballet or *Fa-la*, though not actually so described. It is admirably written, and the treatment of the words *and running in and out* conjures up irresistibly a picture of the rapid pursuit through the two opposing lines of country dancers on the village green. The varied form in which the quaver figure appears has a very happy effect. The passage offers unusually good material for the study of independent part-singing in contradictory rhythm :

The first of these five-part madrigals (No. 16) deals with a patriotic theme, a welcome to James I. The words are mere doggerel and the music is not very inspiring. Though the piece is described as a Madrigal it has hardly any imitative or contrapuntal device. Nothing further is known about Greaves, but it is worth noting that Lady Pierpoint, his patron's wife, was Frances Cavendish, sister of Sir Charles, and cousin of Michael Cavendish. The similarity of the song-books of Greaves and Cavendish has already been referred to, and it is not unlikely that these two composers were personal friends.

The Madrigalian Publications of Thomas Greaves

1604. MADRIGALS FOR FIVE VOICES

included in his volume entitled ' Songs of sundry kinds '

16. England, receive the rightful king.
{ 17. Sweet nymphs, that trip along the English lands (*the first part*).
{ 18. Long have the shepherds sung this song (*the second part*).
{ 19. Lady, the melting crystal of your eye (*the first part*).
{ 20. O that a drop from such a sweet fount (*the second part*).
21. Come away, sweet love, and play thee.

RICHARD ALISON.   Date of birth and death unknown.

In 1606 a volume was published by Richard Alison with the curious title, ' An Howres Recreation in Musicke, apt for Instrumentes and Voyces '.   He was perhaps private musician to his patron, Sir John Scudamore at Holme Lacy.   The music has no particular merit.   Two of the five-part pieces of this Set were reprinted by Thomas Oliphant ; they are constructed more or less on madrigalian design, but do not approach the standard ot the great composers of the School.   Alison's personal history is unknown, except for the fact stated on the title-page of his ' Psalmes of David ', published in 1599, that he was then living in a ' house in the Duke's place neere Alde-gate '.

The Madrigalian Publications of Richard Alison

1606. AN HOUR'S RECREATION IN MUSIC

Songs of four voices

1. The man of upright life (*the first verse*).
2. He only can behold with unaffrighted eyes (*the second verse*).
3. O heavy heart, whose harms are hid (*the first verse*).
4. In hope a king doth go to war (*the second verse*).
5. Though Wit bids Will to blow retreat (*the third verse*).
6. But yet it seems a foolish drift (*the fourth verse*).
7. I can no more but hope good heart (*the fifth verse*).
8. Who loves this life, from love his love doth err.
9. My prime of youth is but a frost of cares (*the first verse*).
10. The Spring is past, and yet it hath not sprung (*the second verse*).

Songs of five voices

11. Rest with yourselves, you vain and idle brains (*the first verse*).
12. For lust is frail where love is ever sound (*the second verse*).
13. Shall I abide this jesting ? (*the first verse*).
14. Can I abide this prancing ? (*the second verse*).
15. The sturdy rock for all his strength (*the first verse*).
16. The stately stag that seems so stout (*the second verse*).
17. What if a day, or a month, or a year ? (*the first verse*).
18. Earth's but a point to the world (*the second verse*).
19. There is a garden in her face (*the first verse*).
20. Those cherries fairly do enclose (*the second verse*).
21. Her eyes like angels watch them still (*the third verse*).
22. Behold, now praise the Lord.
23. O Lord, bow down thine ear.
24. The sacred choir of angels sings.

ROBERT JONES.   Date of birth and death unknown.

Robert Jones was primarily a lutenist-composer, and indeed one of the finest lutenists of his time. He is one of the few musicians of the period who published compositions in both styles. His only volume of Madrigals appeared in 1607 ; but he produced as many as five books of Airs, which will be noticed in a later chapter with the works of the other lutenists. His volume of Madrigals is now one of the rarest of its kind. No complete printed set of the part-books is known ; a MS. set in Brussels is also incomplete. Robert, Earl of Salisbury was Jones's patron. The Set is also unique in including compositions for every number of voices ranging from three to eight. *Sing, merry birds* (No. 7) is very fresh in character. A curious chromatic passage occurs in this madrigal, which suggests the influence of Weelkes and Dowland ; but in contrast to their handling of such passages it must be admitted that Jones gives the impression here of experimenting with material the nature of which he but imperfectly understood :

Another bright and well-written madrigal in this Set is *I come, sweet birds* (No. 8). The subject of birds seems to have made a special appeal to this composer. *Cock a doodle doo* (No. 9) is treated in a humorous vein. Jones was a contributor to the 'Triumphs of Oriana'; but he is another of these musicians of whose personal history little is known to us. In conjunction with Philip Rosseter he was granted a patent in 1610 to train a school of children to be designated 'the children of the revels to the Queen'.

The Madrigalian Publications of Robert Jones

1607. THE FIRST SET OF MADRIGALS OF 3. 4. 5. 6. 7. 8. PARTS
for viols and voices or for voices alone, or as you please

Songs for three voices

1. Thine eyes so bright.
2. She only is the pride of Nature's skill.
3. When I behold her eyes (*the first part*).
4. But let her look in mine (*the second part*).
5. Love, if a god thou art.
6. O I do love, then kiss me.

Songs for four voices

7. Sing, merry birds, your cheerful notes.
8. I come, sweet birds, with swiftest flight.
9. Cock a doodle doo, thus I begin.
10. Shrill-sounding bird, call up the drowsy morn (*the first part*).
11. And when day's fled with slow pace (*the second part*).
12. Here is an end of all the songs.

Songs for five voices

13. Come, doleful owl, the messenger of woe.
14. Sweet, when thou singest (*the first part*).
15. Thou tell'st thy sorrows (*the second part*).

16. When to her lute Corinna sings (*the first part*).
17. And as her lute doth live or die (*the second part*).
18. If I behold your eyes.

Songs for six voices

19. Since your sweet cherry lips I kissed (*the first part*).
20. Then grant me, dear, those cherries still (*the second part*).
21. Stay, wandering thoughts, O whither do you haste ?
22. Your presence breeds my anguish (*the first part*).
23. If those dear eyes that burn me (*the second part*).
24. If you speak kindly to me (*the third part*).

A song for seven voices

25. Are lovers full of fire ? (*the first part*).

A song for eight voices

26. The more I burn, the more I do desire (*the second part*).

1601.   A MADRIGAL FOR SIX VOICES
included as No. 21 in the 'Triumphs of Oriana'.
Fair Oriana, seeming to wink at folly.

HENRY YOULL.   Date of birth and death unknown.

This composer's work has for some reason been almost completely overlooked and forgotten. Yet his Set of Canzonets to three voices contains several attractive pieces. The three-part writing of the madrigalists was, as a rule, laid out upon a smaller design than their other work ; these canzonets are consequently unpretentious, and they do not provide any particular example of profound expression or feeling. But many of them are written in a graceful and easy style and with a good deal of rhythmic strength. The last five numbers in the book are in reality Ballets, although the term Canzonet is employed to describe the entire Set. *Come, merry lads* (No. 20) has a *fa-la* refrain at the end of the first section and *lirum lirum* in the second ; this latter idea was evidently borrowed from Morley. Among the best of Youll's canzonets are *Pipe, shepherds, pipe* (No. 5) and *Of sweet and dainty flowers* (No. 7) which has a pretty phrase to the words *daffa daffa dillic.* Youll seems to have had a special affection for the daffadilly. The opening passage of *Awake, sweet love* (No. 11) is melodious and picturesque ; and *The shepherds' daughters all are gone* (No. 15) is quite attractive. The most effective composition in the Set is, perhaps, *Slow, slow, fresh fount* (No. 8), the words of which are by Ben Jonson. Nothing is known about Youll's biography, but it appears from the dedication of his Canzonets that he was household musician to one Edward Bacon.

The Madrigalian Publications of Henry Youll

1608. CANZONETS TO THREE VOICES

1. Each day of thine, sweet month of May.
2. Come, love, let's walk into the Spring (*the first part*).
3. In yonder dale there are fine flowers (*the second part*).
4. See where this nymph with all her train (*the third part*).
5. Pipe, shepherds, pipe full merrily.
6. Only joy, now here you are.
7. Of sweet and dainty flowers.
8. Slow, slow, fresh fount.
9. In pleasant summer's morning.
10. Once I thought to die for love.
11. Awake, sweet love, 'tis time to rise.
12. Pity, O pity me, mine own sweet jewel.
13. Cease, restless thoughts, to vex my careful mind.
14. Sweet Phyllis, stay, O let some pity move thee.
15. The shepherds' daughters all are gone (*the first part*).
16. But behold where they return along (*the second part*).
17. Say, shepherd, say where is fair Phyllis gone ? (*the first part*).
18. But though poor sheep fair Phyllis thus do mourn (*the second part*).
19. In the merry month of May the fields are decked.
20. Come, merry lads, let us away.
21. Whiles joyful Springtime lasteth.
22. Early, before the day doth spring.
23. Where are now those jolly swains ? (*the first part*).
24. Now the country lasses hie them (*the second part*).

THOMAS RAVENSCROFT. Born *circa* 1585 ; died *circa* 1633.

Three volumes of Thomas Ravenscroft have already been mentioned in connexion with the subject of Rounds and Catches. Although Ravenscroft may have composed some of the pieces contained in these volumes there is no evidence that he was more than the editor of the collections. The first Set was published in 1609 and was entitled ' Pammelia. Musicks Miscellanie. Or, Mixed Varietie of Pleasant Roundelayes, and delightfull Catches, of 3. 4. 5. 6. 7. 8. 10. Parts in one. None so ordinarie as musicall, none so musical, as not to all, very pleasing and acceptable '. This is the earliest English printed collection of this kind of music. It contains exactly a hundred pieces, sacred and secular, and was reprinted in 1618.

Ravenscroft's second volume appeared in the same year as ' Pammelia ' and was called ' Deuteromelia : Or The Second part of Musicks melodie, or melodius Musicke. Of Pleasant Roundelaies ; K. H. mirth, or Freemens Songs. And such delightfull Catches. *Qui canere potest canat.* Catch, that catch can. *Ut Mel Os, sic Cor melos afficit et reficit '*. This Set contained thirty-one numbers, of which *Three blind mice* was No. 13. A good deal of speculation has been indulged in as to the meaning of ' K. H. mirth ' on the title-page. It has been thought by some to stand for ' King Henry's mirth ' ; but it is more likely that ' K. H. ' stands for ' King's Head ' and refers to a house at Greenwich known at a later period to Pepys as ' the great musicke house ', or to a famous tavern of the name in Cheapside.

The third volume was published in 1611 and bore the title ' Melismata. Musicall Phansies. Fitting the Court, Citie, and Countrey Humours. To 3, 4, and 5. Voyces '. It contained twenty-three songs under the following headings : ' Court Varieties,' ' Citie Rounds,' ' Citie Conceits,' ' Country Rounds,' and ' Country Pastimes '.

Ravenscroft published one other volume which contains some pieces of semi-madrigalian character. It was issued in 1614 and entitled 'A Brief Discourse of the true (but neglected) use of Charact'ring the Degrees, by their Perfection, Imperfection, and Diminution in Measurable Musicke, against the

Common Practise and Custome of these Times. Examples whereof are exprest in the Harmony of 4. Voyces, Concerning the Pleasure of 5. usuall Recreations. 1 Hunting. 2 Hawking. 3 Dauncing. 4 Drinking. 5 Enamouring.' This volume included six pieces by John Bennet and two by Edward Peirs, or Pierce, Ravenscroft's former master. Properly speaking, the only numbers which resemble the Madrigal in character are the four in the Dancing section, which are charming fairy-like little pieces, and, to a less extent, Bennet's Hawking song. The rest are laid out on the lines of songs with chorus, and some are no more than tavern-songs.

Ravenscroft was probably born about the year 1585. He received his earliest musical training under Pierce as a chorister at St. Paul's Cathedral. He took the degree of B.Mus. at Cambridge in 1607. From 1618–22 he held an appointment at Christ's Hospital. In one of the prefatory addresses in his 'Brief Discourse' his age is given as twenty-two and reference is made to his youth. It is difficult to believe that he can have been so young in 1614, for he would in that case have been no more than fifteen when he took his B.Mus. degree, and seventeen when he published Pammelia and Deuteromelia. The Latin epigram which refers to his age probably belongs to an earlier date although it was printed in the 1614 volume. Ravenscroft died, as far as can be ascertained, between the years 1630 and 1635. He is best remembered to-day by the sadly garbled versions now in use of his hymn-tunes included in his 'Whole Booke of Psalmes' published in 1621.

The Madrigalian Publications of Thomas Ravenscroft

1609. PAMMELIA. Music's Miscellany.
1609. DEUTEROMELIA. The Second Part of Music's Melody.
1611. MELISMATA. Musical Fancies.

1614. A BRIEF DISCOURSE

Hunting

1. The hunt is up. *Bennet.*
2. Hey trola, trola. *Peirs.*

Hawking

3. Awake, awake, the day doth break. *Ravenscroft.*
4. Sith sickles and the shearing scythe. *Ravenscroft.*
5. Lure, falconers, lure. *Bennet.*

Dancing

6. Dare you haunt our hallowed green ? *Ravenscroft.*
7. Round around, and keep your ring. *Ravenscroft.*
8. By the moon we sport and play. *Ravenscroft.*
9. Round about in a fair ring. *Bennet.*

Drinking
10. Trudge away quickly and fill the
    black bowl.   *Ravenscroft.*
11. Toss the pot, let us be merry.
                        Ravenscroft.
12. Tobacco fumes away all nasty
    rheums.   *Ravenscroft.*

Enamouring
13. What seek'st thou, fool? *Bennet.*
14. My mistress is as fair as fine.
                        Bennet.

15. Love for such a cherry lip.
                        Peirs.
16. Leave off, Hymen, and let us
    borrow.   *Ravenscroft.*
17. Coame, Malkyn, hurle thine
    oyz.   *Ravenscroft.*
18. Yo tell ma zo, but, Roger, I cha
    vound.   *Ravenscroft.*
19. Ich con but zweare.
                        Ravenscroft.
20. A borgen's a borgen. *Bennet.*

ORLANDO GIBBONS.   Born 1583 ; died 1625.

Orlando Gibbons, who published his only Set of madrigals
in 1612, is one of the most important figures among the Tudor
school of English musicians.   Indeed, it is not too much to
say that Byrd, Gibbons, and Purcell are the three greatest
composers in the whole range of English musical history.
Orlando was a younger son of William Gibbons, a member
of the City Waits at Cambridge.   It should be stated that in
Tudor times the Waits were a body of musicians of considerable
skill attached to the corporation of all the leading Boroughs
in the country, their principal duty being to attend upon the
mayor and to perform music before him on state occasions.   Will
Kempe, the famous Elizabethan dancer and comedian, in
his ' Nine days wonder ' praised the Norwich waits in the
following terms : [1] ' Such Waytes fewe Citties in our Realme
have the like, none better ; who besides their excellency in
wind instruments, their rare cunning on the Vyoll and Violin,
theyr voices be admirable, everie one of them able to serve in
any Cathedrall Church in Christendoome for Quiristers.'

Orlando's eldest brother Ellis has been already noticed as
a contributor to Morley's ' Triumphs of Oriana '.   His brother
Edward, who was also several years older than Orlando, was
in Holy Orders and a B.Mus.   He was at one time master of
the choristers at King's College, Cambridge, and subsequently,
according to Boyce and all subsequent historians, he became
Minor Canon and Precentor of Bristol Cathedral, but left
Bristol for Exeter Cathedral, where he became organist and

---

[1] Kempe's Nine days wonder reprinted in *Collectanea Adamantae*, No. 29.

Custos of the College of Priest-Vicars. Further research in the Bristol records proved that he held no appointment whatever at that Cathedral. The civic documents at Oxford have revealed the fact that William Gibbons was living there from about 1580 to 1588, when he returned to his former home at Cambridge. Orlando, without any kind of doubt, was born at Oxford, not Cambridge, in 1583 and baptized there on Christmas Day. He was a chorister at King's in 1596. He became organist of the Chapel Royal in 1604, and of Westminster Abbey in 1623. In 1625 he went with others of the Chapel Royal to attend on Charles I at Canterbury where the King was residing in State awaiting his Queen, whom he had already married by proxy in Paris. During this visit Gibbons died suddenly and was buried in the Cathedral. Among his sons, Christopher alone had any importance as a musician ; he was a chorister at Exeter Cathedral under his uncle, and became organist of Winchester Cathedral, a post which he gave up to join the Royalist army. After the Resoration he held appointments as organist of the Chapel Royal, private organist to Charles II, and organist of Westminster Abbey.

Orlando Gibbons's reputation must be based chiefly upon his Church music, which, for solemn grandeur and perfection of style, stands with the Church music of Byrd on a level to which no other English composer has ever quite attained. Being among the youngest of the great English composers of the polyphonic school, Gibbons was able to profit by the experience of his immediate predecessors, which, at such a period in the development of music, was an unusual advantage. But Gibbons was no mere copyist ; as a genius of the first rank he assimilated all that was best in the style of the older men among his contemporaries, and at the same time was able to superimpose upon that style the stamp of his own originality. Consequently, when compared with that of Tallis and Byrd, the music of Gibbons is obviously of a later date, and yet equally with theirs it belongs to the purely polyphonic type, without the slightest idea of compromise or any suggestion of the rapid transition from that style which was so shortly to be brought about.

In the field of secular vocal music Gibbons did a comparatively small amount of work. His only volume of the kind was, as has been already mentioned, his ' First Set of Madrigals and Mottets of 5. Parts ' which was published in 1612. The title of this volume, in the first place, is unique, for none of the other madrigalists gave the term Motet as an alternative, and it prepares the reader for finding that the contents of the volume are of a serious rather than of a light character.

The whole of this Set stands apart from the rest of the work of the madrigalists, either English or Continental, both as regards the stern severity of the music and the ethical nature of so many of the lyrics. The volume consists of twenty numbers, which, if reckoned as complete compositions, are no more than thirteen in all ; for Nos. 3, 4, 5, and 6 are parts of one whole, and similarly Nos. 17, 18, and 19 belong to each other, while two more of the compositions in the Set are divided into separate sections.

The first composition in the book is the well-known *The silver swan*, which, though quite short and simply written, must be classified as a madrigal of decidedly serious character ; the beautiful effect of the augmented fifth at the words *O death, come close mine eyes* has been entirely eliminated by the editors of all the popular editions of this madrigal, who have substituted D for the first E flat in the Altus-part.

It is impossible to imagine what led to this inexcusable editorial blunder, and it is noteworthy that the edition of the Musical Antiquarian Society was correct in this particular detail. Perhaps the finest thing in this book is the setting of Raleigh's splendid poem *What is our life ?* which Gibbons has wedded to music that matches the words to perfection.

Higher praise could not be bestowed. A fine contrast is produced in this madrigal by the employment of sustained notes at the words :

> Our graves that hide us from the scorching sun
> Are like drawn curtains when the play is done.

And a wonderful climax is reached with the words :

> Thus march we playing to our latest rest.

Gibbons showed a marked partiality for complex rhythms, especially those of triple measure. This feature may be observed particularly in *Fair is the rose* (No. 16), or in *How art thou thralled* (No. 7), where the overlapping triple rhythm at the words *Nature made thee free* seems to be designed for the purpose of emphasizing the idea of freedom or independence. Another exceedingly fine madrigal in this Set is *Now each flowery bank of May* (No. 12), which is treated by Gibbons in a solemn spirit, and which, when closely examined, reveals a wonderful amount of picturesque detail. The gentle sweep of the wind in a scale passage of quavers, running up through all the parts and right across the score, at the words *winds the loved leaves do kiss*, seems almost to forecast the methods of Brahms :

The concluding passage of this madrigal is intensely impassioned, particularly the final six bars or so; the two G naturals on the words *love* and *life* in the last entry of the Quintus (second soprano)-part, which conflict severely with the G sharps both before and after them, and also the last four bars of the Tenor-part, in the high register of the voice, combine in producing an emotional effect which reaches the highest possible pitch.

Gibbons makes constant use of the chord with the augmented fifth so frequently mentioned in these pages, but one example of a very unusual treatment of this chord, especially as regards its resolution, may be quoted from *Now each flowery bank* :

The whole of this passage has a delightfully elusive effect resulting from the repeated postponement of any finality of cadence; the composer clearly intended to convey the idea of the everflowing stream; the little ripple in the Tenor-part is a remarkably delicate touch of the illustrator's brush, characteristic of the subtlety of feeling which Gibbons so often displayed.

Space will not permit of a detailed study here of the whole of this Set of madrigals, each of which is a masterpiece in its own style; but, besides those already touched upon, *Dainty fine bird* (No. 9) and *Ah, dear heart* (No. 15) must be specially mentioned as being among the finest compositions of their kind.

To compare Gibbons, as a madrigal-writer, with the other leaders of the English School is not easy, because his conception of what a Madrigal might be and the terms in which he expressed himself in this class of composition are entirely different from those of any other of the Tudor composers. His severity is different in kind from that of Byrd and he is at the same time far more emotional ; indeed he may perhaps be considered to be among the most emotional of all the madrigalists. On the other hand, he lacks something of the suppleness of Wilbye, and he attempts nothing in the direction of the gayer fields of beauty, the nearest approach being *Trust not too much, fair youth* (No. 20).

In actual performance no madrigals are so difficult to interpret satisfactorily as those of Gibbons. Most of them demand exceptional care in the treatment of the individual voice-parts, and the rhythms are often extremely complex, while some of the details of the workmanship call for very close examination on the part of the conductor. It may be here suggested that more copious marks of expression are called for in these than in almost any other madrigals, while it is also probable that each individual conductor would desire to work with special expression-marks of his own for the purpose of giving his personal reading of this music. In the madrigals of Gibbons there is unlimited scope for variety and for individuality of interpretation. It will probably be found that a slow *tempo* will be demanded by the character of the music almost throughout this Set.

The Madrigalian Publications of Orlando Gibbons

1612. THE FIRST SET OF MADRIGALS AND MOTETS OF
5 PARTS.

1. The silver swan.
2. O that the learned poets of this time.
⎰ 3. I weigh not Fortune's frown nor smile (*the first part*).
⎱ 4. I tremble not at noise of war (*the second part*).
⎰ 5. I see Ambition never pleased (*the third part*).
⎱ 6. I feign not friendship where I hate (*the fourth part*).
⎰ 7. How art thou thralled, O poor despised creature (*the first part*).
⎱ 8. Farewell, all joys ! (*the second part*).

    9. Dainty fine bird, that art engaged there.

    { 10. Fair ladies, that to love captived are (*the first part*).

    { 11. 'Mongst thousands good one wanton dame (*the second part*).

    12. Now each flowery bank of May.

    13. Lais, now old, that erst attempting lass.

    14. What is our life ? a Play of passion.

    15. Ah, dear heart, why do you rise ?

    16. Fair is the rose, yet fades with heat and cold.

    (17. Nay, let me weep though others' tears be spent (*the first part*).

    { 18. Ne'er let the sun with his deceiving light (*the second part*).

    (19. Yet if that age had frosted o'er his head (*the third part*).

    20. Trust not too much, fair youth.

CHAPTER XIX

JOHN WARD — FRANCIS PILKINGTON — HENRY LICHFILD —
THOMAS VAUTOR—MARTIN PEERSON—THOMAS TOMKINS
—JOHN HILTON—PETER PHILIPS

JOHN WARD. Date of birth unknown ; died *circa* 1640.

JOHN WARD published his 'First Set of English Madrigals to
3. 4. 5. and 6. parts' in 1613. This volume contains twenty-eight
compositions—six numbers for three, four, and five voices respectively, and ten for six voices. This Set deserves a high
place among the works of the English madrigalists. It is in his
six-part work that Ward was at his best, and he appears to have
been conscious of this, if we may judge from the proportionately
large number of such songs in the Set. The lyrics which this
composer chose for his purpose are of especial excellence, and
the authorship of a large proportion of them can be identified.
The first two numbers are a setting of Sidney's *My true love
hath my heart,* and the sonnet is here set in its entirety ; it has
been printed in many well-known anthologies in incomplete
form. The music in this case has no outstanding features, but
is nevertheless melodious and attractive, and is neatly rounded
off at the conclusion by the recapitulation of the opening phrase
of the music in accordance with that of the words of the poem.
Ward seems to have had a special preference for the poems of
Sidney and Drayton ; he also used words by each of the two
Davisons. Another attractive three-part number is *Go, wailing
accents* (No. 5), set to Francis Davison's words. All the three-
part madrigals in the Set are within the range of female voices.

The four-part section is the least interesting part of the book.
O my thoughts (No. 8) opens melodiously, but has rather a weak
ending ; and *How long shall I ?* (No. 12) is marred by a too
prolonged passage of a conventional character at the words
where first mine eyes. Among the five-part numbers *Sweet
Philomel* (No. 13) is a thoroughly characteristic bit of madrigal-
writing ; *Flora, fair Nymph* (No. 15) and *Hope of my heart*

(No. 17) should also be noticed : in the first of these a very
strong effect is produced at the words *And die I shall* by the
employment of the chord of C minor on the second strong position
of the bar as a group of passing notes, while D is sustained in
the upper voice until the concord is reached again in the following bar. In *Hope of my heart* a chromatic passage is introduced
at the words *But cruel without measure.* Perhaps the most
attractive of the five-part numbers in this Set is *Upon a bank
with roses set* (No. 18) ; the words are by Drayton and lend
themselves to well-contrasted effects. In the closing bars of
this madrigal there is an interesting double-suspension somewhat similar to the much-quoted example in Bateson's *Hark !
hear you not ?* (Set I, No. 22).[1]

Ward's use of suspensions is a special characteristic of his
work. A noteworthy example may be cited from the very fine
six-part madrigal *Out from the vale of deep despair* (No. 21) ;
it occurs at the words *Daphne's cruelty hath lost,* and involves the
simultaneous employment of six different notes in the scale :

Attention may be directed incidentally to the augmented
second in the Altus-part in this phrase ; this is not an isolated
example of such a progression in Ward's work. Other remarkable discords are to be found in this same madrigal as well as in

[1] See p. 258.

several others of the six-part numbers. One further example may be quoted showing the simultaneous use of six different notes in the scale ; this example is from *If the deep sighs* (No. 23), another of Drayton's poems :

Occasionally Ward duplicated his suspensions in a manner that was in direct violation of academic rule. This peculiar feature in his work is somewhat similar to Farnaby's use of consecutive fifths, and it was evidently introduced because the composer aimed at that particular effect and liked it, and not because he lacked the ability to avoid a grammatical error. As an example of this peculiarity the following bars may be quoted from *If the deep sighs* :

The whole of these ten six-part madrigals are fine works. The best known of these is *Die not, fond man* (No. 25), but, although it is deservedly popular, it is by no means the finest ; it displays traces of conventionality here and there. Ward showed a preference for the serious type of subject, and perhaps the best of these madrigals is *If the deep sighs* (Nos. 23 and 24).

It is of great length, and is in fact one of the very longest of the English madrigals ; but it is treated with great dignity, and the severity of the subject is occasionally relieved by the introduction of lighter material. The opening of the second half is especially beautiful, notably the setting of the words, *Nor not a river weeps not at my tale. I have entreated and I have complained* (No. 26) is set to words by Walter Davison and is a fine example of madrigal-writing ; it ends with a beautiful passage :

tears . . . can-not pierce her heart, not pierce her

heart, nor sighs, nor sighs

her ears.

Ward was apparently a member of the household of Sir Henry Fanshawe. He died before 1641. Nothing is known of his personal history. In Adrian Batten's organ-book, in which several little notes are inserted giving the appointments held by the various composers, Ward is described by contrast as a ' gentillman '. This seems to imply that he was an amateur musician.[1]

---

[1] Batten's organ-book at St. Michael's College, Tenbury, fol. 64*b*.

The Madrigalian Publications of John Ward

1613. THE FIRST SET OF ENGLISH MADRIGALS

Songs of three voices

1. My true love hath my heart (*the first part*).
2. His heart his wound received (*the second part*).
3. O say, dear life, when shall these twin-born berries ?
4. In health and ease am I.
5. Go, wailing accents, go.
6. Fly not so fast, my only joy and jewel.

Songs of four voices

7. A satyr once did run away for dread.
8. O my thoughts, my thoughts, surcease.
9. Sweet pity, wake, and tell thy cruel sweet.
10. Love is a dainty mild and sweet.
11. Free from Love's bonds I lived long.
12. How long shall I with mournful music stain ?

Songs of five voices

13. Sweet Philomel, cease thou thy songs awhile (*the first part*).
14. Ye sylvan nymphs, that in these woods (*the second part*).

15. Flora, fair nymph, whilst silly lambs are feeding.
16. Phyllis the bright, when frankly she desired.
17. Hope of my heart.
18. Upon a bank with roses set about.

Songs of six voices

19. Retire, my troubled soul, rest and behold.
20. Oft have I tendered tributary tears.
21. Out from the vale of deep despair.
22. O divine love, which so aloft can raise.
23. If the deep sighs of an afflicted breast (*the first part*).
24. There's not a grove that wonders not my woe (*the second part*).
25. Die not, fond man, before thy day.
26. I have entreated and I have complained.
27. Come, sable night, put on thy mourning stole.
28. Weep forth your tears and do lament.

FRANCIS PILKINGTON. Born *circa* 1562 ; died 1638.

Francis Pilkington was one of those few lutenist-composers who published works in the two distinct styles that were in vogue in his time. His first publication belongs to the lutenists' class and will be noticed in the following chapter. Pilkington subsequently forsook the ' Air ' for the Madrigal and published two Sets of ' Madrigals and Pastorals ', issued respectively in the years 1613 and 1624. In these two Sets is some music of considerable interest, and *O softly-singing lute* (Set II, No. 24) is quite first-class. As a madrigal-writer Pilkington may best be compared with Michael East, although differing from him in technical details of style ; for, like East, he proved himself able to write in the true madrigalian manner with a full mastery of its idiom and technique, while his music, also, is generally of a bright nature without showing very marked individuality or any profound depth of feeling and imagination.

Pilkington set to music several lyrics which had already been used by other madrigalists ; for example, *I follow, lo, the footing* (Set I, No. 2) ; *Sovereign of my delight* (Set II, No. 1) and *Stay heart, run not so fast* (Set II, No. 4). Each of these was set by Morley at an earlier date, but the inevitable comparison is vastly in favour of Morley. Thus, in *I follow, lo, the footing*, Pilkington exhibited little of Morley's subtle imagination and humour. His treatment of the words *proud of herself* in this madrigal will serve to illustrate the statement. At that point Morley introduced in the Tenor-part a triple rhythm of more stately measure than that of the other voices, and he thus imparted a suggestion of haughty superiority which cannot be mistaken. Again, in this same composition Pilkington employed a rapid quaver figure for the words *will run me out of breath till I have caught her*, yet he failed to convey that vivid impression which is inseparable from Morley's handling of the same words, both as regards the breathless race and its termination. But to compare Pilkington with so great a giant is perhaps unfair, for he is undoubtedly to be accounted, at least, a worthy member of this great School of musicians. On the other hand, unlike most of the English madrigalists whose technique in vocal writing approached near to perfection, there are among Pilkington's madrigals some instances of rather awkward and unvocal passages. For example, the following phrase occurs in the Cantus-part of *Crowned with flowers* (Set II, No. 15) :

Hard by a fount of crys - tal.

No. 16 of the second Set is an 'Elegy on the death of his worshipful friend Master Thomas Purcell of Dinthill, Esq., in Salop'. It is stated that the coat-of-Arms on the monument of Henry Purcell, the composer, identifies him with the Shropshire Purcells ; too much value must not be placed on this class of evidence, but if it be so Pilkington's elegy is probably the earliest musical reference to this great name, and it is note-

worthy that this Thomas Purcell of Dinthill should figure as
the friend of so important a contemporary musician.

Francis Pilkington was probably in some way connected
with the Lancashire Pilkingtons, but no proof of this is forth-
coming. In an exhaustive genealogical study Colonel John
Pilkington proves that the composer cannot be identical with
a Francis Pilkington who was his contemporary and certainly
a member of the Lancashire family. The composer's father
was at one time in the service of the Stanleys, and this may
account for Francis coming to Chester. He was for many
years connected with Chester Cathedral, first of all as a lay-
clerk and subsequently as a Minor Canon, having been ordained
by the Bishop of Chester in 1614. He was appointed Precentor
of Chester in 1623 and at that time also held the living of Holy
Trinity in that town. His first Set of madrigals was dated rather
quaintly ' from my mansion in the monastery of Chester the
25 day of September 1612 '. He took the B.Mus. degree in
1595, having at that date studied music for sixteen years. In
the dedication of his final volume in 1624 he mentions his
' now aged Muse '. The known facts taken together make it
probable that the date of his birth was between the years 1560
and 1565. His death took place in 1638.

The Madrigalian Publications of Francis Pilkington

1613. THE FIRST SET OF MADRIGALS AND
PASTORALS OF 3. 4. AND 5. PARTS

Of three voices

1. See where my love a-maying goes.
2. I follow, lo, the footing.
3. Pour forth, mine eyes, the fountains of your tears.
4. Stay, O nymph, the ground seeks but to kiss.
5. Dorus, a silly shepherd swain.
6. Is this thy doom ?

Of four voices

7. Amyntas with his Phyllis fair.
8. Here rest, my thoughts.
9. Why should I grieve that she disdains ?
10. The messenger of the delightful Spring.

11. Have I found her ? O rich finding !
12. What though her frowns and hard entreaties kill ?
13. Love is a secret feeding fire.
14. Why do I fret and grieve ?
15. All in a cave a shepherd's lad.

Of five voices

16. Sing we, dance we on the green.
17. Under the tops of Helicon.
18. Sweet Phillida, my flocks as white.
19. My heart is dead within me.
20. No, no, no, it will not be.
21. When Oriana walked to take the air.
22. Now I see thou floutest me.

1624. THE SECOND SET OF MADRIGALS AND
PASTORALS OF 3. 4. 5. AND 6. PARTS

Of three voices

1. Sovereign of my delight.
2. Yond hill-tops Phoebus kissed.
3. Wake, sleepy Thyrsis, wake.
4. Stay, heart, run not so fast.
5. Ye bubbling springs, that gentle music makes.
6. Your fond preferments.

Of four voices

7. Menalcas in an evening walking was.
8. Coy Daphne fled from Phoebus (*the first part*).
9. Chaste Daphne fled from Phoebus (*the second part*).
10. If she neglect me.
11. Palaemon and his Sylvia forth must walk.
12. You gentle nymphs, that on these meadows play.

Of five voices

13. Chaste Syrinx fled, fear hasting on her pace.
14. Come, shepherds' weeds, attend my woeful cries.
15. Crowned with flowers, I saw fair Amaryllis.
16. Weep, sad Urania, weep.
17. O gracious God, pardon my great offence.
18. Go, you skipping kids and fawns.
19. Care for thy soul.
20. Drown not with tears, my dearest love.

Of six voices

21. Dear shepherdess, thou art more lovely fair (*the first part*).
22. Cruel Pabrilla, with thine angry look (*the second part*).
23. A fancy (*for the viols*).
24. O softly-singing lute.
25. O praise the Lord, all ye heathen.
26. Surcease, you youthful shepherdesses all.
27. A pavane (*for instruments*).

HENRY LICHFILD.   Date of birth and death unknown.

Henry Lichfild's only Set of madrigals was published in 1613 and consisted of twenty numbers, all of which are for five voices. This volume is not to be reckoned among the most important of the madrigal Sets, but the music throughout is interesting and of a good average level of merit. Lichfild wrote for the most part in a cheerful mood, though rarely showing that unrestrained feeling of gaiety which is expressed in other madrigals by frequent runs of quavers. He did not attempt the more serious kind of subject and was, perhaps, aware of his own limitations. Yet his writing was polished and vocal, and his work has a well-deserved place among the madrigal-writings of the great Elizabethans.

Perhaps the best piece in the Set is *I always loved to call my lady Rose* (No. 7). It opens with a simple rhythm treated homophonically and has a great charm ; it breathes the true madrigalian spirit in every bar. Another bright piece of work with a straightforward rhythm is *O come, shepherds, all together* (No. 8), inclining a little to convention towards the conclusion. *Ay me, when to the air* (No. 11) opens with a beautifully melodious phrase in the Cantus-part interwoven with the Quintus. The closing line *But with their Echo call me fool* is treated in the manner which all the madrigalists loved ; the word *fool*, on the final common chord, follows the last *echo* after a general silence of a minim's duration.

Lichfild seems to have been specially fond of the name of Daphne, which comes in as many as seven of his madrigals; it is introduced in a remarkable manner with a persistent triple rhythm in the last line of *Alas, my Daphne, stay* (No. 10).

Other interesting madrigals in the Set are *Injurious hours* (No. 18), with its curious creeping effect in the latter section, *Ay me ! that life should yet remain* (No. 5), and *Whilst that my lovely Daphne* (No. 19). This last named is somewhat in the style of the madrigals in the ' Triumphs of Oriana,' but ending with the words *Long live my lovely Daphne*.

The personal history of this composer is buried in obscurity except for the fact that he was in the service of Lady Cheyney, or Cheney, of Toddington House, a few miles from Luton in Bedfordshire. This fine house was left by Lord Cheney to his widow in 1587 ; she lived there till her death in 1614. She left Lichfild a legacy of £20.

The Madrigalian Publications of Henry Lichfild

1613. THE FIRST SET OF MADRIGALS OF 5. PARTS

1. All ye that sleep in pleasure.
2. Shall I seek to ease my grief ?
3. The shepherd Claius, seeing (*the first part*).
4. First with looks he lived and died (*the second part*).
5. Ay me ! that life should yet remain.
6. O my grief ! were it disclosed.
7. I always loved to call my lady Rose.
8. O come, shepherds, all together.
9. Sweet Daphne, stay thy flying.
10. Alas, my Daphne, stay but hear.
11. Ay me ! when to the air I breathe my plaining.
12. Arise, sweetheart, and come away to play.
13. When first I saw those cruel eyes (*the first part*).
14. If this be love to scorn my crying (*the second part*).
15. Cruel, let my heart be blessed.
16. A silly sylvan kissing heaven-born fire (*the first part*).
17. The sylvan justly suffered (*the second part*).
18. Injurious hours, whilst any joy doth bless me.
19. Whilst that my lovely Daphne.
20. My heart, oppressed by your disdaining.

THOMAS VAUTOR. Born *circa* 1590 ; date of death unknown.

Thomas Vautor, who in 1619 published his ' First Set : Beeing Songs of divers Ayres and Natures, of Five and Sixe parts : Apt for Vyols and Voyces ', is another madrigal-composer who has been allowed to slip into general neglect. This volume contains a good many madrigals of interest, although they cannot be compared with those of the great leaders of the School. It seems that Vautor was connected with Leicestershire ; he was domestic musician in the household of Sir George Villiers, father of the famous Duke of Buckingham. Lady Villiers was a Beaumont of Glanfield Hall and connected with the Beaumonts of Stoughton Grange. It was in memory of one of the Stoughton Beaumonts that Vautor wrote his Elegy *Weep, weep, mine eyes* (No. 16). The surname of Vautor is very uncommon and has not the appearance of English origin. It is not unlikely that it is a corruption of some Huguenot name, possibly of Vautier or even of Vautrollier ; and that leads to the further possibility that Thomas Vautor was a near relative of Thomas Vautrollier, the Elizabethan printer. But this is no more than conjecture. Vautor graduated B.Mus. at Oxford in 1616, and it may be supposed that he was born about the year 1590. The date of his death is not known.

The first three numbers in Vautor's Set are Ballets. In the first of these, *Come forth, sweet nymph,* the regular rhythm is broken by a delightful triple at the words *Dalida makes me sing.* The unusual time-signature, 6·1, that is here employed, was used also by Byrd ; it signifies six crotchets to the semibreve. The time-signature $_3\phi_2$, which Vautor used in *Shepherds and nymphs* (No. 22), is seldom to be found elsewhere in the madrigal-books. *O merry world* (No. 10) is a gay type of madrigal. *Dainty sweet bird* (No. 18) is also characteristic of this composer, but it compares poorly with the wonderful setting of the same words by Gibbons. There are certain points of similarity which suggest that Vautor was, consciously or unconsciously, influenced by Gibbons's setting. Thus the opening phrase is nearly identical in outline :

And in the concluding bars the similarity is even more
noticeable :

Yet Vautor did also write with an individuality of style, and
in some respects his idiom was more modern than that of the
other English madrigalists.   These characteristics are exemplified in *Sweet Suffolk owl* (No. 12), which is designed on quite
important lines.   One phrase which especially arrests the
attention, as being quite unlike anything in the work of such
composers as Wilbye or Weelkes, is that which Vautor used at
the words *with feathers like a lady bright* ; the whole phrase is
recited on one full chord reiterated homophonically in quavers
in all the voices simultaneously, and the same effect is repeated
a few bars later.   Another feature of this madrigal is the
recapitulation of the telling section *Te whit te whoo*, which
brings the composition to a close.

The final madrigal in this Set, *Shepherds and nymphs* (No. 22)
is framed on the lines of the ' Triumphs of Oriana ', and it holds
its own in comparison with many of those in that famous
collection.   The composer used a very good ' bell ' phrase at the
words *both bon-fires and bell-ringers*.   In spite of the passages

quoted from *Dainty sweet bird*, it must be admitted that Vautor aimed at originality of style, and that he usually achieved his purpose in that direction.

The Madrigalian Publications of Thomas Vautor

1619. SONGS OF DIVERS AIRS AND NATURES
OF FIVE AND SIX PARTS

Songs of five voices

1. Come forth, sweet nymph, and play thee.
2. Sing on, sister, and well met.
3. Ah sweet, whose beauty passeth all my telling.
4. Mother, I will have a husband.
5. Fairest are the words that cover deep'st conceit.
6. Cruel Madam, my heart you have bereft me.
7. Never did any more delight to see.
8. Lock up, fair lids, the treasures of my heart (*the first part*).
9. And yet, O dream, if thou wilt not depart (*the second part*).
10. O merry world, when every lover with his mate.
11. Sweet thief, when me of heart you reft.

12. Sweet Suffolk owl, so trimly dight.
13. Thou art not fair for all thy red and white (*the first part*).
14. Yet love me not, nor seek not to allure (*the second part*).
15. Mira cano, sol occubuit.
16. Weep, weep, mine eyes; salt tears due honour give.

Songs of six voices

17. Blush, my rude present, blushing yet this say.
18. Dainty sweet bird, who art encaged there.
19. Unkind, is this the meed of lover's pain?
20. Melpomene, bewail thy sisters' loss (*the first part*).
21. Whilst fatal sisters held the bloody knife (*the second part*).
22. Shepherds and nymphs, that trooping.

MARTIN PEERSON. Born *circa* 1580 ; died 1650

Martin Peerson is a composer who ought not to be entirely passed over in connexion with the English Madrigal School, although he is not, strictly speaking, to be classed as a pure madrigal-writer.   Hardly any of the compositions in his two published Sets can really be styled Madrigals; the large majority of them are of the nature of duets or songs, with a chorus or refrain in which additional voices take part.   However, the influence of the madrigalists does show itself in a marked degree upon Peerson's music, so that he occupies an interesting position on transitional ground between the madrigalian era and the Restoration period.

Peerson was born about the year 1580, and in early manhood

he became ' Master of the children ' in St. Paul's Cathedral. He died in 1650 and was buried in the Chapel of St. Faith in the Cathedral. He left a substantial legacy to the poor of the parish of Dunnington in the Isle of Ely, and this circumstance seems to suggest that it was his birthplace, for he does not appear to have had any subsequent connexion with Dunnington after taking up his appointment at St. Paul's.

His first published volume appeared in 1620 and was entitled ' Private Musicke, Or the First Booke of Ayres and Dialogues, Contayning Songs of 4. 5. and 6. parts, of severall sorts, and being verse and Chorus is fit for Voyces and Viols.' The title itself indicates the transitional character of the music. Some of the pieces are more or less madrigalian in style, but most of them are of the verse and chorus type mentioned in the title, and many of them contain short instrumental interludes. *Upon my lap my Sovereign sits* (No. 12) is, for instance, for two voices and accompaniment. *Sing, Love is blind* (No. 18) is much more modern in design than the Madrigal ; it ends with a pretty *hey nonny no* treated in the style of harmonized melody rather than in imitative counterpoint. The last piece in the volume was composed as early as 1604, although it was not published until 1620 ; it was written ' for the King and Queenes entertaynment at High-gate on May day ' in that year to words by Ben Jonson. This illustrates the practice of the composers of those days in waiting to publish their music until they had compiled a sufficient number of pieces to fill a volume ; it can never be assumed with certainty that the date of the publication of a particular madrigal coincides even approximately with the date of its composition.

Peerson's second Set was published in 1630 and contained twenty-five compositions of various kinds. It bore the following curious title, ' Mottects or Grave Chamber Musique, Containing Songs of five parts of severall sorts, some ful, and some Verse and Chorus. But all fit for Voyces and Vials, with an Organ Part ; which for want of Organs, may be performed on Virginals, Bass-Lute, Bandora, or Irish Harpe.' The organ accompaniment was an innovation in this kind of music ; and indeed the Virginal had not been named as an alternative to the lute or other instruments for the purposes of accompaniment before Peerson's

earlier volume in 1620. The term Motet was employed by
Peerson in the same sense as that in which Gibbons used it ;
but, in spite of the title, some of the pieces in this volume are
set to words of a light and amorous nature ; for example,
Cupid, my pretty boy (No. 10).

The whole of the poems in Peerson's 1630 volume, with the
exception of the Elegy at the conclusion which was set twice to
independent music, are drawn from the *Caelica* Sonnets of Fulke
Greville, Lord Brooke. This poet died in 1628, two years before
Peerson's Set was published, and it was in his memory that the
two settings of the Elegy were composed.

The Madrigalian Publications of Martin Peerson

1620. PRIVATE MUSIC, OR THE FIRST BOOK
OF AIRS AND DIALOGUES

Of four voices

1. Open the door ! who 's there within ?
2. Resolved to love, unworthy to obtain.
3. Ah, were she pitiful as she is fair.
4. Disdain, that so doth fill me.
5. O precious Time, created by the might.
6. Can a maid that is well bred ?
7. O I do love, then kiss me.
8. Since just disdain began to rise.
9. At her fair hands how have I grace entreated !
10. Now Robin, laugh and sing.
11. Hey the horn, the horn-a.
12. Upon my lap my Sovereign sits.
13. Lock up, fair lids, the treasure of my heart.
14. Love her no more, herself she doth not love.
15. Come, pretty wag, and sing (*the first part*).

Of five voices

16. Then with reports most sprightly (*the second part*).
17. Pretty wantons, sweetly sing.
18. Sing, Love is blind.
19. What need the morning rise ?
20. Gaze not on Youth ; let Age contain (*the first part*).
21. True pleasure is in chastity (*the second part*).
22. The spring of joy is dry.

Of six voices

23. Is not that my fancy's Queen ?
24. See, O see, who comes here a maying ?

1630. MOTETS, OR GRAVE CHAMBER MUSIC
containing songs of 5 parts of several sorts

1. Love, the delight of all well-thinking minds (*the first part*).
2. Beauty, her cover, is the eye's true pleasure (*the second part*).
3. Time fain would stay that she might never leave her (*the third part*).
4. More than most fair (*the first part*).
5. Thou window of the sky (*the second part*).
6. You little stars that live in skies (*the first part*).
7. And thou, O Love, which in those eyes (*the second part*).

{ 8. O Love, thou mortal sphere of powers divine (*the first part*).
{ 9. If I by nature, wonder, and delight (*the second part*).
  10. Cupid, my pretty boy, leave off thy crying.
  11. Love is the peace whereto all thoughts do strive.
  12. Self-pity's tears, wherein my hope lies drowned.
  13. Was ever man so matched with a boy ?
  14. O false and treacherous Probability.
{ 15. Man, dream no more of curious mysteries (*the first part*).
{ 16. The flood that did, and dreadful fire that shall (*the second part*).
{ 17. Who trusts for trust, or hopes of love for love (*the first part*).
{ 18. Who thinks that sorrow felt (*the second part*).
  19. Man, dream no more of curious mysteries.
  20. Farewell, sweet boy, complain not of my truth.
  21. Under a throne I saw a virgin sit.
{ 22. Where shall a sorrow great enough be sought ? (*the first part*).
{ 23. Dead, noble Brooke shall be to us a name (*the second part*).

for six voices

{ 24. Where shall a sorrow great enough be sought ? (*the first part*).
{ 25. Dead, noble Brooke shall be to us a name (*the second part*).

THOMAS TOMKINS. Born 1572 ; died 1656

Thomas Tomkins published in 1622 what was, in the stricter use of the term, the last volume of first-rate importance in the great series of English madrigals which began with Byrd's ' Psalms, Sonnets, and Songs ' in 1588. In spite of its late date this volume must be reckoned among the most valuable contributions to the series. It is consequently very remarkable that Tomkins's music should have experienced such complete neglect, as has been the case, ever since the popularity of madrigal-singing declined in his own lifetime. Except for one or two recent reprints, none of the work of this very notable English musician is known to his own countrymen, and it is not improbable that a large number of musicians of the present day have never even heard of his name.

According to his own statement in the dedication of his ' Songs ' in 1622, Tomkins was born in Pembrokeshire. The surname was entirely foreign to West Wales in the sixteenth century, and the only known record of it is to be found in the archives of St. David's Cathedral. There can, in consequence, be no room for doubt in connecting Thomas the composer with the family, two members of which held musical positions at St. David's. These were Thomas Tomkins who was organist of the cathedral in 1571, and his son Thomas, who, though still a chorister boy, and possibly no more than seven or eight years of age, was appointed a lay-clerk in 1577 with the purpose of increasing his father's stipend.[1] Further information as to the Tomkins family is supplied by the pedigree in the Worcestershire Visitation of 1634,[2] which bears the autograph signature of the composer, and also that in the Visitation of Herefordshire in 1683.[3] From these and other sources of evidence the following facts may be evolved : Thomas Tomkins, the elder, was the son of Ralph Tomkins, of Lostwithiel in Cornwall, where the family had owned property for some generations ; he disposed of this property in early life and became organist of St. David's Cathedral, where he had two sons by his first marriage, to both of whom he gave the name of Thomas, as is shown in the official visitation pedigrees. The elder of these boys was the chorister who became a lay-clerk in 1577 ; he was summarily dismissed in 1586, went to sea and lost his life with Sir Richard Grenville in the *Revenge* in 1596. His brother Thomas was the composer. He was certified to be aged 78 in June 1650.[4] He was married about 1598 to Alice, daughter of —— Hassard, who is, doubtless, to be identified with the widow of his predecessor, Nathaniel Pattrick ; and his son Nathaniel, ultimately a Canon of Worcester, was born in 1598 or 1599. He became organist of Worcester Cathedral about this date and took the B.Mus. degree at Oxford in 1607. In 1621 he was appointed one of the organists of the Chapel Royal, and in 1628 he succeeded Ferrabosco as Composer-in-ordinary to Charles I. While in this position he wrote the large number of Church Services and Anthems which were published after his death under the title of *Musica Deo sacra*. He died in 1656 and was buried at Martin Hassingtree in Worcestershire.

Meanwhile his father married a second time and had several other sons, several of whom were distinguished musicians. The eldest of this second family was John, who was born in 1586 and became organist of St. Paul's Cathedral. Later in life the father took Holy Orders and became Minor Canon—subse-

---

[1] Chapter Records of St. David's Cathedral.
[2] MSS. in the College of Arms.　　[3] Ibid.　　[4] Domestic State Papers P.R.O.

quently Precentor—of Gloucester Cathedral about the year
1595; in 1596 he was Vicar of St. Mary-de-Lode, Gloucester,
holding this living together with the minor-canonry. He died
in 1626, having resigned the Precentorship about a year earlier.[1]

These facts have been set out here at some length, partly
because they provide a good deal of new information, and
partly because the authorship of *The fauns and satyrs*, the
Oriana madrigal which bears the name of Thomas Tomkins,
depends upon them. The question of the authorship of this
madrigal cannot be settled with complete certainty, but it is
clear that the younger Tomkins was at least 25 years old
in 1601, when the ' Triumphs ' were published, and was already
organist of Worcester Cathedral ; there is also no evidence
that his father was a composer. It therefore seems reasonable
to assign the authorship of the Oriana madrigal to the Worcester
Tomkins, the composer of the 1622 Set of Songs.

These ' Songs of 3. 4. 5. and 6. parts '—the term ' Madrigal '
is not actually employed—consist of twenty-eight compositions.
Four of them are set to scripture words, and these, with the
exception of *David's Lament for Absalom* (No. 19), do not quite
reach the same standard as the rest of the volume. Nine of the
secular numbers have a *fa-la*, or equivalent refrain, but of these
only a small minority can be regarded as Ballets in the strictest
sense. It says much for the inventive genius of Tomkins that
he was able to add something new to the *fa-la* form when it
might have been thought that the last word in its development
had been said by Morley and Weelkes. The most conventional
of these *fa-las* is *To the shady woods* (No. 13) ; but in most of
the others there is some distinctive rhythmic figure of a novel
kind, and *See, see the shepherds' Queen* (No. 17) is constructed
in three sections as compared with the two sections of the older
Ballet. Tomkins also showed a tendency to abandon the dance
rhythm, which, quite apart from the *fa-la*, was an essential
feature in this form in Morley's time ; a noticeable example
of this is to be seen in *Too much I once lamented* (No. 14), which
was dedicated to his ' ancient and much reverenced Master,
William Byrd ', and which, apart from the *fa-la*, is quite severe

---

[1] The author is indebted to Sir Ivor Atkins, organist of Worcester Cathedral,
for some of the fresh details concerning this composer.

in character and very far removed from dance-measure. Similar in style is the remarkable *O let me live for true love* (Nos. 7 and 8), which is elaborately laid out as regards design, and shows some very original harmonization, notably in the *fa-las* that follow the opening phrase of the second half of the piece. Among the most beautiful of the madrigals in this fine Set is *Weep no more, thou sorry boy* (Nos. 10 and 11), the beauty of which increases towards the end. The following phrase from this number could hardly be surpassed :

A little further is this beautiful passage :

and the madrigal concludes with series of sequences the harmonies of which must have been regarded as very original at the time of the publication of this volume. The passage should be sung rather slowly and with pathos :

The originality of Tomkins's harmonies may be further illustrated by a brief excerpt from another very fine madrigal, *Was ever wretch tormented ?* (No. 12). The sequence of $\frac{6}{4}$ chords employed here is especially interesting, while the low position of all the voices is, of course, designed with particular reference to the words at this point of the poem :

One more quotation from this Set may perhaps be allowed :
the closing passage of *When I observe those beauty's wonderments*
(No. 23) is intensely beautiful and may be compared even with
the best work of Wilbye :

There appear to have been two editions of this Set of Tomkins's,
for among the surviving copies of this work there are two
noteworthy variants on the title-page ; in one case the date
1622 is printed at the foot of the page, but in the other case
this is replaced by a line and the formula *Cum priuilegio*. This
fact seems to have remained unnoticed. In consequence the
writer of the article on Tomkins in the ' Dictionary of National
Biography ' states that the Set is undated, whereas Rimbault
and other writers give the date 1622. Assuming the undated
edition to be the earlier of the two, it is still necessary to assign
this date to it, because Heather is described as *Doctor* Heather
in the dedication of No. 24 of the Set, and he did not take the
D.Mus. degree until May 1622. It seems likely that this Set of
Madrigals gained immediate popularity and that a second
edition had to be issued in the same year, the date then being
added in the place of *Cum priuilegio* on the title-page.

The Madrigalian Publications of Thomas Tomkins

1622. SONGS OF 3. 4. 5. AND 6. PARTS

Songs of three parts
1. Our hasty life away doth post.
2. No more I will thy love importune.
3. Sure, there is no god of Love.
4. Fond men, that do so highly prize.
5. How great delight from those sweet lips.
6. Love, cease tormenting.

Songs of four parts
{ 7. O let me live for true love (*the first part*).
{ 8. O let me die for true love (*the second part*).
9. Oyez ! has any found a lad ?
{ 10. Weep no more, thou sorry boy (*the first part*).
{ 11. Yet again, as soon revived (*the second part*).
12. Was ever wretch tormented ?

Songs of five parts
13. To the shady woods now wend we.
14. Too much I once lamented.
15. Come, shepherds, sing with me.
16. Cloris, whenas I woo.
17. See, see the shepherds' Queen.
18. Phyllis, now cease to move me.
19. When David heard that Absalom was slain.
20. Phyllis, yet see him dying.
21. Fusca, in thy starry eyes.
22. Adieu, ye city-prisoning towers.

Songs of six parts
23. When I observe those beauty's wonderments.
24. Music divine, proceeding from above.
25. Oft did I marle how in thine eyes.
26. Woe is me, that I am constrained.
27. It is my well-beloved's voice.
28. Turn unto the Lord our God.

1601. A MADRIGAL FOR FIVE VOICES
included as No. 10 in the ' Triumphs of Oriana '.

The fauns and satyrs tripping.

Tomkins's Set is unique in one particular, for, besides following the practice observed by all the other madrigalists of dedicating his volume to some personal friend or patron (in this case to Lord Pembroke), he also made a separate dedication of each of the twenty-eight pieces in the Set. The names are of sufficient interest to be quoted in detail :

1. To my deare Father Mr. Thomas Tomkins.
2. To Mr. William Walker.
3. To Mr. Humfrey Witby.
4. To my Brother Mr. Nicholas Tomkins.
5. To Master William Crosse.
6. To Master Thomas Day.
7. To Doctor Douland.
8. To Master John Daniell.
9. To Master John Coprario.
10. To my Brother Peregrine Tomkins.
11. To my Brother Robert Tomkins.
12. To my Brother Giles Tomkins.
13. To Mr. Robert Chetwode.

14. To my ancient and much rever-
    enced Master, William Byrd.
15. To Mr. Nathaniel Giles.
16. To Mr. Orlando Gibbons.
17. To Mr. John Steevens.
18. To Mr. Henry Molle.
19. To Mr. Thomas Myriell.
20. To Mr. Nicholas Carlton.
21. To Mr. Phinees Fletcher.
22. To Mr. William White.
23. To Mr. Thomas Warwicke.
24. To Mr. Doctor Heather.
25. To Master John Ward.
26. To my Brother John Tomkins.
27. To Mr. Doctor Ailmer.
28. To my sonne Nathanael Tomkins.

JOHN HILTON.   Born 1599 ; died 1657

As late as 1627 John Hilton, the younger, published his Set
of 'Ayres, or, *Fa las* for Three Voyces'. The merest glance at the
dates given in the preface of the Musical Antiquarian Society's
reprint of this volume in 1844 makes it quite obvious that this
John Hilton was not to be identified with the contributor to
the 'Triumphs of Oriana' who bore the same name.[1] It is
strange that neither Rimbault nor Oliphant appears to have
noticed this, nor yet the writer of the notice of Hilton in the
'Dictionary of National Biography', though he nevertheless
observed some discrepancies. The younger Hilton was born
in 1599 and is now proved to be the son of the organist of
Trinity College, Cambridge. He took his B.Mus. degree at
Cambridge in 1626, but he appears to have been a pupil of
Dr. William Heather, the founder of the Chair of Music in
Oxford University.   He died in 1657 and was buried at
St. Margaret's, Westminster, of which church he was for many
years Organist and Parish Clerk.

Although the alternative term Air is employed in the title-
page of this Set there is only one piece in it which is not actually
a Ballet, namely *When Flora frowns* (No. 17). The volume as
a whole is disappointing ; the ballets are very conventional
and cannot be compared with those of Morley, Weelkes, or
Tomkins ; and this is all the more noticeable seeing that
Tomkins published *Fa-las* of such remarkable distinction only
five years earlier than Hilton. The best composition in the
Set is, perhaps, *Leave off, sad Philomel, to sing* (No. 11).

---

[1] See p. 245.

The Madrigalian Publications of John Hilton

1627. AIRS OR FA-LAS FOR THREE VOICES

1. To sport, our merry meeting.
2. My mistress frowns when she should play (*the first part*)
3. You lovers that have loves astray (*the second part*).
4. Phoebe tells me when I woo.
5. Celia's wound and mine were one.
6. Dear, may some other, since not I?
7. Though me you did disdain to view.
8. Love wounded me but did not touch.
9. The woodbine, Flora, doth decay.
10. I heard a withered maid complain.
11. Leave off, sad Philomel, to sing.
12. O had not Venus been beguiled.
13. Tell me, dear, fain would I know.
14. Faint not, lovers, for denials.
15. Gifts of feature and of mind.
16. As Flora slept and I lay waking.
17. When Flora frowns I hope for peace.
18. Love laid his yoke upon me.
19. Now is the Summer springing.
20. Come, sprightly mirth, like birds in the Spring.
21. Come, love, let's crown this famous night.
22. Hero, kiss me or I die (*the first part*).
23. Quickly send them unto me (*the second part*).
24. If it be love to sit and mourn.
25. Fly, Philomel, to deserts fly.
26. Who master is in Music's art.

PETER PHILIPS, date of birth unknown; died 1625

The subject of the Tudor madrigalists could not be said to have been fully discussed without any mention of Peter Philips. This composer was an Englishman by birth, but spent all his life abroad; consequently, although he must certainly be accounted one of the best English composers of the period, yet his style was in every detail moulded upon the Italian design and showed no trace of English influence. For this reason it would not be correct to reckon him as belonging to the English Madrigal School. For the same reason, too, the work of William Costeley lies outside the scope of the present volume; he was a Scotsman by birth, but spent his life almost entirely in France. Nevertheless Philips was a very eminent as well as a very voluminous composer, excelling chiefly in ecclesiastical music. But he was also an important contributor to madrigal-literature, and he published at least four Sets of madrigals, some of which went through several editions within a few years. The first of these was entitled *Melodia Olympica di diversi Eccellentissimi Musici a iv, v, vi, et viii voci,* and was published at Antwerp in 1591. This was followed in 1596 by

Il Primo Libro di Madrigali a sei voci. His *Madrigali a otto voci* was published in 1598, and *Il secondo Libro di madrigali a sei voci* in 1603. Philips wrote in a highly polished style, showing an absolute mastery of technique. Such dissonances as we find in the work of Byrd, Weelkes, Kirbye, and Wilbye are never to be found in the smooth writing of Philips. There is no trace of the experimental tendency, which led the English School to employ augmented chords and progressions or other harmonic innovations ; neither do we find anything of the severe character which, for example, Orlando Gibbons displayed in his madrigals ; nor again that complexity of rhythm for which many of the English School showed a partiality. Yet if the specially English features are absent from the music of this Englishman, we must still praise the excellence of his attainments in a foreign style, for, without doubt, as an all-round musician he takes very high rank among European composers, both in England and on the Continent, at the close of the sixteenth century. Philips's madrigals were written almost entirely to Italian words.

The following are characteristic examples of Philips's smooth and massive style : *Questa che co begl' occh' allum' il mondo cieco* (No. 1 of his eight-part Set) ; *Echo, Figlia dei bosch'e de le valli*, in two sections (Nos. 20 and 21 of the same Set) ; and nothing could be more delightful than *Dispiegate guancie amate* which Mr. Barclay Squire has reprinted. One English madrigal by Peter Philips was included by Morley in his ' Madrigals to five voyces Celected out of the best approved Italian Authors ' published in 1598. The words begin *The nightingale that sweetly doth complain* (Nos. 19 and 20) ; it is of considerable length and is beautifully written. It is noteworthy that for the words *to learn by proof in this case that I run* are set with a run of crotchets where Morley himself and other English madrigalists would undoubtedly have used quavers ; and the example serves to emphasize the divergent influence of the training that was characteristic of the different Schools to which these composers belonged.

The date of Philips's birth is not known. He left England in early life, and having been ordained in the Church of Rome, he was appointed to a canonry at Bethune in Flanders towards the end of the sixteenth century. In 1610 he became a Canon of St. Vincent in Soignies, and he died there in 1625.

CHAPTER XX

THE ENGLISH LUTENIST-COMPOSERS

SINCE the term Madrigal has been commonly employed to describe compositions of Dowland, Ford, and other famous lutenists of the period, it will be evident that a book which purports to deal with the subject of the English madrigalists and their works could not be regarded as complete if the lutenists should be entirely ignored. Moreover, a few of the lutenists' Airs in their harmonized form for four voices approach so closely to the madrigal-style as sometimes to be almost indistinguishable from the simpler compositions which have an indisputable claim to the title. This is particularly the case with some of the Airs of Pilkington, and very occasionally with those of Dowland. But it is not here proposed to examine all the lutenists' work in such detail as that of the madrigalists, and some of these composers will receive no more than a passing notice.

The form and construction of the lutenists' Airs has been already considered in a former chapter ;[1] but it may be repeated that they were much more regular in rhythmic outline than the Madrigals ; that they were harmonized for the most part on homophonic rather than polyphonic principles ; and that a lute-part was invariably printed with the music. This lute-part was intended primarily to be used for the purpose of accompanying the highest voice-part when rendered as solo-song ; but sometimes the composers extended this principle and made any single one of the voice-parts available for use as solo-song with the lute accompaniment. The lute might also be used for accompanying the combined voices, but it was rarely regarded as an indispensable feature in the performance when sufficient voices were available for the rendering of all the parts. Very occasionally it was excluded

[1] See p. 60.

from such employment by reason of the introduction of variant harmonies, which, although suitable and effective in accompanying the solo-voice, might conflict sharply with the combined harmony of the voices. A part for bass viol was added.

The system of tablature commonly employed by the English lutenists was as follows : A stave of six lines was used ; this stave had no connexion whatever with the stave of ordinary musical notation, but represented the six strings of the lute in a semi-pictorial fashion. On the finger-board of the instrument a series of ivory frets were fixed, and the pressure on the string by the player's finger behind any of these frets shortened its length by a measured proportion and so raised the pitch of the string. Each fret was designed to raise the pitch by a semitone. The particular fret to be ' stopped ' in this manner, with the object of producing any required note of music, was indicated by a letter of the alphabet printed in the tablature immediately above the string to which it applied. These letters have no reference at all to the names of the notes. Thus the letter *a* denoted the ' open ' string, and each succeeding letter represented an added semitone in the rising chromatic scale. The distinctive style of the Elizabethan *e* enables the eye quickly to differentiate it from *c* where italics of modern type might lead to confusion. The six strings of the lute were known as the treble, small mean, great mean, counter-tenor, tenor, and bass, and all but the treble were strung double. The normal tuning in England was to the notes :

The sixth or bass string was frequently tuned to F instead of G. A seventh string, ordinarily tuned to D, was often added below the bass string ; but to avoid confusion to the eye it occupied no permanent place on the stave, but was introduced when occasion required on exactly the same principle as that by which notes are introduced with leger lines in ordinary notation. The following diagram will serve as a key for translating lute-tablature into ordinary notation :

		a	b	c	d	e	f	g	h
Treble	(G)	a	b	c	d	e	f	g	h
Small mean	(D)	a	b	c	d	e	f	g	h
Great mean	(A)	a	b	c	d	e	f	g	h
Counter-tenor	(F)	a	b	c	d	e	f	g	h
Tenor	(C)	a	b	c	d	e	f	g	h
Bass	(G)	a	b	c	d	e	f	g	h

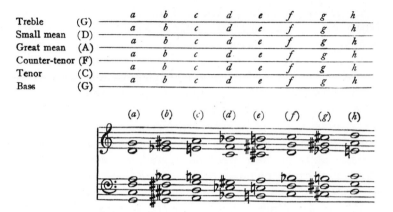

The sustaining value of the notes or chords was shown by a system of signs placed above the stave. These signs, ⌐ ⋈ ⋈ ⋈ ⋈, represented severally the semibreve, minim, crotchet, quaver, and semiquaver ; dots of augmentation, bearing their ordinary signification, were added when required. The signs were used as sparsely as possible ; thus if no sign appears over a note its length is governed by the sign last used. For example, a group of four successive crotchets would have the ⋈ over the first of the group only. It will be obvious that this system necessitated the introduction of some kind of barring, and allusion to this matter has already been made in a former chapter. The regularity of the barring varied considerably ; sometimes it adhered fairly closely to the time-signatures, but at others it followed the less regular rhythms of the music or of the verbal phrases, and occasionally bar-lines were entirely absent for a prolonged period.

For the purpose of indicating the particular moment at which the notes were to be struck this system of tablature was an exact one ; but as regards the harmonic structure of the music it left room for some uncertainty and ambiguity, much being left to the imagination of the listener, such imagination being itself based upon a conventional experience as regards the resolution of certain discords and other harmonic details. One illustration will serve to explain this point. (The passage is from Dowland, Bk. I, No. 20).

Literally translated this reads :

With the full harmonic outline developed and displayed this becomes :

The pairs of consecutive fifths in the above passage are characteristic of the disregard for scientific harmonic progression which is frequently involved owing to the limitations of the lute. Such progressions can, of course, be easily and quite legitimately avoided by a somewhat freer adaptation of the literal text of the tablature ; but it will be readily recognized that transcription and arrangement of the lute-part for modern use on a pianoforte must always call for a large measure of discretion and taste.

JOHN DOWLAND.   Born 1562 ; died 1626

By far the most important of the lutenist-composers was John Dowland, who indeed holds a very high place among the most distinguished English musicians of all periods. He was a man of remarkable personality, and it is probably not too much to say that in his own time no other musician in Europe was so widely known, not only for the genial nature which brought him friends in the many countries in which he travelled, but also on account of his rare genius both as a performer on the lute and as a composer. Among his many friends was the famous Italian madrigalist Luca Marenzio. Dowland appears to have studied under Marenzio in Italy,[1] and in the ' Address to the Courteous Reader ' of his ' First Booke of Songes or Ayres ', published in 1597, he alludes to a letter from this famous Italian composer.

Dr. Grattan Flood, in an important article upon Dowland which adds a finishing touch to Mr. Barclay Squire's valuable researches into this composer's history,[2] has finally disposed of the tradition that he was born in Westminster. He was in fact born in Ireland at Christmastide 1562, possibly at Dalkey, Co. Dublin, where his father John Dowlan is known to have lived at a later date. Richard Dowland, sexton of Christ Church Cathedral, Dublin, may have been his brother. The surname is commonly found in Ireland in the form of Dolan. The father died in 1577, and about a year later the boy came to England. In 1580 he went to Paris as a page in the train of Sir Henry Cobham[3] and during this period he became a convert to the Roman Catholic faith. His stay in Paris lasted three years. On his return he was married, and his son Robert was born in 1586. He took the degree of B.Mus. at Oxford in 1588, and in 1592 was one of the contributors to East's 'Whole Booke of Psalmes'. In 1594, after failing, perhaps for religious reasons, to obtain appointment as one of the Queen's musicians, Dowland went to Italy, as already stated, to study under Marenzio, and remained on the Continent for at least two years ; but on his return, after spending a short time in England, he seems to have resided as a graduate in Trinity College, Dublin,[4] having once more become a Protestant.

Dowland produced his ' First Booke of Songes or Ayres of fowre partes with Tableture for the Lute ' in 1597. This book immediately became immensely popular, and went through more

[1] Salisbury Papers, vol. v, p. 269. Hist. MSS. Commission.
[2] Gentleman's Magazine, 1906, pp. 287–91.
[3] Salisbury Papers, vol. v, p. 447. Hist. MSS. Commission.
[4] Mahaffy's Particular Book of Trinity College, p. 236.

editions in quick succession than any other publication of Tudor music, the fifth edition appearing in 1613. Dowland had by this time laid the foundation of that great reputation which won the applause of so many of the poets of the early seventeenth century. In 1598 he was appointed lutenist to Christian IV, King of Denmark, and resided at Elsinore, with one short interval in 1601, until the year 1609, when he finally returned to his native country. He had in the meantime published his second and third ' Books of Airs ', in the years 1600 and 1603 respectively.

On his final return to England Dowland lived the life of a disappointed man. Having enjoyed an unusual degree of popularity on the Continent, he found that he had been superseded and partially forgotten among his fellow countrymen. Moreover, he appears to have spent his income freely and with a light-hearted gaiety, so that his loss of popularity coincided with straitened means. Further circumstances helped to sadden and embitter his life : he professed dislike of many modern tendencies of musical development, although what this expression exactly could have meant is difficult to conjecture, coming as it did from the pen of the composer of such a song as *From silent night* (' A Pilgrimes Solace ', No. 10) with its amazingly modern harmonic developments. And he also nourished a keen resentment against the lutenists of a younger generation on the ground that they imitated his style and arrogated to themselves the credit for it. In the preface to his final publication, ' A Pilgrimes Solace ', which appeared in 1612, he indulged in a general complaint against the older generation who 'say what I do after the old manner ', and also against ' the young men, professors of the Lute, who vaunt themselves to the disparagement of such as have been before their time (wherein I myself am a party) that there never was the like of them '. At this time Dowland held the appointment of lutenist to Lord Walden at Audley End, and later he was one of the six lutenists to Charles I. Dowland died in London, and the actual date of his death is given as January 21, 1626, in the papers of the Dublin family of Forster to whom Dowland seems to have been related. The date is consistent with an entry in the Audit Office Declared Accounts in the

Record Office ; [1] this entry records the payment of his salary
as the king's lutenist for the quarter ending at Christmas 1625
and for twenty-six days of the following quarter.   Dowland
dedicated one of the songs in 'A Pilgrimes Solace' to John
Forster of Dublin.   The place of his burial remains unknown.
His son Robert succeeded him as one of the royal lutenists.
Matthew Dowland, buried at St. Margaret's, Westminster, in
1628, may have been a son or brother of John.

Dowland's greatness showed itself in several directions.
In the first place he was a melodist of the very first order,
standing among the greatest of the world's song-writers.   His
' First Book of Airs ' represented an entirely new departure.
This publication formed the foundation of the English school
of lutenist-composers, a school which had no parallel on the
Continent ; while in his later books of airs, notably ' A Pilgrimes
Solace ', Dowland evinced that same spirit which characterized
so many of the great poets and musicians of that period, in
that he was searching for new forms, and for fresh combinations
of instruments and voices for the purpose of expressing his
ideas.   And he was an innovator in yet another direction ; for
in the chromatic treatment of his harmonies he was, at the
very outset of his career, no less original than Weelkes, while
the song *From silent night*, published in 1612, must be placed
with Weelkes's *O Care, thou wilt despatch me* (Set III, Nos. 4
and 5) as one of the musical marvels of the Elizabethan age.
The chromatic scale passage in this song, which is for solo-
voice accompanied with the lute and with treble and bass
viols, is closely reminiscent of the phrase employed by Weelkes
towards the close of his *Cease, sorrows, now* (Set I, No. 6) and
also of Dowland's own *All ye whom Love or Fortune* (Book I,
No. 14) ; but in this later song Dowland indulged in still
more elaborate chromatic development and rivalled Weelkes
in introducing an A sharp as a definite part of the harmonic
structure.   There are also some other surprisingly modern
features in this song, from which the following few bars may
be quoted :

[1] Audit Office Decld. Accts., Bundle 392, No. 65.

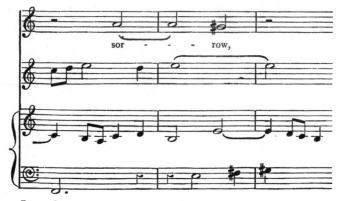

In order to convey a more complete idea of the nature of the originality of Dowland's writing, this further illustration will be found interesting : it forms the concluding passage of *When the poor cripple* (No. 16 of ' A Pilgrimes Solace ') :

Dowland's use of chromatic harmonies constituted one of the grave charges which Burney saw fit to bring against him at a period in which so much false and ignorant prejudice was engendered with reference to the Tudor composers. But his music was not always of a chromatic character ; the beauty of many of his songs rests upon their simplicity, purity of melody, and perfection of verbal phrasing as in *Come away, come, sweet love* (Book I, No. 11) ; *Rest awhile* (Book I, No. 12) ; *Awake, sweet love* (Book I, No. 19) ; *White as lilies* (Book II, No. 15) ; *Shall I sue* (Book II, No. 19) ; *By a fountain* (Book III, No. 12) ; *I must complain* (Bk. III, No. 17) ; *Were every thought an eye* (Book IV, No. 6). But whether he was chromatic or diatonic, grave or gay, his songs almost without exception are of the very finest quality. Nothing could be finer, for instance, than *Burst forth, my tears* (Book I, No. 8) ; *Toss not, my soul* (Book II, No. 20) ; *Weep you no more, sad fountains* (Book III, No. 15) among many others.

Dowland may reasonably be regarded as the greatest song-writer that this country has yet produced, not excepting even Purcell. He was also, as we may imagine, a fine singer, as well as being the most accomplished lutenist in Europe, and it can cause no surprise that he earned such fame and created so deep an impression wherever his travels led him, accompanying himself on the lute whilst he sang his own exquisite songs.

Of the many commendatory verses which refer to him by name the most frequently quoted is that from Barnfield's miscellany, ' The Passionate Pilgrim '. Those lines are too well known to call for repetition here, but the present notice may fittingly be concluded with an epigram written by Dowland's fellow lutenist the poet Campian :

Tho: Campiani Epigramma de instituto Authoris.

> Famam posteritas quam dedit Orpheo,
> Dolandi melius Musica dat sibi ;
> Fugaces reprimens archetypis sonos ;
> Quas et delicias praebuit auribus,
> Ipsis conspicuas luminibus facit.

Publications by Dowland for voices and lute

1597. The first book of Songs or Airs of four parts.
1600. The second book of Songs or Airs of 2, 4, and 5 parts.
1603. The third and last book of Songs or Airs.
1610. Three Airs contributed to ' A Musical Banquet ', edited by Robert Dowland.
1613. A Pilgrim's Solace, wherein is contained musical harmony of 3, 4, and 5 parts.

MICHAEL CAVENDISH.   Born *circa* 1565 ; died 1628

The history of this composer has already been dealt with in connexion with his work as a madrigalist. His volume contains as many as twenty Airs with lute accompaniment ; the first fourteen are to be ' expressed with two voyces and the base Violl or the voice and Lute only '. The other six are for four voices with the usual alternative for solo use. These Airs are of an attractive character and show an accurate sense of verbal accentuation on the part of the composer. As previously mentioned, this work has been entirely unknown until recently, when a copy unexpectedly appeared in a London sale-room and was fortunately secured for the British Museum.

Publications by Cavendish for voices and lute
1598. Airs in Tablatory to the Lute.

THOMAS MORLEY.   Born 1558 ; died 1603

This famous madrigalist published one volume of the lutenist class. It includes twenty-one songs for solo-voice with accompaniment for the lute and bass-viol. There are also a Pavane and a Galliard at the end of the book. The only known exemplar is now in the Folger Museum at Washington, D.C. The last seven songs are missing, but two of these are in MS. at Christ Church, Oxford. No. 6 of the Set is the well-known setting of Shakespeare's *It was a lover and his lass*. *Mistress mine* (No. 8) should not be confused, as it frequently has been, with Shakespeare's *O mistress mine*, the words being quite different.

In his ' Address to the Reader ' Morley explained that he was but a beginner in this kind of composition, which he termed ' lute ayres ', and he mentioned in the dedication that the songs ' were made this vacation time '. This volume was not actually the composer's first experiment in writing songs for the lute, because he arranged the first fifteen of his five-part canzonets ' tablaturewise for the lute ' so that in the absence of other singers the Cantus-part might be sung as a solo with lute accompaniment.

As an exception to the general rule followed in the present

chapter, the table of contents of this rare and important volume is printed here in full :

Publications by Morley for voice and lute

TABLE OF CONTENTS

PHILIP ROSSETER. Born *circa* 1575 ; died 1623

Rosseter's only volume of works was published in 1601 in conjunction with his intimate friend Thomas Campian, although Rosseter's name alone appeared on the title-page. This volume which, strictly speaking, consists of two books of Airs, contains nothing but songs for solo-voice with accompaniment for lute, orpharion, and bass-viol. Each composer contributed twenty-one songs, and the words of the entire volume are the work of Campian. Rosseter was born about the year 1575. In the latter part of his life he was chiefly occupied with theatrical work. In 1610 a patent was granted to him in conjunction with his brother-lutenist Robert Jones and two others, to train a school of children who were to be designated the ' children of the revels to the Queen '. Rosseter died in Fetter Lane on May 5, 1623, and was buried at St. Dunstan's, Fleet Street.

Publications by Rosseter for voice and lute

THOMAS CAMPIAN.   Born 1567 ;   died 1620

Next to Dowland, Campian is the most prominent personality
of the English lutenists.   He excelled in writing Airs for the
single voice rather than for combined voices, and confined
himself chiefly to that form of expression.   It has been said
of Campian that he was in the best sense an amateur.   By
profession he was qualified as a physician and held the degree
of M.D. ;   it is probable that this distinction was conferred
upon him by some foreign University, for although he was
educated at Cambridge he took no degree of any kind there.
Yet he did at some time in his life practise medicine, and it
was in the capacity of medical adviser that he obtained leave
to visit Sir Thomas Monson in the Tower of London in 1617
while he was imprisoned there on the charge of murdering
Sir Thomas Overbury.

Campian is best known to English people by his charming
lyric poetry, and it was as a poet that he first came before
the notice of his contemporaries, for a book of his Latin
epigrams and elegiacs was published in 1595.   The consideration
of Campian's poetry lies outside the scope of the present
volume, but it should be mentioned that he was among those
who held the opinion that classical metres were to be preferred
to rhyming verse as a medium for poetical expression.   In
1602 he wrote a treatise on the Art of English Poesie in which
he condemned the ' childish titilation of riming '.   Without
discussing the subject further it may be said that this contro-
versy illustrates but one more aspect of that eager endeavour
of the Elizabethans to discover the most suitable forms,
whether new or old, in which they could most aptly express
their thoughts.

It was fortunate for English literature that Campian was
endowed with a gift for musical composition in addition to
poetry ;   for it must have been abundantly evident to him
that lyric verse was far better suited to musical setting than
lines constructed upon the rules of the classical metres.   Consequently, in spite of any convictions which he held upon the
point, he was constrained to turn to lyric verse when he came
to express himself in the dual capacity of poet and composer.

Apart from his songs Campian published in 1613 a book on counterpoint, which was entitled ' A New Way of Making Foure parts in *Counter-point*, by a most familiar, and infallible Rule ', and included discourses on Keys, Closes, and Concords.

Campian was born on February 12, 1567, and baptized at St. Andrew's, Holborn. He died on March 1, 1620, and was buried at St. Dunstan's, Fleet Street. On his death-bed he bequeathed all his property to his friend Philip Rosseter, and it is pleasant to reflect that these two close friends lie buried near the same spot. Many new and interesting facts connected with the life of this musician-poet are fully set out in Mr. Percival Vivian's admirable edition of his literary works.

The spelling of Campian's name with the second *a* in the place of an *o* has been adopted in the present volume on the ground that it is invariably so spelt in the original edition of all four of his Books of Airs, whether on the title-pages or dedications ; and the Latinized form of the name, as used by the poet himself, was *Campianus*.

Publications by Campian for voice and lute

1601. A book of Airs to be sung to the lute (published in conjunction with Rosseter).
1607. Songs for a mask in honour of Lord Hay and his bride.
1613 (?). Two books of Airs to be sung to the Lute and viols.
1613. Songs for a mask at the marriage of Princess Elizabeth.
1613. Songs for a mask at Caversham House.
1613. Songs for a mask at the marriage of Robert, Earl of Somerset.
1617 (?). The third and fourth Books of Airs.

The actual dates of the first and second, and of the third and fourth Books of Airs are not known. The dates 1610 and 1612 respectively were given by Rimbault in his *Bibliotheca Madrigaliana* and the same dates were quoted in the ' Dictionary of National Biography ' *sub* Campion. The first and second books must have been published later than 1612, for the death of Prince Henry is alluded to in them. The third and fourth books contain a reference, in the dedication, to the Overbury Plot, and cannot have been published before Sir Thomas Monson's innocence was established early in 1617.

ROBERT JONES.   Date of birth and death unknown

Robert Jones has already been noticed among the madrigal-composers, but he occupies a more important position as a lutenist. As a performer he seems to have been one of the best lute-players of his day. He published as many as five books of Airs with lute accompaniment. Several beautiful songs are to be found in these books, although few of them can be compared with those of Dowland. One of his compositions, *Farewell, dear love* (Book I, No. 12), is frequently mentioned as having been alluded to by Shakespeare in *Twelfth Night*.[1] The fact that some of the words of this song were introduced by Shakespeare in that passage does not necessarily carry with it any reference to Jones's work. The music of this piece is not of outstanding interest. Of the 'Ultimum Vale, or the Third Booke of Ayres' the only known exemplar is in the Library of the Royal College of Music, and there is also but one exemplar remaining of 'The Muses' Gardin for Delights, Or the fift Booke of Ayres'; this was discovered by Mr. Barclay Squire in Lord Ellesmere's library at Bridgewater House. It is now in the Huntington Library, Pasadena, California.

Publications by Jones for voices and lute

1601. The First Book of Airs.
1601. The Second Book of Songs and Airs.
1608. Ultimum Vale, or the Third Book of Airs.
1609. A Musical Dream, or the Fourth Book of Airs.
1611. The Muses' Garden for delight, or the Fifth Book of Airs.

THOMAS GREAVES.   Date of birth and death unknown

Nothing is known of the personal history of Thomas Greaves beyond the fact that he was lutenist to Sir Henry Pierpoint at the time when he published his 'Songes of sundrie kindes' in 1604. This book has already been mentioned in connexion with Greaves's work as a madrigalist, the last six compositions which it contains being Madrigals. The book opens with nine Airs to be sung to the lute and bass-viol.

[1] Act II, Sc. 3.

Publications by Greaves for voice and lute

1604. Airs to be sung to the lute and bass-viol (included in Songs of Sundry Kinds).

FRANCIS PILKINGTON. Born *circa* 1562; died 1638

Pilkington was one of the few musicians who published compositions in the two distinct styles of his time. His two Madrigal Sets have already been noticed in their due order, together with an outline of his personal history. His 'Booke of Songs or Ayres' is for four voices with lute-tablature, and, like Dowland's Sets, was intended either for solo-voice with lute accompaniment or for four unaccompanied voices. Pilkington's Airs are far more contrapuntal in character than those of the other lutenists, and they often approach the Madrigal style so closely as to be indistinguishable from the simpler kind of Madrigal.

Publications by Pilkington for voices and lute

1605. The first book of Songs or Airs of 4 parts with tablature for the lute.

TOBIAS HUME. Date of birth unknown; died *circa* 1645

Hume, who published some Airs with compositions of other kinds in 1605, was an officer in the army, and eventually rose to the rank of colonel. He spent the latter days of his life as one of the Brethren of the Charterhouse. In 1642 he presented a petition to Parliament to employ him for ' the business in Ireland ' claiming that if he could be supplied with a hundred instruments of war which he should give directions to be made, he would ' ruin the rebels within three months '. Hume was an amateur musician of some skill both as a composer and as a performer on the viol da gamba. His first volume consisted mainly of instrumental pieces, but it included a few ' Songes to bee sung to the Viole, with the Lute '. A subsequent publication, quaintly entitled ' Captain Humes Poeticall Musicke ', included no songs with lute accompaniment.

Publications by Hume for voice and lute

1605. Songs to be sung to the viol with the lute (included in a volume of Instrumental Airs, &c.).

JOHN BARTLET. Date of birth and death unknown

Nothing is known about Bartlet beyond the fact that he was in the service of Sir Edward Seymour and that he took the degree of B.Mus. at Oxford in 1610. In 1606 he published a volume of songs of three kinds which he called a ' Triplicitie of Musicke '. The first section consisted of fourteen songs for four voice-parts in which the instrumental accompaniment was an indispensable feature ; this accompaniment was for lute or orpharion and viol da gamba. The second section included four songs for treble duet with lute and viol ; and the book ended with three songs for solo-voice accompanied by the lute and viol da gamba.

Publications by Bartlet for voices and lute

1606. A book of Airs with a triplicity of music.

JOHN COOPER (COPRARIO). Born *circa* 1580 ;
died *circa* 1650

This lutenist spent some years in the early part of his life in Italy, where he changed his surname to Coprario in deference to Italian feeling. On returning to England he retained this name. He was musical instructor to the children of James I, and subsequently Composer-in-ordinary to Charles I. His first publication consisted of some songs for the treble voice, with accompaniment for lute and bass-viol, written on the occasion of the death of Lord Devonshire. Six of these were for a single voice and the seventh was a duet. Cooper's other published compositions were also produced in circumstances of a personal nature. One was a Set of solo-songs of mourning for the untimely death of Prince Henry, the words of which were written by Campian. The other took the form of a contribution to the mask at the marriage of Robert, Earl of Somerset, to which Campian also contributed.

Publications by Cooper for voices and lute

1606. Funeral tears for the death of Lord Devonshire.
1613. Songs of mourning for the death of Henry Prince of Wales.
1614. Airs sung in the mask at the marriage of Lord Somerset.

JOHN DANYEL. Date of birth and death unknown

Little is known of John Danyel, who is thought to have been the brother of Samuel Daniel, the poet. He took the degree of B.Mus. at Oxford in 1604. Later in life he was one of the Court musicians to Charles I. His published volume consisted of twenty-one solo songs.

Publications by Danyel for voice and lute
1606. Songs for the lute, viol and voice.

THOMAS FORD. Born *circa* 1580 ; died 1648

In 1607 Thomas Ford published his volume of ' Musicke of Sundrie Kindes, Set forth in two Bookes '. The second of these books contained nothing but instrumental pieces, many of which have very lively names ; for example, *The wild goose chase* (No. 9), *Whip it and trip it* (No. 15), and *A snatch and away* (No. 17). The first of the two books consisted of ten ' Aries for 4. Voices to the Lute, Orphorion, or Basse-Viol ' ; and it ends with a ' Dialogue for two Voices ' with lute accompaniment.

This set of ten Airs is one of the most beautiful of the lutenists' publications, for Ford's work, simple as it is, may be compared with that of Dowland for beauty of melody. It is another of those Sets intended for alternative use either as solo-song with lute accompaniment or for four unaccompanied voices. *Not full twelve years twice told* (No. 1) is among the most beautiful of these songs ; one exquisite phrase may be quoted from it :

My course was short, the long-er is my rest,

Other attractive numbers in this set are *What then is love?* (No. 2), *Go, Passions, to the cruel fair* (No. 5), and *There is a lady sweet and kind* (No. 9).   No. 8 is the well-known *Since first I saw your face.*   This lovely song has been unfortunately handled by editors of a past generation, who have altered and modernized the text in certain places ;   this is particularly the case at the words *shall we begin to wrangle,* where most reprints give an F sharp in the bass ;   this gratuitous alteration of the text necessitates further tampering with the tenor part. In the following bar F sharp is not indicated in the voice-part of the original edition, but that F sharp was intended by the composer is clearly shown in the lute-tablature.   The correct text is as follows :

Little is known of Ford's personal history.   He was one of the musicians on the staff of Henry Prince of Wales, having among his colleagues the younger Ferrabosco.   Subsequently he became one of the musicians of Charles I.   Ford died in November 1648 and was buried at St. Margaret's, Westminster.

The splendid set of manuscript part-books in the Fellows' library at Winchester College, mentioned in a former chapter,[1] contains ten three-part madrigals written in a later hand than the rest of the book and dating about the years 1600–10 ; these are described as ' Mr. Ford's three parts '.   They are not of much merit and therefore it seems unlikely that they are the work of Thomas Ford.   Ford was not an uncommon name at that period.

· See p. 38.

Publications by Ford for voices and lute

1607. Music of Sundry Kinds set forth in two Books, the first whereof are Airs for four voices to the lute, orpharion, or bass viol.

ALFONSO FERRABOSCO. Born *circa* 1580 ; died 1628

Although this musician was of Italian extraction, as his name implies, yet he must be reckoned among the English composers, seeing that he was born in England and spent his whole life in this country. He was the son of Alfonso Ferrabosco, who settled in England in the middle of the sixteenth century and who had published a Set of madrigals in Venice as early as 1542. It was he who engaged in the friendly musical contests with Byrd of which Peacham and Morley gave descriptions. The younger Ferrabosco was born at Greenwich about the year 1580, and he became musical instructor to Henry Prince of Wales. He subsequently succeeded Coprario, or Cooper, as Composer-in-ordinary to Charles I. His book of Airs, published in 1609, was dedicated to the Prince and contained commendatory verses by Campian, Nathaniel Tomkins, and Ben Jonson. Ferrabosco was associated with Jonson and Inigo Jones in the production of Masks. Jonson was evidently a personal friend of his, for he also wrote some introductory lines to another publication by Ferrabosco entitled ' Lessons for 1. 2. and 3. Viols ', while several lyrics in his Book of ' Ayres ' are by Jonson. Ferrabosco died in March 162⅞ and was buried at Greenwich. The singer of the name of Ferrabosco mentioned occasionally by Samuel Pepys was possibly Alfonso's daughter ; but John, organist of Ely, was almost certainly his son. A valuable account of the Ferrabosco family, with special reference to Alfonso the younger, by Mr. Godfrey Arkwright, was printed in Robin Gray's ' Studies in Music ', pp. 199–214.

Publications by Ferrabosco for voice and lute

1609. Book of Airs.

WILLIAM CORKINE. Date of birth and death unknown

William Corkine published two volumes of songs with lute and bass viol accompaniment in 1610 and 1612 respectively. These books also included several dances for the instrument called the lyra-viol. Nothing is known of Corkine's biography.

Publications by Corkine for voice and lute

1610. Airs to sing and play to the lute and bass-viol.
1612. Second book of Airs.

JOHN MAYNARD. Date of birth and death unknown

This lutenist seems at one time to have been in the service of Lady Joan Thynne of Cause Castle in Shropshire ; and he also held the position of lutenist at St. Julian's School in Hertfordshire. Nothing else is known about him. His published volume was in two sections ; the first consisted of twelve songs with lute and viol da gamba accompaniment ; and the second section included twelve Pavans and Galliards for the lute. The songs, which were entitled 'The xii. Wonders of the World', were severally addressed to different characters : the Courtier, the Divine, the Soldier, the Lawyer, and so on. The words of the 'twelve wonders' were written by Sir John Davies.

Publications by Maynard for voice and lute

1611. The twelve wonders of the world. Set and composed for the viol da gamba, the lute and the voice.

JOHN ATTEY. Date of birth unknown ;
died *circa* 1640

Little is known about Attey except that he died at Ross about the year 1640. The popularity of the air with lute accompaniment waned rapidly in the second decade of the seventeenth century, when it was being superseded by the new type of song that owed its origin to the composers of the new Italian school, with whom the first attempts at opera were diverting attention from the older methods of expression. One effect of the new movement was to cause a lull in the fashion for lute-playing and lute music, which prevailed until the revival of the French lute-school in the latter part of the century.

Attey's volume was published after a considerable interval since any similar work had appeared, and it was definitely the last of this remarkable series of lutenists' compositions, which had begun with the publication of Dowland's first book exactly a quarter of a century earlier. Attey's Airs, like those of Dowland, were set for four voices as well as for solo-song ; so that the series which had in the meanwhile included such a large proportion of Airs for solo-voice exclusively, ended with the same type of composition as that with which it began. The work of the lutenists, when considered solely from a musical point of view, is of far less importance than that of the madrigalists, but it has a peculiar interest which is derived from the fact that it represents an art-form that originated in England, and that it remained, until it fell into disuse, an exclusively English product.

Publications by Attey for voices and lute
1622. First book of Airs of four parts with tablature for the lute.

WALTER PORTER. Born about 1590 ; died 1659

The work of Walter Porter calls at least for some comment in a volume that purports to deal with English secular vocal music of the madrigalian era. Yet Porter should not, strictly speaking, be classed either as a madrigal-writer or among the lutenist-composers. His compositions are styled ' Madrigales and Ayres ', but a large number of instruments occupy an essential place in their performance, and none of the songs are strictly madrigalian in character. The full title of this volume, which was published in 1632, reads as follows : ' Madrigales and Ayres. Of two, three, foure, and five Voyces, with the continued Base, with Toccatos, Sinfonias and Rittornellos to them. After the manner of Consort Musique. To be performed with the Harpsechord, Lutes, Theorbos, Base Violl, two Violins, or two Viols.'

It is not necessary to add anything to the composer's description in order to show the nature of this work and how

far it lies removed from the true polyphonic school. Yet
Porter's volume contains much that is of considerable interest.
In the first place, much of the music is printed with regular
bars, or, in Porter's own words, 'set forth with Division',
thus providing an early example of this innovation which
so shortly afterwards became a universal custom.   Another
peculiarity of this volume is that Porter, unlike all the madrigalists, stated definitely in the table of contents the particular
class of voice for which each part was designed.

In his address 'To the Practitioner' at the beginning of the
volume the composer stated, 'I have made the singing Base
also a thorow Base, in which you are not to sing but where
there are words or this signe :‖: of Repetition'.   It is worth
while to mention that this is the earliest printed instruction
upon this point, although the practice of writing passages
which had no words and which were intended to be played
on instruments, instead of being sung, goes back quite half
a century before Porter's volume appeared ; Byrd, for instance,
adopted it in his 1588 set.

A marked peculiarity of Porter's style was the use of
rapidly reiterated notes upon one syllable of the words,
a practice which he undoubtedly borrowed from Monteverde,
who used it very frequently and who certainly originated it.
Porter is believed to have been a pupil of Monteverde, and his
style goes far to support the conjecture.   Some doubt has been
expressed as to the effect which Monteverde intended to
produce by this curious device ; but that it was a form of
vibrato, or *tremolo*, is made perfectly clear by Porter, who in
this 'address to the practitioner' explains : 'In the Songs
which are set forth with Division, where you find many Notes
in a place after this manner ♩♩♩♩ in rule or space,
they are set to expresse the *Trillo*.' He adds that he has retained
this and other Italian terms in order to avoid any uncertainty
of meaning.   The two following examples may be quoted to
illustrate this curious mannerism in Porter's work :

From *O praise the Lord* (No. 1).

Ye   that ful - fil, ful - fil his com-mand - ment

From *Farewell, once my delight* (No. 15).

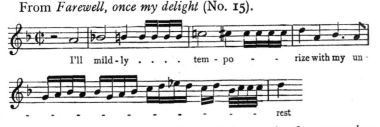

I'll mild-ly . . . . tem - po - - rize with my un -

- - - - - - - - - rest

The only known copy of this work is now in the possession of Mr. S. R. Christie-Miller of Burnham Court, Bucks.[1]

Porter was a tenor singer and a gentleman of the Chapel Royal; he subsequently became master of the choristers of Westminster Abbey. He died in 1659 and was buried at St. Margaret's, Westminster, on November 30 of that year. Two years before his death he published another volume entitled 'Mottets of Two Voyces for Treble or Tenor and Bass. With the Continued Bass or Score: To be performed to an Organ, Harpsycon, Lute or Bass-Viol'.

As Porter's volume of madrigals and airs is so scarce, the table of contents is sufficiently interesting to print here in full:

[1] In December 1919 the Burnham library was dispersed, and Porter's book was purchased for the British Museum.

22. Young Thyrsis lay in Phyllis' lap   Of 5 voices.
23. Thy face and eyes and all thou   Of 3.   Alto, Tenor, and Bass.
    hast.
24. Tell me, Amyntas, Cloris cries.   Of 2.   Alto, and Tenor.
25. I saw fair Cloris walk alone.   Of two Trebles.
26. Death, there is no need of thee.   Of 4.   Treble, Alto, Tenor, and Bass
27. Like the rash and giddy fly.   Of 3.   Two Trebles, and a Bass.
28. Wake, sorrow wake.   Of 5 voices.
    (An Elogie to the Right Honor-
    able Lady the lady Arrabella
    Steward).

APPENDIX A

Biographical synopsis of the composers of the English madrigal and lute schools.

The page numbers refer to the principal notice.

Name		Page.	Date of Birth.	Place of Birth.	Date of Death.	Place of Death.	Place of Burial.	Professional Position.
Alison, Richard	...	265	...	...	...	...	...	Lived in Duke's Place, Aldgate.
Attey, John	...	324	...	...	c. 1640	Ross, co. Hereford	...	...
Bartlet, John	...	320	...	...	...	...	...	In service of Sir Edward Seymour.
Bateson, Thomas	...	256	c. 1570	...	1630	Dublin	? Dublin	Organist Chester Cathedral and Ch. Ch. Cathedral, Dublin.
Bennet, John	...	242	...	...	...	...	...	...
Byrd, William	...	158	1543	? Lincolnshire	July 4, 1623	? Stondon, co. Essex	Stondon	Organist Lincoln Cathedral, St. Paul's Cathedral, and Chapel Royal.
Campian, Thomas	...	316	Feb. 12, 1567	St. Andrew's, Holborn	March 1, 1620	London	St. Dunstan's, Fleet Street	...
Carlton, Richard	...	250	c. 1558	...	...	...	...	Precentor Norwich Cathedral, Vicar of Bawsey-cum-Glosthorp.
Cavendish, Michael	...	236	c. 1565	Cavendish Overhall, co. Suffolk	July 5, 1628	St. Mary Aldermanbury, London	...	...
Cobbold, William	...	246	Jan. 5, 1560	St. Andrew's, Norwich	Nov. 7, 1639	Beccles	Beccles, co. Suffolk	Organist Norwich Cathedral.
Cooper (Coprario) John	...	320	c. 1580	...	c. 1650	...	...	Instructor to children of James I and Composer in Ordinary to Charles I.
Corkine, William	...	324	...	...	...	...	...	...
Danyel, John	...	321	...	...	...	...	...	...
Dowland, John	...	307	Dec. 1562	? Dalkey, co. Dublin	Jan. 21, 1626	...	...	Lutenist to Christian IV, King of Denmark, Lord Walden, and Charles I.
East, Michael	...	251	c. 1580	? London	c. 1640	? Lichfield	...	Organist Lichfield Cathedral.

Name.	Page.	Date of Birth.	Place of Birth.	Date of Death.	Place of Death.	Place of Burial.	Professional Position.
Farmer, John ...	240	c. 1565	...	c. 1605	? London	...	Organist Ch. Ch. Cathedral, Dublin.
Farnaby, Giles ...	232	c. 1560	...	c. 1600	? London	St. Alphege, Greenwich	Lived in London.
Ferrabosco, Alfonso (the younger)	323	c. 1580	Greenwich	March 1628	Greenwich	...	Composer in Ordinary to Charles I.
Ford, Thomas ...	321	c. 1580	...	Nov. 1648	London	St. Margaret's, Westminster.	Musician to Henry Prince of Wales and to Charles I
Gibbons, Ellis ...	245	c. 1575	Cambridge	? 1602	? Salisbury	...	Organist Salisbury Cathedral.
Gibbons, Orlando ...	272	1583	Cambridge	June 5, 1625	Canterbury	Canterbury Cathedral	Organist Chapel Royal and Westminster Abbey.
Greaves, Thomas ...	264	...	...	...	...	...	Lutenist to Sir Henry Pierpoint at Holm, co. Notts.
Hilton, John (the elder) ...	245	...	...	c. 1608	? Cambridge	...	Organist Trinity College, Cambridge.
Hilton, John (the younger) ...	300	1599	? Cambridge	March 1657	London	St. Margaret's, Westminster.	Organist St. Margaret's, Westminster.
Holborne, William ...	232	...	...	...	...	...	
Holmes, John ...	245	c. 1575	...	March 25, 1638	Salisbury	...	Organist Winchester Cathedral and Salisbury Cathedral.
Hume, Tobias ...	319	...	...	April 16, 1645	Charterhouse, London	...	...
Hunt, Thomas ...	246	...	...	...	...	...	Household musician to Sir Thomas Kytson at Hengrave Hall, co. Suffolk.
Johnson, Edward ...	247	...	...	...	...	...	
Jones, Robert ...	266	...	...	...	...	...	
Kirbye, George ...	225	c. 1565	? Bury St. Edmunds	Oct. 1634	Whiting Street, Bury St. Edmunds	St. Mary's, Bury	Household musician to Sir Robert Jermyn at Rushbrooke Hall, co. Suffolk.
Lichfild, Henry ...	286	...	...	...	...	...	In service of Lady Cheney at Toddington House, co. Beds.
Lisley, John ...	247	...	...	...	...	...	
Marson, George ...	245	...	...	...	...	...	
Maynard, John ...	324	...	...	...	...	...	Lutenist at St. Julian's School, Hertford.

Name							
Milton, John	246	c. 1563	? Stanton St. John, co. Oxon.	March 1647	London	St. Giles', Cripplegate	Organist St. Paul's Cathedral and Chapel Royal.
Morley, Thomas	177	1558	...	1603	London	...	...
Mundy, John	224	c. 1560	? London	June 29, 1630	Windsor	St. George's Chapel	Organist Eton College and St. George's Chapel, Windsor Castle.
Nicolson, Richard	246	c. 1570	...	1639	Oxford	...	Organist Magdalen College, Oxford.
Norcome, Daniel (Nurcombe)	245	1576	Windsor	c. 1620	Windsor	...	Minor Canon of Windsor.
Pattrick, Nathaniel	231	c. 1565	? Worcester	March 1595	Worcester	St. Michael's, Worcester	Organist Worcester Cathedral.
Peerson, Martin	290	c. 1580	? Dunnington, co. Cambs.	1650	London	St. Paul's Cathedral	Master of the children of St. Paul's.
Philips, Peter	301	...	...	1625	Soignies	? Soignies	Canon of St. Vincent, Soignies.
Pilkington, Francis	283	c. 1562	...	1638	? Chester	...	Precentor Chester Cathedral and Vicar of Holy Trinity, Chester.
Porter, Walter	325	...	...	Nov. 1659	London	St. Margaret's, Westminster	Master of the Choristers, Westminster Abbey.
Ravenscroft, Thomas	270	c. 1585	...	c. 1633	? London	...	Organist Christ's Hospital, London.
Rosseter, Philip	315	c. 1575	...	May 5, 1623	Fetter Lane, London	St. Dunstan, Fleet Street	...
Tomkins, Thomas	293	c. 1573	St. David's, co. Pembroke	1656	...	Martin Hassingtree, co. Worc.	Organist Worcester Cathedral.
Vautor, Thomas	288	c. 1590	...	...	...	...	Household musician to Sir George Villiers.
Ward, John	279	...	...	c. 1640	...	...	In service of Sir Henry Fanshawe.
Weelkes, Thomas	191	c. 1575	...	Nov. 30, 1623	St. Bride's, London	St. Bride's, Fleet Street	Organist Winchester College and Chichester Cathedral.
Wilbye, John	209	1574	Diss, co. Norfolk	Sept. 1638	Colchester	Holy Trinity, Colchester	Household musician to Sir Thomas Kytson at Hengrave Hall, co. Suffolk.
Youll, Henry	268	...	...	...	...	...	Household musician to Edward Bacon.

APPENDIX B

The following index may be found convenient for purposes of reference. It constitutes a complete list of all the English madrigals printed in the Elizabethan part-books. The compositions of the lutenist-composers, for example Dowland and Ford, are not included here, nor are those of Martin Peerson, since these are not in a strict sense madrigals. Settings of words from the Psalms or other passages from the Bible, whether metrical or not, are also omitted from this Index. Those madrigals are marked with an asterisk which were printed in the original editions in separate sections or parts ; and those printed here in italics are the second or subsequent parts of such compositions.

It should here be repeated that the composers apparently desired to leave it optional to perform separately the single sections of those madrigals which they deliberately divided into two or more parts and numbered independently in their volumes or ' Sets '.

Love is a secret feeding fire	Pilkington i. 13
Love is the fire that burns me	Bateson ii. 1
Love laid his yoke upon me	Hilton 18
Love learns by laughing first to speak . . .	Morley i. 21
Love me not for comely grace	Wilbye ii. 12
*Love, shooting among many	Farnaby 13–14
Love shooting at another	Farnaby 14
Love took his bow and arrow . . .	Morley v. 5
Love would discharge the duty	Bateson i. 2
Love would discharge the duty . . .	Byrd ii. 34
Love wounded me but did not touch . . .	Hilton 8
Love's folk in green arraying . . .	Morley v. 4
Lullaby, my sweet little Baby	Byrd i. 32
Lure, falconers ! give warning to the field . .	Bennet Br. Dis. 5
Make haste, ye lovers, plaining	Weelkes i. 17
Mars in a fury	Weelkes iv. 6
*Melpomene, bewail thy sister's loss . . .	Vautor 20–21
Menalcas in an evening walking was . . .	Pilkington ii. 7
Merrily, my love and I	Bateson i. 27
Methinks I hear Amphion's warbling strings . .	Weelkes iv. 4
Mira cano, sol occubuit	Vautor 15
Miraculous Love's wounding ! . . .	Morley iv. 5
'Mongst thousands good one wanton dame . .	Gibbons 11
Mopsie, leave off to love	East i. 12
Mother, I will have a husband . . .	Vautor 4
Mourn now, my soul, with anguish . . .	Kirbye 8
Much it delighted to see Phyllis smiling . .	Cavendish 23
Music divine, proceeding from above . .	Tomkins 24
Music some thinks no music is	Bateson i. 28
Must I part, O my jewel ? . . .	Kirbye 21
My bonny lass she smileth	Morley iii. 7
*My flocks feed not	Weelkes i. 2–4
My heart is dead within me . . .	Pilkington i. 19
My heart oppressed by your disdaining . .	Lichfild 20
My heart, why hast thou taken ? . .	Morley Ital. canz. 8
My Hope a counsel with my Love . .	East i. 10
My lady's coloured cheeks were like the roses .	Farnaby 1
My lovely wanton jewel	Morley iii. 12
My mind to me a kingdom is . . .	Byrd i. 14
My mistress after service due . . .	Bateson ii. 2
*My mistress frowns when she should play .	Hilton 2–3
My nymph, the dear, and her my dear . .	Morley v. 11
My peace and my pleasure	East iii. 3
My Phyllis bids me pack away . . .	Weelkes i. 24
*My prime of youth is but a frost of cares .	Alison 9–10
*My prime of youth is but a frost of cares .	East i. 18–19
My prime of youth is but a frost of cares .	Mundy 17
My tears do not avail me	Weelkes i. 23
My throat is sore, my voice is hoarse . .	Wilbye i. 27
*My true love hath my heart . . .	Ward 1–2
*Nay let me weep, though others' tears be spent .	Gibbons 17–19
Ne'er let the sun with his deceiving light .	Gibbons 18
Never did any more delight to see . . .	Vautor 7
No haste but good, yet stay !. . . .	East iv. 18
No more I will thy love importune . .	Tomkins 2
No, no, Nigella !	Morley iii. 6
No, no, no, it will not be . . .	Pilkington 20
No no, she doth but flout me . . .	Morley ii. 12
No, no, though I shrink still . . .	Weelkes v. 11
Noel, adieu, thou Court's delight . .	Weelkes iv. 10

APPENDIX C

Reference to the Original Editions in the Principal Libraries.

A = Altus.
B = Bassus
C = Cantus.
C1 = Cantus Primus.

C2 = Cantus Secundus.
Ct = Contra-tenor
M = Medius
Q = Quintus.
S = Superius.

Sx = Sextus.
T = Tenor.
Tr = Triplex.
imp. = imperfect.

I. MADRIGAL SETS

Abbreviated Description.	Brit. Mus.	Bodl. Lib., Oxford.	Camb. Univ. Lib.	Royal Coll. of Music.	Ch. Ch., Oxford.
Alison 1606. C1, C2, A, T, B .	K. 3. m. 1	Antiq. e. E. 1696	...	I. C. 34	...
C1 (imp.)	55. b. 20 (14)	...	...	I. D. 14 (2)	449–54
Bateson 1604. C, A, T, B, Q, Sx.	K. 3. h. 3	...	...	...	...
C, A, B, Sx, Q (imp.)	...	...	...	...	...
A, T, B, Q	...	...	...	...	...
Bateson 1618. C, A, T, B, Q, Sx.	K. 3. g. 7	[MS.] Mus. Sch. E. 470–3	...	I. D. 14 (3)	449–54
A, T, B, Q	...	[MS.] Mus. Sch. E. 470–3	...	...	...
Bennet 1599. C, A, T, B .	K. 3. h. 5	[MS.] Mus. Sch. E. 453–7	...	I. C. 37	449–54
Byrd 1588. S, M, Ct, T, B .	K. 2. f. 1	85. d. 8	...	I. D. 1 (1)	489–94
another copy	...	...	...	...	...
M, Ct, T, B	...	...	Syn. 5. 58. 1	...	...
S .	...	...	Syn. 6. 58. 10	...	...
Ct .	...	Douce MM. 361	...	...	...
M .	55. b. 20 (1)	...	Syn. 6. 6⁴	...	...
B .	...	...	...	...	...
Byrd 1588, 1590 edition	...	...	...	...	...
S (imp.), M, T, B .	K. 2. f. 2	...	...	...	...
B .	D. 101. d	...	...	...	...

Byrd 1589. S, M, Ct, T, B, Sx	K. 2. f. 3	[MS.] Mus. Sch. E. 453–8	...	I. D. 2	489–94
S, T, B, Sx	K. 3. h. 7	...	...	...	...
S	...	...	Syn. 6. 58. 12	...	...
Byrd 1589, 1610 edition	...	...	...	...	...
S, Ct, T, B (imp.), Sx	K. 2. f. 10	...	...	...	...
S	...	...	S. S. S. 35. 16	...	...
Ct.	...	...	...	...	...
Byrd 1611. C1, C2, Ct, T, B, Sx.	K. 2. f. 11	Douce MM. 361	...	I. D. 1 (2)	489–94
C2, Ct.	...	[MS.] Mus. Sch. E. 453–8	...	...	...
Carlton 1601. C, A, T, B, Q	K. 3. h. 8	Douce MM. 361	...	...	141–5
C, A, T (imp.), B, Q	...	...	...	...	...
C, T	...	...	...	...	...
East 1604. C, A, T, B, Q	K. 2. d. 3*	[MS.] Mus. Sch. E. 435–7	...	I. D. 3	225–30
C, A, T, B	K. 2. d. 3*	...	...	I. D. 6	...
B	...	...	...	...	...
East 1606. C, A, T, B, Q	K. 2. d. 4	[MS.] Mus. Sch. E. 435–7	...	I. D. 7	225–30
C, B, Q (imp.)	K. 2. d. 5	...	...	...	...
East 1610. C, A, T, B, Q, Sx	K. 3. h. 11	[MS.] Mus. Sch. E. 453–8	...	I. D. 14 (4)	449–54
C, A, T, B	...	[MS.] Mus. Sch. E. 547–50	...	...	...
B, Sx	...	...	...	...	...
East 1618 (4th Set) C, A, T, B, Q, Sx	K. 2. d. 5*	...	...	I. D. 14 (5)	449–54
C, B, Sx	...	...	...	...	...
C	K. 2. d. 6	...	Syn. 6. 61. 18	...	...
East 1618 (5th Set). C, B, Q	...	...	...	I. D. 14 (10)	...
East 1624. C, A, T, B, Q, Sx	K. 2. d. 6*	...	...	I. B. 10	...
B, Sx	...	...	...	...	...
East 1638. C1, C2, A, B	K. 2. d. 7	...	...	II. E. 5	455–8
Farmer 1599. C, A, T, B	K. 3. m. 7	...	...	I. D. 8	449–54
Farnaby 1598. C, A, T, B.	K. 8. d. 5	...	...	...	...
Gibbons 1612. C, A, T, B, Q	K. 3. h. 12	[MS.] Mus. Sch. E. 453–7	...	I. D. 14 (6)	449–54
another copy	...	...	...	...	708–12
Hilton 1627. C, A, B.	K. 3. h. 13	[MS.] Mus. Sch. E. 511 a–c	...	...	449
B.	...	...	...	...	1111
Holborne 1597	...	...	...	I. D. 12	...
Jones 1607.[1] C, A, T, B, Q, Sx	...	...	C. 11. 13[2]	...	...
C. B.	K. 3. h. 16	Douce MM. 361	...	...	...
Kirbye 1597. C1, C2, T, B, Sx	K. 1. e. 6	...	...	...	...
A.	...	...	...	...	...

[1] In the Royal Library at Brussels.

I. MADRIGAL SETS (*continued*)

Abbreviated Description.	Brit. Mus.	Bodl. Lib., Oxford.	Camb. Univ. Lib.	Royal Coll. of Music.	Ch. Ch., Oxford.
Lichfild 1613. C, A, T, B, Q.	K. 8. f. 5.	...	...	I. D. 13	...
C (imp.), A, B	...	...	...	...	...
Morley 1593. C, A, B	K. 3. i. 7	...	...	...	...
A	...	...	...	...	...
B	C. 8. i. 12	Douce HH. 216 MM. 361	...	I. D. 21 I. D. 14 (9) II. E. 39	...
Morley 1593, 1606 edition	...	...	...	...	...
another copy	K. 3. i. 10	...	...	...	...
Morley 1593, 1631 edition	K. 3. i. 12	...	...	...	...
Morley 1594. C, A, T, B	K. 3. i. 13	...	...	...	...
another copy	...	...	...	...	...
B	K. 3. m. 11	Malone 975	Syn. 6. 60. 6²	I. D. 14 (8)	...
Morley 1594, 1600 edition	...	Douce MM. 361	...	...	...
T, B	K. 3. i. 4	...	...	I. D. 19	242–6
T	K. 3. i. 5	...	...	...	...
Morley 1595 (Ballets). C, A, T, B, Q	...	Mus. 19. e. 3	...	...	...
another copy	...	Douce MM. 361	...	...	...
C	...	Douce MM. 361	...	...	...
A	K. 3. 16	Mus. 19. e. 2	...	...	...
Q	K. 3. i. 8	...	...	...	...
Morley 1595 (Ballets), 1600 edition	...	...	...	...	...
C, B.	K. 3. m. 10	...	...	I. D. 14 (12)	...
Morley 1595 (Canzonets). C, A	K. 3. 19	...	...	...	...
Morley 1595 (Canzonets), 1619 edition	...	Ashm. 1670	Syn. 5. 59. 2	...	...
C	...	...	...	...	...
Morley 1597. C, A, T, B, Q, Sx	K. 3. i. 15	[MS.] Mus. Sch. E. 453–8 Malone 974 Douce MM. 361	Syn. 6. 60. 6³	I. D. 20	449–54
A (imp.)	...	...	...	...	...
Morley 1601 (Triumphs). C, A, T, B, Q, Sx, 1st ed. (Bright Phoebus)	...	...	...	...	...
1601, 2nd ed. (With angel's face)	...	...	...	...	...
another copy	...	...	...	...	...
A	...	...	...	...	...
? which edition B	...	...	...	...	...

Mundy 1594. S, M, Ct, T, B .	K. 2. a. 3	Mus. 2. e. 2-6			489–94
Ct .	...	Douce MM. 361			...
T .			Syn. 6. 59. 4		...
Pilkington 1613. C, A, T, B, Q .	K. 2. d. 10				...
Pilkington 1624. C, A, T, B, Q, Sx .	K. 2. d. 11				...
B .	C. 156			I. D. 21	449–54
Tomkins 1622. C, A, T, B, Q, Sx .	...	[MS.] Mus. Sch. E. 453–8			...
C, A, T, B .	K. 3. k. 7	[MS.] Mus. Sch. E. 547–50			...
C, Sx, T, B .	K. 3. k. 8				...
Vautor 1619. C, A, T, B, Q, Sx .	K. 3. k. 11			I. D. 14 (1)	135–40
Ward 1613. C, A, T, B, Q, Sx .	K. 3. k. 15	[MS.] Mus. Sch. E. 453–8	Syn. 7. 61. 89		...
A (imp.) .	...				...
Weelkes 1597. C1, C2, A, B, Q, Sx .	55. b. 20 (5 and 8)	[MS.] Mus. Sch. E. 470–3		I. D. 26	...
C2, A, B, Q .	K. 3. k. 14				...
A, Q, Sx, B .	55. b. 20 (7 and 15)	[MS.] Mus. Sch. E. 453–7		I. D. 27	...
C1, A .	...				...
Weelkes 1598. C, A, T, B, Q .	K. 3. k. 16	Malone 970			449–54
C, A .	...				...
Weelkes 1600. 5 voices, C, A, T, B, Q .	K. 3. k. 16	Malone 970		I. D. 28	449–54
Weelkes 1600. 6 voices, C, A, T, B, Q, Sx .	...				...
except T all imp.—A, T, B, Q .	55. b. 20 (9 and 10)				...
C .	K. 3. k. 13	Douce MM. 361		I. D. 14 (11)	...
Q, Sx .	...	Malone 971			...
Weelkes 1608. C, A, B .	K. 3. k. 17	Douce WW. 96		I. D. 29	...
B .	55. b. 20 (6)	Malone 972			...
Wilbye 1593. C, A, T, B, Q, Sx .	K. 3. k. 18	[MS.] Mus. Sch. E. 453–8		I. D. 30	...
A .	55. b. 20 (16)				...
Wilbye 1609. C, A, T, B, Q, Sx .	K. 3. k. 21				...
A .	...				...
Youll 1608. C, T, B .	...	Antiq. e. E. $\frac{1608}{1}$	Syn. 6. 60 (1–3)		...
B .	...				...

II. MISCELLANEOUS

Abbreviated Description.	Brit. Mus.	Bodl. Lib., Oxford.	Camb. Univ. Lib.	Royal Coll. of Music.	Ch. Ch. Oxford.
Amner 1615. C, A, T, B, Q, Sx	K. 3. h. 2.	[MS.] Mus. Sch. E. 453–8	Syn. 6. 61. 11–14	...	...
T, B, Q, Sx			Syn. 8. 61. 34		
Leighton 1614	K. 1. i. 9	...		I. G. 5	...
Morley 1597 (Italian). C, A, T, B	K. 3. i. 10	...	Syn. 5. 59. 2	I. D. 14 (7)	913–8
C	...				
Morley 1598 (Italian). C, A, T, B, Q	K. 3. i. 14	Douce MM. 361	...	...	...
A	...	?			
Peerson 1620		Douce MM. 361			
imperfect		Douce MM. 361			
Peerson 1630. C, A, Ct, T, B	K. 2. d. 12		...	...	449–54
Porter 1632	K. 2. d. 13	...			818–23
Porter 1657	K. 8. f. 20	[MS.] Mus. Sch. d. 349ᵃ⁻ᵇ			818–23
another copy	K. 4. h. 7	...			878–80
another copy					
Ravenscroft Pammelia 1609	K. 1. e. 9	Tanner 303	...	I. D. 36	...
another copy	K. 3. k. 3	...		II. E. 42	
1618 edition		Douce M. 702		II. E. 41 (1)	
Ravenscroft Deuteromelia 1609	K. 1. e. 10	Tanner 303		II. E. 41 (2)	
Ravenscroft Melismata 1611	K. 1. e. 11	Tanner 303		II. E. 41 (3)	
another copy	...	4 M. 33. Art.			
another copy		Douce M. 83			
Ravenscroft Brief Discourse 1614	K. 1. e. 7	Tanner 303		II. E. 41 (4)	
another copy	K. 1. e. 8	...			
Watson 1590. S, A, T, B, Q, Sx	K. 3. k. 12	30. d. 8		I. D. 25	342–5
Whythorne 1571. Tr, M, Ct, T, B	...	...		...	
Tr, M, Ct, B					
Whythorne 1590	K. 4. c. 2	Douce W.W. 62		...	
T	...	...			
Whythorne 1590	K. 4. c. 3	Douce W. subᵗ. 30			
B	...	Malone 977			
Yonge 1588. C, A, T, B, Q, Sx	K. 3. k. 19	[MS.] Mus. Sch. E. 453–8		I. D. 32	913–18
C, A, T, B				I. D. 33	
C, Q (imp.)	...			I. D. 35 (1)	
Sx				I. D. 34	
Yonge 1597. C, A, T, B, Q. Sx	K. 3. k. 20	[MS.] Mus. Sch. E. 453–8		I. D. 35 (2)	913–18
C, A, Q, T, B	...	...			

III. LUTENISTS' BOOKS OF AIRS

Abbreviated Description.	Brit. Mus.	Bodl. Lib., Oxford.	Camb. Univ. Lib.	Royal Coll. of Music.	Ch. Ch., Oxford.
Attey 1622	K. 8. h. 8	...	...	...	...
Bartlet 1606	K. 8. h. 3	...	...	...	...
Campian with Rosseter 1601	K. 2. i. 3	...	...	...	868
Campian 1st and 2nd books undated	K. 2. i. 1	...	...	I. G. 35	...
Campian 3rd and 4th books undated	K. 2. i. 2	...	...	...	...
Cavendish 1598	K. 2. i. 20	...	...	...	...
Coprario 1606	K. 2. g. 7	...	...	...	...
Coprario 1613	K. 2. g. 8	B. 5. 12. Art.	...	...	...
imp.	...	...	Q. 10. 24 ² (D)	...	...
Corkine 1610	K. 8. h. 4	...	...	...	...
Corkine 1612	K. 8. h. 5	...	...	...	...
Danyel 1606	K. 2. g. 9	...	...	...	...
Dowland 1597	K. 2. i. 4	...	...	...	...
Dowland 1597, 1600 edition	K. 2. i. 5 (1)	...	...	...	...
Dowland 1597, 1606 edition (imp.)	K. 2. i. 6	...	...	...	834
Dowland 1597, 1613 edition	K. 2. i. 13	...	...	I. G. 20	...
Dowland 1600	K. 2. i. 5 (2)	...	...	I. G. 21	...
Dowland 1603	K. 2. i. 5 (3)	...	...	...	...
Dowland 1612	K. 2. i. 10	...	...	...	...
R. Dowland, Mus. Banquet, 1610	K. 2. i. 9	B. 5. 12. Art.	...	I. G. 22	...
Ferrabosco 1609	K. 8. h. 2	...	...	I. G. 41	...
Ford 1607	K. 9. a. 19	...	...	...	...
Greaves 1604	K. 9. a. 18	...	...	...	...
Hume 1605	K. 2. g. 10	...	...	...	...
Hume 1607	K. 2. g. 11	...	...	...	...
Jones 1600	K. 9. a. 17 (1)	...	...	...	...
Jones 1601	K. 9. a. 17 (2)	...	...	I. G. 23	...
Jones 1608	K. 2. g. 2	...	...	...	...
Jones 1609	...	...	...	...	...
Jones 1611 [1]	...	...	...	...	...
Mason and Earsden 1618	K. 8. h. 7	B. 5. 12. Art.	...	...	...
Maynard 1611	K. 8. h. 6	...	...	...	...
Morley 1600 [2]	...	...	...	...	...
Pilkington 1605	K. 2. i. 11	...	...	...	...
Rosseter with Campian 1601	K. 2. i. 3	...	...	...	...

[1] Formerly in the Bridgewater House Library; now in the Huntington Library at Pasadena, California. A photographic facsimile is in the British Museum.

[2] Formerly in the Halliwell Phillips collection; now in the Folger Museum at Washington, D.C

Z

INDEX OF MUSICAL ILLUSTRATIONS

GENERAL INDEX